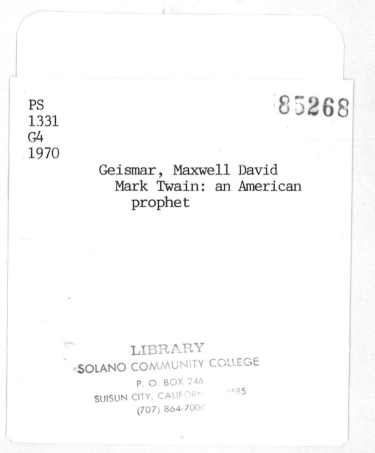

Mark Twain: an American Prophet

# Books by Maxwell Geismar

## THE NOVEL IN AMERICA

Writers in Crisis: The American Novel, 1925–1940
(*Studies of Ring Lardner, Ernest Hemingway, John Dos Passos,*
*William Faulkner, Thomas Wolfe, John Steinbeck*)
The Last of the Provincials: The American Novel, 1915–1925
(*Studies of H. L. Mencken, Sinclair Lewis, Willa Cather,*
*Sherwood Anderson, F. Scott Fitzgerald*)
Rebels and Ancestors: The American Novel, 1890–1915
(*Studies of Frank Norris, Stephen Crane, Jack London,*
*Ellen Glasgow, Theodore Dreiser*)
American Moderns: From Rebellion to Conformity
Henry James and the Jacobites
Mark Twain: An American Prophet
Ring Lardner and the Portrait of Folly

## EDITOR

The Ring Lardner Reader
The Walt Whitman Reader
The Portable Thomas Wolfe
Sherwood Anderson: Short Stories
Jack London: Short Stories
Mark Twain and the Three R's

# AN AMERICAN PROPHET

## MAXWELL GEISMAR

edited and abridged by
MAXWELL GEISMAR

**McGraw-Hill Book Company**

New York • St. Louis • San Francisco • London • Düsseldorf
Kuala Lumpur • Mexico • Montreal • Panama • São Paulo
Sydney • Toronto • Johannesburg • New Delhi • Singapore

Library of Congress Catalog Card Number: 71-108681

First McGraw-Hill Paperback Edition, 1973.

Reprinted by arrangement with the Houghton Mifflin Company.

07-023081-1

2 3 4 5 6 7 8 9 MU MU 7 9 8 7 6 5 4

A selection from this book appeared in the March 1970 issue of
*Scanlan's Monthly,* copyright © 1970 by Scanlan's Literary
House, Inc.

Thanks are due to Harper & Row, Inc., Publishers, for permis-
sion to quote illustrative passages from the following books:
"The Mysterious Stranger" from *The Mysterious Stranger and
Other Stories* by Mark Twain. Copyright 1916 by Harper &
Brothers; copyright renewed 1944 by Clara Clemens Gabrilowitsch. *Europe and Elsewhere* by Mark Twain. Copyright
1923, 1951 by The Mark Twain Company. *Mark Twain's Autobiography,* Vol. I and Vol. II, edited by Albert Bigelow Paine.
Copyright 1924 by Clara Gabrilowitsch; copyright renewed
1952 by Clara Clemens Samossoud. *Mark Twain in Eruption,*
edited by Bernard DeVoto. Copyright 1922 by Harper & Brothers; copyright renewed 1940 by The Mark Twain Company.
*Letters from the Earth* by Mark Twain, edited by Bernard De-
Voto. Copyright © 1938, 1944, 1946, 1959, 1962 by The Mark
Twain Company.

To my wife Anne

# *Author's Note*

I am glad to welcome the paperback edition of *Mark Twain: An American Prophet,* first published in 1970.

This is an abridged version of that first publication. It originally appeared as a book of 564 pages and has now been condensed, purely for reasons of space, in order to bring the paperback edition down to a reasonable size and price. Mostly what I have omitted, with sorrow, have been the marvelous quotations and statements of Mark Twain himself of which, when I first came across them, I became so enamored that I had to write a book about them: a book which in my own mind would explain and describe the remarkable literary personage who expressed these thoughts.

I have also condensed much of the critical discussion of Twain scholarship and Twain criticism of the last twenty-five years. Some readers of the original book felt I should have done this anyhow; and one kindly academic soul instructed me that if I would omit this discussion of Twain's critics then indeed I would have written the "definitive" book on Twain. I did not tell him that I thought I *had* written the definitive book on Twain, and that the Twain scholarship of the contemporary scene was fascinating to me as a primary symptom of the cold war epoch and the cold war culture.

In this period the obviously secondary talent of Henry James, for example, has been elevated far beyond its value—though the Jamesian Cult, according to its more intelligent spokesmen, has already begun to wane. And the obviously primary talent of Mark Twain—who must be considered along with Melville and Whitman not merely as one of the three great nineteenth century American talents, but as among the three geniuses of our literature —has been systematically down-graded. The present study of Mark Twain, both in this paperback and in its original hardcover edition, attempts to correct that contemporary impression, and to see Twain in his true and most original light, as he flourished to the very end of his life  and was revered and adored in the minds and hearts of his fellow countrymen. I know these sentiments and these words may sound strange in the age of the anti-hero and alienation. But they are true about Mark Twain in his own period; and they remain true about him today. As I've said elsewhere, he reminds us of great literature because he *is* great literature.

Maxwell Geismar

Harrison, New York
Independence Day, 1973

In tribute to Mark Twain's Eve,
edenic divine native artist

"Fiat justitia ruat coelum"
— *The Noble Savage*

# CONTENTS

Mark Twain: an American Prophet

# ONE

# FACTUAL

This is a critical study of Mark Twain's literary career in which I have used autobiographical material to clarify certain issues of Twain's work, certain works of his in which personal background was relevant, or certain phases and periods of his work in general. Since I have used this material for the purpose of clarifying his "real life" (that is to say, his literary work) rather than for its own sake, and have used it partially in places, and in other places perhaps familiarly, in the sense of taking it for granted, it occurred to me that it might be helpful to present some kind of factual summary of Twain's life at the outset.

He was born Samuel Langhorne Clemens on November 30, 1835, in Florida, Missouri. His family came from the good southern stock which emigrated westward in those days; his father was a man of cultivation and dignity (and a certain aloofness) who was always on the edge of material comfort and always falling below it. The family was poor but respectable; the mother was a central influence to whom Sam Clemens paid ample and affectionate tribute. In 1839 they moved to Hannibal, Missouri, the scene of Twain's enfabled romances of western childhood and of a later violent and black despair as to both his own dreams and frontier democracy.

In 1847 the father died (just when he was about to achieve some worldly success again), and Sam Clemens left school, which he never much praised, to become a printer's apprentice in the shop of his even more grandiose but ill-fated brother Orion. From 1855 to 1856 he wandered around the country as a journeyman printer in St. Louis, New York, Philadelphia, Keokuk, and Cincinnati, and he began some journalistic work. (His career so far was typical, and paralleled that of another orphic spirit of his own day, Walt Whitman, whom Twain in effect never knew or mentioned.) The years from 1857 to 1860 were the years of piloting on the Mississippi which formed another central strand of Twain's early experience, and which were molded into the chronicle of frontier river life, following after and not unrelated to Herman Melville's epic of the whaling trade.

The Civil War destroyed Mississippi shipping; at the war's start Clemens was a Southern volunteer who promptly resigned, along with his regiment, when news of General Grant's presence was rumored. In July, 1861, he left with his brother Orion for the Nevada territory where he prospected on and off for silver, struck it rich, lost his money, and became a reporter for the Virginia City *Territorial Enterprise* and then, moving west because of a duel which he had no heart for, for the San Francisco *Morning Call.* In 1866 he made a fateful visit to the Sandwich Islands, now Hawaii, which proved his vision of an earthly paradise, provided another central theme for his writing, and started him out on the lecture platform. In 1867 he traveled to Europe and the Holy Land as correspondent for the San Francisco *Alta California,* and just two years later, using the material from this trip, he published his famous travel book, *The Innocents Abroad,* which established his literary reputation and sold one hundred thousand copies.

This was the apprenticeship of a genius in the annals of world literature; from being in effect a proletarian vagabond Sam Clemens overnight became a culture hero to which he promptly added a legendary marriage to an American coal heiress from upper New York state.

In 1870 he married Olivia Langdon and they moved to Buffalo, where their first son, Langdon, was born. (He died in 1872.) They were planning and building the Hartford mansion which was to be their true home; in 1871 they moved there; and their daughter Susy was born in 1872, and Clara in 1874. Meanwhile Clemens was publishing a series of famous early books, *Roughing It, The Gilded Age, The Adventures of Tom Sawyer.*

Their third daughter, Jean, was born in 1880. They were always taking trips to Europe, and in London Twain was lionized. The eighties brought forth more big books, among them *Life on the Mississippi, The Adventures of Huckleberry Finn,* along with that curious chronicle, *A Connecticut Yankee in King Arthur's Court.* By then, however, Clemens, who always gambled, who was a child of the nineteenth century and lived to regret it, was involved in the business and scientific ventures which broke his life in half. At first it was his publishing house which made a fortune on General Grant's *Memoirs,* and gradually went broke. And then there was the fabulous Paige typesetter, reputedly the most expensive machine ever made, on which Twain squandered every cent he had made, and Livy's fortune too. (They were living to the tune of one hundred thousand dollars a year, about half of which Clemens spent on his "inventions.") At fifty, at the peak of his fame, he went bankrupt in a society where most men of his age never made it back again.

Mark Twain did, by the grace of God and a Standard Oil tycoon named Henry H. Rogers. Fortune's favorite child was not abandoned yet — though the terrible financial crisis led indirectly perhaps (or so the Clemenses may have believed) to the death of their beloved Susy while they were away from her on a lecture tour, and to Livy's own nervous collapse, lingering illness, and death. With the end of Mark Twain's domestic idyll, his private garden of innocence and love and play (Twain's favorite ancestors were Adam and Eve), he entered the second and most severe trauma of his mature life. But that is enough for you to know about the facts of the situation; here let the book take over the story. And what a remarkable story it is: of success and failure, of innocence and corruption, of good and evil, of the great spiritual peaks and deep abysses which accompanied Mark Twain's life and career.

But he lived it through; he survived it all. Like the great book of his old age, the *Autobiography* — one of the great books of our letters — he would have many editions, and perhaps the final one is yet to come. In his affinity with the animal world, Mark Twain's behavior was sometimes catlike; but he did not really have nine lives. He had something better, the double soul of a great artist.

That is to say, he did not have the split personality which is commonly attributed to him, nor all the frustration and repression and mental conflict which goes along with that. He had a soul both pagan and civilized, but a civilizational soul which did not repress or replace the pagan one, but lived together with it, harmoniously or acridly, as it may be, but together, always fused and joined in Clemens' central artistic vision: the double aware

of its loss and rejoicing in its heritage. (Among depth psychologists Freud knew this, but it was Otto Rank who pursued it to
final meanings — and Mark Twain was Rank's favorite writer.)
All writers have this to some degree; it is the special province
of art and the artist. But few have had it so openly, freshly,
and actively as Clemens, and it is the secret of his whole
achievement.

That is why, literally, he is such a pleasure and a delight to
read; because to him life and art *were* pleasure, or at least art
was, at its best. That is why the early Sam Clemens refused to
work any more than he had to, and why the later Clemens refused to write when he did not enjoy the writing. He is one of
the great "daylight writers" of the world, as you'll see, who
transcended all the torments, horrors, fears, pain, and illness in
the black night of our existence.

It will become clear, too, that I do not accept certain other
fixed concepts of Mark Twain criticism extending from the
twenties to the seventies. It is obvious that the grand historian
of our literature, Van Wyck Brooks, did not understand
Twain's humor and falsely used this great artist as an example
of native genius being broken and destroyed by American materialism. The remarkable thing about Mark Twain is that his
great financial and social success never touched his heart or
temperament. Nor was he seriously affected by the Victorian
censorship to which he yielded ironically on occasion; but rather
the reverse. The underground sexuality of his nature, sometimes
hidden or suppressed, emerged in full force in his later work,
and in the *Autobiography* itself.

Was he also a writer, broken in mid-course, who will be remembered only for those idylls of frontier youth, and who
turned away from the society of his period to live in some historical fantasy-land? (Justin Kaplan, in the latest biography of

Mark Twain.) On the contrary, a whole area of Twain's social criticism of the United States has been repressed or avoided by Twain scholars precisely because it is so bold, so brilliant, satirical, and prophetic. He was one of the most mature American artists precisely because he had, so to speak, such a long, deep childhood. Those whose childhood is cut short or is never lived through fully: those are the ones who never fully mature, and remain caught in the pubescent or adolescent emotional states throughout their lives. To become old, one has first to be young; and to be truly young is never to become completely old. It was not mere whimsy that led Livy to call Clemens "Youth," but the recognition of a deep strain in his temperament.

Was Twain just a personal, anecdotal, intimate "humorist," as was said at the start of his career and as Charles Neider says again in the most recent edition of Twain's last book? Never was a writer more interested in the whole world around him, or more involved in every detail of it. The "I" of Whitman and Twain alike was not the "Big Me" of the autistic personality. It was the primitive and animistic "I" (to a large degree that of Eastern and Asiatic religious philosophy) of an organism which does not even recognize its own separation from the world around it, which *is* that world, while being most clearly itself. Just as nothing human is alien to it, so it is immersed in everything which is human. Curiosity — and what he called the "unobstructed eye" — is a dominant feature of Twain's temperament. He could never stop looking at the world, and at the "damned human race" which he viewed with such ridicule, wrath, and laughter. Because he too belonged to that race, and worse he could say of no man.

Two concluding notes. I have used the names of Mark Twain and Samuel Clemens almost interchangeably throughout this book, but that of Sam Clemens when I am talking of the man behind the artist, or when talking of him more personally, perhaps, or affectionately. Upon a few occasions I have used the name "Sam" by itself, but rarely, or never, I think, have I used the name "Mark" by itself, perhaps for some curious reason of personal taste which I have not myself been able to understand.

And finally: I know I have quoted from Clemens in great detail in terms of a formal literary study. I did this because I never thought it was excessive, and I could never bring myself to stop quoting some passages. (Though what is printed here I have pruned sharply, much to my private regret, from the original block of quotations.) It is not just that when Mark Twain is good, he is too good *not* to quote. But also, much of the material reprinted here has been buried in his more obscure books, some of it appearing in almost unknown books. And I thought it better to rescue and to collect here all those prose passages, from whatever source, which seem today as sharp and fresh and pristine; or as appropriate and brilliant and penetrating, as sophisticated and satiric and entertaining as when the ink first flowed from such a pen, divine and diabolical.

# TWO

# A PAGAN PURITAN

Even the beginning was auspicious. His early short story "The Celebrated Jumping Frog of Calaveras County" was printed and became the title story of a volume of Twain's newspaper sketches published in 1867.

The story was a typical example of the frontier tall tale, but what marked it off was that it was already a parody of a parody. Twain was interested in the form of the sketch, and that is to say, in the garrulous narrator whose stream of consciousness is continuously nonselective. The "Frog" is still entertaining and a good example of its genre, but the young author, coming across a translation of it in the *Revue des Deux Mondes,* felt a need to translate the French back into English in a new version called "The Frog Jumping of the County of Calaveras."

"It there was one time here an individual known under the name of Jim Smiley . . ." Who was the man "the most fond of to bet which one have seen, betting upon all that which is presented, when he could find an adversary; and when he not of it could not, he passed to the side opposed. All that which convenienced to the other, to him convenienced also; seeing that he had a bet, Smiley was satisfied. And he had a chance! a chance even worthless; nearly always he gained." The revised version of the "Frog" went on to Smiley's animals: the queer birds, dogs, horses of the original tale, and the frog himself. "Eh bien! this Smiley nourished some terriers and rats and some cocks of combat, and some cats, and all sorts of things; and with his rage of betting one no had more of repose. He trapped one day a frog and him imported with him [*et l'emporta chez lui*] saying that he pretended to make his education. You me believe if you will, but during three months he not has nothing done but to him apprehend to jump [*apprendre à sauter*] in a court retired of her mansion [*de sa maison*]."

Already Sam Clemens, this "rude frontier genius," was displaying his wit, his verbal play, and that kind of humor, both in the original "Frog" and the revised "Frog," which had no counterpart (until the days of Ring Lardner) in the national letters. And barely two years later, with his first travel book, *The Innocents Abroad,* in 1869, he was suddenly catapulted into a national prominence beyond his wildest dreams. He had wanted to be a journalist, a lecturer, an entertainer who would make people laugh; now he was suddenly a popular writer on the way to money, fame, and social position.

In New York Clemens attended Henry Ward Beecher's Plymouth Church less for religious reasons than to observe the platform style of the famous minister; and it was Beecher's church that initiated the "pilgrimage" to the Holy Land which Twain covered as the *Alta California*'s foreign correspondent before writing his book. The enduring secret of *The Innocents Abroad,* of course, lies in the fact that it was the first American travel book, realistic, satirical, homely, debunking, to set itself off against a whole tradition of foreign "romance" in this genre; a romance literature of travel exemplified at that very moment by the Jamesian "dream of Europe." Conversely, Twain was at his best just when he quoted and parodied the conventional travel books about the scene he was visiting; this was a very cosmopolitan, a highly sophisticated country bumpkin from the wild west who paid mock homage to the hallowed shrines of Old World culture.

On these excursions, he was trying to write not what he ought to feel, as he said, but what he did feel. To be sure, *The Innocents Abroad* contains many sections of padded material or plain filler, of more or less conventional gambits of comedy, of dragging and belabored narrative. As in almost all Twain's work from start to last, the quality is uneven; and it is precisely in this rough literary terrain that you fall upon the priceless literary episodes and prose passages.

For all the semblance of a genial old-fashioned American tale of travel entertainment, too, the *Innocents* was at base a radical document which presaged the future career of Mark Twain. It was perhaps even more radical in its "innocence" than some of the middle Twain would be, though not the later or the last Twain at all. As usual, after the trip was over, Sam Clemens started with the thing that was closest to him: in this case the "Old Travelers," whom he met in France. "But still I love the Old Travelers. I love them for their witless platitudes; for their supernatural ability to bore; for their delightful asinine vanity; for their luxuriant fertility of imagination; for their startling, their brilliant, their overwhelming mendacity!" In France there was the description of the cancan. "I placed my hands before my face for very shame. But I looked through my fingers. They were dancing the renowned 'Can-can.' A handsome girl in the set before me tripped forward lightly to meet the opposite gentleman — tripped back again, grasped her dresses vigorously on both sides with her hands, raised them pretty high, danced an extraordinary jig that had more activity and exposure about it than any jig I ever saw before, and then, drawing her clothes still higher, she advanced gaily to the center and launched a vicious kick full at her *vis-à-vis* that must infallibly have removed his nose if he had been seven feet high . . . That is the Can-can. The idea of it is to dance as wildly, as noisily, as furiously as you can; expose yourself as much as possible if you are a woman; and kick as high as you can, no matter which sex you belong to."

Along with his insistence on factuality and materiality, Clemens had a natural affinity for the flesh; this astute realist was close to the primitive bases of life. Thus the *Innocents* pays its tribute to pretty women everywhere, to animal life always; and here too Clemens initiated a lifelong admiration, at once esthetic, moral and social, for the dark-skinned peoples of the earth. Yet in all his moments of worship and devotion there was always a satiric sting. "Ah, the grisettes! I had almost forgotten. They are another romantic fraud." In Paris Twain noted directly that "all through this Faubourg St. Antoine, misery, poverty, vice, and crime go hand in hand, and the evidences of it stare one in the face from every side. Here the people live who begin the revolutions. Whenever there is anything of that kind to be done, they are always ready. They take as much genuine pleasure in building a barricade as they do in cutting a throat or shoving a friend into the Seine. It is these savage-looking ruffians who storm the splendid halls of the Tuileries, occasionally, and swarm into Versailles when a king is to be called to account."

Wasn't there a note of veiled admiration here, too, when compared, say, with the mincing nightmares of "anarchism" in *The Princess Casamassima*? In Genoa, Clemens was impressed by

the ladies again. "I scanned every female face that passed, and
it seemed to me that all were handsome; I never saw such a
freshet of loveliness before." He noticed the female attendants
at the Italian public baths. "I am an unprotected male, but I
will preserve my honor at the peril of my life!" — and here
came the highly charged and controversial commentary on
the Old Masters and the Catholic religion. The gory paintings
of the Savior were repugnant to Twain's democratic esthetics,
and he disdained the huge, coarse frescoes of suffering martyrs.
"It could not have diminished their sufferings any to be un-
couthly represented. We were in the heart and home of priest-
craft — of a happy, cheerful, contented ignorance, superstition,
degradation, poverty, indolence, and everlasting unaspiring
worthlessness."

But it is interesting that he blamed the people themselves —
"How can men, calling themselves men, consent to be so degraded and happy?" — as much as their institutions. (And
he was still unaware of the paradox contained in their "happiness.") In Venice, indulging in a deliberately deadpan low-
browism which produced fine pages of satire on the conventional art-snobbery of his period, he confessed his own taste for
the Renaissance art which dealt with the affairs of men in this
world. Considering Clemens' lack of background, of formal
education, of knowledge of Old World culture, there is already
a remarkable sense of history in these sections of *The Innocents
Abroad,* just as there is a nice analysis of the Catholic clerical
organization. "As far as I can see, Italy, for fifteen hundred
years, has turned all her energies, all her finances, and all her
industry to building up a vast array of wonderful church edifices,
and starving half her citizens to accomplish it. She is to-day
one vast museum of magnificence and misery . . . It is the
wretchedest, princeliest land on earth."

In his early mood of nineteenth-century materialistic progress, no doubt Clemens stressed the achievements of Morse,
Fulton, Jenner, and Daguerre at the expense of "Roman sloth,
Roman superstition, and modern Roman boundlessness of ignorance." But the first volume of *The Innocents Abroad* was an
eloquent defense of the American democracy which, abandoning its own roots, corrupting its own aspirations in the
Gilded Age, was just then turning toward that dream of European nobility and "culture" which Twain attacked. Reading
over this classical travel book today, we notice how steadily it
builds its power from a mild and genial tone at the opening to
its closing satire on the Old World's social misery, princely castes,
and religious superstition. "From the sanguinary sports of the
Holy Inquisition; the slaughter of the Colosseum; and the dismal tombs of the Catacombs," said he, "I naturally pass to the
picturesque horrors of the Capuchin Convent." And how skill-
fully Clemens mixed these passages of social satire and parody
with a brilliant kind of personal humor. "I never felt so fer-
vently thankful, so soothed and tranquil, so filled with a blessed
peace, as I did yesterday when I learned that Michael Angelo
was dead." So much for Europe — in which Clemens, however, was destined to spend more of his mature life than he did
in America; and the second volume of *The Innocents Abroad*
turned to the East and the Holy Land itself.

In Constantinople he was even more appalled at Eastern
misery and disease. "A beggar in Naples who can show a foot
which has all run into one horrible toe, with one shapeless nail
on it, has a fortune — but such an exhibition as that would not
provoke any notice in Constantinople. The man would starve
. . . Who would pay any attention to attractions like his
among the rare monsters that throng the bridges of the Golden
Horn and display their deformities in the gutters of Stamboul?"

The Mosque of Saint Sophia was the rustiest old barn in hea-
thendom; the Turks were dirty pagans, and if Clemens was incited by European Catholicism, he was not greatly impressed
by Mohammedanism. "Mosques are plenty, churches are
plenty, graveyards are plenty, but morals and whiskey are
scarce. The Koran does not permit Mohammedans to drink.
Their natural instincts do not permit them to be moral. They
say the Sultan has eight hundred wives. This almost amounts
to bigamy." This was tongue in cheek, of course, and he was
aroused by the "incendiary" travel books on the Mideast, along
with the food. "When I think how I have been swindled by
books of Oriental travel, I want a tourist for breakfast." There
is another hilarious diatribe against the celebrated Turkish
baths as a malignant swindle; in the ruins of Sebastopol, they
took home the fragments of a Russian general for a souvenir.
Yet, received by the Czar at Yalta, this democrat was rather
taken in by the charm of Russian royalty — at least when compared with ordinary life in Asia, in Smyrna. "Everywhere there
is dirt, everywhere there are fleas, everywhere there are lean,
broken-hearted dogs; every alley is thronged with people; wherever you look, your eye rests upon a wild masquerade of extravagant costumes" — while the muezzin's cry called the "faithful vagabonds" to prayer, and superior to everything was the combination of Mohammedan stenches.

He was struck by the Armenian women, though, as he had
been by the peasant girls in Yalta, and as he was by the ancient
history of Ephesus. "We speak of Apollo and of Diana — they
were born here; of the metamorphosis of Syrinx into a reed —
it was done here; of the great god Pan — he dwelt in the caves
of this hill of Coressus; of the Amazons — this was their best-
prized home; of Bacchus and Hercules — both fought the war-
like women here; of the Cyclops — they laid the ponderous

marble blocks of some of the ruins yonder — of Homer — this was one of his many birthplaces . . ." The *Innocents* is a diary of what the early Sam Clemens hated and liked; and if there was much more of the former than the latter in his book, it was also true that the intensity of his admirations made up for their lack of range.

In the approach to the Holy Land itself, the women of Beirut added an interest to Twain's travels by covering their faces and exposing their breasts. And here again he spoke of animals as though he was one. How does a camel look? "When he is down on all his knees, flat on his breast to receive his load, he looks something like a goose swimming; and when he is upright he looks like an ostrich with an extra set of legs . . . They are not particular about their diet. They would eat a tombstone if they could bite it . . . I suppose it would be a real treat for a camel to have a keg of nails for supper." The holy traveler also had a horse by the name of Jericho. "He is a mare. I have seen remarkable horses before, but none so remarkable as this. I wanted a horse that could shy, and this one fills the bill. I had an idea that shying indicated spirit. If I was correct, I have got the most spirited horse on earth . . . He has only one fault. His tail has been chopped off or else he has sat down on it too hard, some time or other, and he has to fight the flies with his heels" — and so on until Jericho is one of the characters taking the trip.

Battered old parodies of animals that they are, they are usually in better shape than their masters.

Clemens found the Syrians to be naturally goodhearted and intelligent but horribly poor and ground down by their rulers. "If ever an oppressed race existed, it is this one we see fettered around us under the inhuman tyranny of the Ottoman empire. I wish Europe would let Russia annihilate Turkey a little —

not much, but enough to make it difficult to find the place again without a divining-rod or a diving-bell."

Ancient and nostalgic evils vanished to make place for new and future evils in the prophetic strain of Mark Twain; and there are times in the *Innocents* when one is torn between the social injustices and the pleasure evoked by Clemens' denunciations of them. The Ottoman Empire was his special peeve here, but he had enough spirit left to turn upon something much closer: his fellow Christian pilgrims who were beating their horses to death in a frenzied attempt to reach Damascus before the Sabbath day. "Nothing could move the pilgrims. They *must* press on. Men might die, horses might die, but they must enter upon holy soil next week, with no Sabbath-breaking stain upon them. Thus they were willing to commit a sin against the spirit of religious law, in order that they might preserve the letter of it. I am talking now about personal friends; men whom I like; men who are good citizens; who are honorable, upright, conscientious: but whose idea of the Saviour's religion seems to me distorted."

Meanwhile he had come across a whole new vein of comic writing. The retelling of Biblical legends in Twain's ironical, poker-faced, flat western country style is another feature of the *Innocents* which a whole line of American humorists, and perhaps particularly Ring Lardner, would use and adapt to their own needs. In the holy shrines of Jerusalem, Clemens erupted into passages of irony and parody:

The great feature of the Mosque of Omar is the prodigious rock in the center of its rotunda. It was upon this rock that Abraham came so near offering up his son Isaac — this, at least, is authentic — it is very much more to be relied on than most of the traditions, at any rate. On this rock, also the angel stood and threatened Jerusalem, and David persuaded him to spare the city. Mohammed was well acquainted with this stone. From it he ascended to heaven. The stone tried to follow him and if the angel Gabriel had not happened by the merest good luck to be there to seize it, it would have done it. Very few people have a grip like Gabriel — the prints of his monstrous fingers, two inches deep, are to be seen in that rock today . . . This rock, large as it is, is suspended in the air. It does not touch anything at all. The guide said so. This is very wonderful . . .

But notice that this pantheistic Mark Twain could endow even a stone with a remarkable personality. Then there is the central aphorism of *The Innocents Abroad*. "There are some things which, for the credit of America, should be left unsaid, perhaps; but these very things happen sometimes to be the very things which, for the real benefit of Americans, ought to have prominent notice."

And then there was the final blast — scandalous at the time — at the whole boatload of Christian pilgrims; the folly of the entire trip to the Holy Land. Very early, Sam Clemens started out to bite the hand that fed him. Yet it made for an exciting end to a book which still remains, in these high spots, a vital, fresh and interesting kind of travelogue, one which is still popular and still read today. For Twain had already become a master stylist without appearing to know it. Here was that natural, personal, simple, informal western "country-style" of prose — appearing just like the "conversation" or table talk it never was — which as early as 1869 had transformed the American language. While in the same years both Howells and Henry James were trying to "refine" the English language, and while a full century later our contemporary academic prose was full of lingering anachronisms, Twain, after Thoreau, had dealt formal English a mortal blow. How sharp and fresh and brilliant is the prose style of *The Innocents Abroad* as you read it now. In fact Twain's next book, *Roughing It,* published in 1872, if entirely different in scene and tone, was another such travelogue as the *Innocents,* with the language even more native and homelier. Starting out to be the recital of Clemens' first trip west into Nevada and California, about nine years earlier, *Roughing It* was also, in its best moments, a classical account of a frontier society.

After the prefatory note in *Roughing It,* where Twain lamented the fact that information poured out of him "like the precious ottar of roses out of the ottar," the chronicle launched into a handsome description of the western stage coaches. The book's opening note, which Twain was to develop on that celebrated Mississippi raft, was one of pagan pleasure; the pure enjoyment of life.

> The stage whirled along at a spanking gait, the breeze flapping curtains and suspended coats in a most exhilarating way; the cradle swayed and swung luxuriously, the pattering of the horses' hoofs, the cracking of the driver's whip, and his "Hi-yi! g'lang!" were music; the spinning ground and the waltzing trees appeared to give us a mute hurrah as we went by . . . and as we lay and smoked the pipe of peace and compared all this luxury with the years of tiresome city life that had gone before it, we felt that there was only one complete and satisfying happiness in the world, and we had found it.

Very early, Twain sounded this note of escape and asylum from the burden of the nineteenth-century civilization whose commerce and science he elsewhere appeared to celebrate. This was already a flying womb, so to speak, in whose "cradle" Sam Clemens lolled and luxuriated. And here he mixed the marvelous descriptions of the western frontier with the profiles of the heroic Overland stage drivers. These "great and shining digni-

taries" were early prototypes of the Mississippi pilots; this favorite son of the wild west was the envy of hostlers and station-
keepers alike. "When they spoke to him they received his
insolent silence meekly . . . when he opened his lips they all
hung on his words with admiration . . . when he discharged
a facetious insulting personality at a hostler, that hostler was
happy for the day; when he uttered his one jest — old as the
hills, coarse, profane, witless, and inflicted on the same audience, in the same language, every time his coach drove up there
— the varlets roared and slapped their thighs . . . And how
they would fly around when he wanted a basin of water, a gourd
of the same, or a light for his pipe! — but they would instantly
insult a passenger if he so far forgot himself as to crave a favor
at their hands. They could do that sort of insolence as well
as the driver they copied it from — for, let it be borne in mind,
the Overland driver had but little less contempt for his passengers than he had for his hostlers."

There are the crude scenes of the Overland stations; the barren settings, the rough and coarse human types, the bad food
mixed with dead flies: scenes of human desolation to contrast
with the portraits of the Overland coach drivers and of the
western animals. To the jackrabbit, Clemens added the ante-
lope, the wolf, the prairie dog, the coyote. These were the
western democratic souls too, along with the frontiersmen; our
very own domestic animals, and how well Twain knew them.
"The coyote is a long, slim, sick and sorry-looking skeleton with
a gray wolf skin stretched over it, a tolerable bushy tail that forever sags down with a despairing expression of forsakenness and
misery, a furtive and evil eye, and a long, sharp face with
slightly lifted lip and exposed teeth. He has a general slinking
expression all over. The coyote is a living, breathing allegory of
Want. He is *always* hungry. He is always poor, out of luck and

friendless. The meanest creatures despise him, and even the fleas would desert him for a velocipede. He is so spiritless and cowardly that even while his exposed teeth are pretending a threat, the rest of his face is apologizing for it. And he is *so* homely!" This was prose again, and, since the coyote's only answer to life was to run, there is a comic description of the coyote pretending to let a dog catch up with him.

The trick was the personifying and the "humanizing" of the animals whom Twain described with a sense of perfect familiarity, but in this western paradise — this western inferno — animal and human life existed in a kind of natural equality. (But there is a distinction between the "civilized" town animals and the wild animals.) Like Melville before him and Dreiser after him, Clemens had the primitive writer's sense of physical grace and vitality, of pure animal dignity even when, as in the coyote's case, it was notable for its absence. And to these early frontier heroes *Roughing It* added the division agents of the western Overland. There were only eight of these division kings who ruled supreme by law of club and pistol over the station-keepers, hostlers, outlaws, and fugitives of the west; and, moving from the pony express of four hundred gallant horses and eighty riders delivering the United States mail to the black hills of Fort Laramie where the Indian raiders still persisted, *Roughing It* reached an early peak of eloquence with the advent of the outlaw Slade. (But the whole opening section of the book is lyrical, hilarious, brilliant; as fresh and interesting today as when it was first written.) Slade was another of the division managers — "A high and efficient servant of the Overland, an outlaw among outlaws, and yet their relentless scourge, Slade was at once the most bloody, the most dangerous, and the most valuable citizen that inhabited the savage fastnesses of the mountains." As an outlaw, he had been picked by the Overland to protect the company against the other outlaws. And "we had gradually come to have a realizing sense of the fact that Slade was a man whose heart and hands and soul were steeped in the blood of offenders against his dignity; a man who awfully avenged all injuries, affronts, insults or slights of whatever kind — on the spot if he could, years afterward if lack of earlier opportunity compelled it; a man whose hate tortured him day and night till vengeance appeased it."

Working directly, and openly, from a local history of the desperadoes which he recreated in his own vein, Clemens wrote a chapter on this type of democratic hero-villain; villains whose villainy captivated their western chronicler. Slade with his "history-creating revolver" and his energetic administration of the Overland became the absolute ruler of a "very paradise of outlaws and desperadoes. There was absolutely no semblance of law there. Violence was the rule. Force was the only recognized authority. The commonest misunderstandings were settled on the spot with the revolver or the knife. Murders were done in open day and with sparkling frequency and nobody thought of inquiring into them . . ." Nor did Mark Twain himself have much thought here as to what kind of future culture would emerge from "this hive of horse thieves and assassins," or what imprint this frontier violence would leave upon the American character. If violence and force, without semblance of law, were at the root of the frontier code, the early Clemens was more concerned with their esthetic color than with their cultural implications. So, too, while Twain's early fictional portraits are not complex, his first two travel books proved his talent for reporting and documentaries, his sense of scene and atmosphere, his capacity to take in the world around him sharply and fully. This was a fusion of journalism, philosophy, poetry, and drama, of mixed emotions ranging sharply from lyricism to satire, comedy and broad farce, in which Twain was really modeling an altogether new literary form: the prose epic of travel, or the American picaresque.

The eventual death of Slade at the hands of a group of Montana vigilantes, the condemned outlaw's hunger for his wife, his mixed nature of childlike courage, savagery, tears, and passion — this was meat for the primitive bard in Clemens, while his pen flourished again on the Rocky Mountain passes and peaks. "These Sultans of the fastness were turbaned with tumbled volumes of cloud, which shredded away from time to time and drifted off fringed and torn, trailing their continents of shadow after them; and catching presently on an intercepting peak, wrapped it about and brooded there — then shredded away again and left the purple peak, as they had left the purple domes, downy and white with new-laid snow." This "plain style" managed to achieve its complex effects in language not altogether unlike that of Hemingway's famous Gulf Stream descriptions some sixty years later.

There were skeletons of mules, oxen, and men along the western route of *Roughing It,* monuments of the huge emigration of the past, and during a great rain Clemens' coach lost the road and almost fell into a gully. "I have always been glad that we were not killed that night. I do not know any particular reason, but I have always been glad." There is a chapter on the Mormons, newly established at Salt Lake City. Clemens was fascinated by their society, their history, their peculiar institutions, and their power, as by the Mormon Bible which was so pretentious, slow, and sleepy, such an insipid mass of inspiration. "It is chloroform in print. If Joseph Smith composed this book, the act was a miracle — keeping awake while he did it was, at any rate." But this satire was as nothing compared with the venom of Twain's attack on the Goshoot Indians who were, if anything,

worse than the Digger Indians. As a disciple of Fenimore
Cooper, he said, and a worshiper of the Red Men, "even of the
scholarly savages in the *Last of the Mohicans*," he found the
Goshoots so repulsive as to make him question all his former
ideas about the American Indians. "It was curious to see how
quickly the paint and tinsel fell away from him and left him
treacherous, filthy, and repulsive — and how quickly the evidences accumulated that wherever one finds an Indian tribe he
has only found Goshoots more or less modified by circumstances and surroundings — but Goshoots after all." Was this
plain realism on the part of Clemens, or plain ignorance and
prejudice on the part of an artist who in the course of the very
same book would be outraged by the treatment of the Chinese
in California and intoxicated by Polynesian beauty? For a
writer like Twain, who was so early attracted by the Negro slaves
and their descendants, was there even an element of frontier
guilt in his hatred of the Indian? *

But such ambiguities hardly concerned the young Sam Clemens who simply wrote as he felt, and whose western travelogue
had now reached the end of its journey to Carson City, Nevada.
In literary terms, too, one notices there are no "central characters" in *Roughing It,* and no central human relationships, just
as there is no plot line except the trip itself, and no narrative
structure except that of the picaresque. There is barely a mention of Clemens' brother Orion under whose tutelage the original trip was taken. There is only a narrator — but a narrator

---

* The whole frontier thesis in American culture, as first expounded by Frederick
Jackson Turner in the 1920s, and endlessly discussed by academic historians
ever since, is obviously false, since the "Frontier in American History" was the
*white man's* frontier which expanded itself only by the destruction of the Indian
culture which it replaced — which was established, that is to say, and, as
D. H. Lawrence pointed out, through the genocide on which American culture
rested.

whose vision has entered so completely into that of the narrative scene itself as to erase even the sense of a narrator. This was Mark Twain's primary narcissism; a total identification of ego and world in which the ego, as with Walt Whitman's mystic "I," was primitively submerged into the world and part of it, without any bounds of separate personality. This is the art of *Roughing It.*

In what is really the central part of the book, the silver-mining life in Nevada, the logic of the pistol is a primary fact and the description of Carson City amounts to a nightmare. No wonder Clemens discovered Lake Tahoe as another watery Eden far from "civilization," and this episode has overtones of a western *Walden,* surrounded by all the vice and corruption and violence of the mining town. Typically, however, it was Samuel Clemens who set fire to his island retreat, and typically this satanic spirit voiced no guilt for his crime in these pages. In 1858 the silver lodes had been discovered, the Californians had flocked in to become a majority over the original Mormon government, and President Lincoln had sent out Governor Nye. But what is curious about the time of Clemens' visit there in 1863 is how remote the Civil War was from Carson City and Clemens' mind alike. He had deserted from his southern regiment without compunction; the regiment itself had "disbanded" upon hearing that General Grant was in the vicinity; and in *Roughing It,* while he was mildly pro-Union, the great moral issues of slavery and abolitionism were never touched upon. The stupidity and corruption of the Nevada legislature were much closer to his heart.

The first volume of the travelogue closed with the description of the moment when the silver mines were discovered. "Plainly this was the road to fortune. The great 'Gould and Curry' mine was held at three or four hundred dollars a foot when we arrived; but in two months it had sprung up to eight hundred. The 'Ophir' had been worth only a mere trifle, a year gone by, and now it was selling at nearly *four thousand dollars a foot!*" There followed a list of other fabulous mines being opened up. "I would have been more or less than human if I had not gone mad like the rest." And he did. "I confess, without shame, that I expected to find masses of silver lying all about the ground." And it became a raging fever. "Of all the experiences of my life, this secret search among the hidden treasures of silver-land was the nearest to unmarred ecstasy . . . It was a delirious revel." And with what irony Clemens relived the fabulous fortune-hunting of his youth. "We had not less than thirty thousand feet apiece in the 'richest mines on earth,' as the frenzied cant phrased it — and were in debt to the butcher. We were stark mad with excitement — drunk with happiness — smothered under mountains of prospective wealth — arrogantly compassionate toward the plodding millions who knew not our marvelous canon — but our credit was not good at the grocer's. It was the strangest phase of life one can imagine. It was a beggars' revel."

Between the descriptions of such fevered frenzy, Twain felt obliged in *Roughing It,* as he had in *Innocents Abroad,* to insert a series of western tall tales, some of them funny and some not. They are a form of padding in the book which mainly must be endured or skipped until we realize that Clemens has abandoned mining in favor of milling. "That is to say, I went to work as a common laborer in a quartz-mill, at ten dollars a week and board." But he never worked any longer than he had to, inheriting what he called "the nomadic instinct" from distant Arabian ancestors. Experiencing, as Jack London did, the "pit" of manual labor, Clemens was determined never to work at all unless he had to. The whole meaning of life was just this sense of *escape* from work, of leisure and pleasure as the goal of life. Like Whitman who, perhaps unknown to Twain, had invited his readers to "loaf" with him; like Dreiser "mooning about" in the days of his youth, Clemens also remembered "my slothful, valueless, heedless career." These great anti-puritanical writers all agreed on the value of no value in their experience; the direction of no direction, in a childlike voyage through life for the sake of life — in a hapless mood of discovery, excitement, and enjoyment very different from that of stern dedication to discipline, toil, responsibility, and "maturity."

Mark Twain was perhaps the clearest example of them all, and he had an element of the Dostoevskian Gambler in him too. Out there in Carson City they did find their blind lead and Clemens was worth a million dollars for ten days, while his mind was obsessed by visions of much wealth — until they forgot to work their claim, as required by law, and lost it. Destiny was saving this artist for other purposes.

But taking her time about it. Moving away from the narrator's speculative insanity, the second volume of *Roughing It* gives a lurid picture of the "flush days" in Nevada, a unique picture of what was surely one of the gamiest periods of frontier "culture." "Virginia had grown to be the 'livest' town, for its age and population, that America had ever produced. The sidewalks swarmed with people . . . The streets themselves were just as crowded with quartz-wagons, freight-teams, and other vehicles. The procession was endless. So great was the pack, that buggies frequently had to wait half an hour for an opportunity to cross the principal street. Joy sat on every countenance, and there was a glad, almost fierce, intensity in every eye, that told of the money-getting schemes that were seething in every brain . . . Money was as plenty as dust; every individual considered himself wealthy, and a melancholy countenance was nowhere to be seen. There were military companies, fire companies, brass-bands, banks, hotels, theaters, 'hurdy-gurdy houses,' wide-open gambling-palaces, political pow-wows, civic processions, street-fights, murders, inquests, riots, a whiskey-mill every fifteen steps . . ." Here, too, surrounding the fabulous Comstock lode, were all the frauds and tricks, the wildcat claims, the doped mines. The North Ophir was salted with melted half dollars; while the renowned tragedian, McKean Buchanan, quit the stage for a mining fortune which turned out to be nil. Again there was a reign of violence where not merely the editors of local newspapers but the printers carried guns. "The first twenty-six graves in the Virginia cemetery were oc-cupied by *murdered* men," as Clemens reported, and nobody was respected until he had shot his man. Death was by the visi-tation of God, and "to attempt a portrayal of that era and that land, and leave out the blood and carnage, would be like por-traying Mormonism and leaving out polygamy." But this was a society of equality in Nevada where for a time "the lawyer, the editor, the banker, the chief desperado, the chief gambler and the saloon-keeper occupied the same level in society." And "to be a saloon-keeper and kill a man was to be illustrious."

Clemens stressed the violence of this primitive frontier more than the sexual mores.* "The saloons were overburdened with custom; so were the police courts, the gambling dens, the broth-els, and the jails — unfailing signs of high prosperity in a mining region," while "vice flourished luxuriantly during the

---

* What is most curious for a writer so essentially autobiographical and con-fessional as Clemens is the absolute taboo he succeeded in throwing around his early sex life in this free frontier world. There are stories and rumors about his heavy drinking during this period, but despite all of Clemens' self-descriptions, and his obvious affinity for women, his pagan sense of pleasure and the flesh, and despite massive Twain scholarship, there is, as regards his sexual experiences or lack of them, a complete silence, and blank. Later on too, Clemens was very open about his physical affection for Livy, and there are certain strains of apparent sexual guilt, but this area remains highly secret, closed off.

heyday of our flush times." But here he was flat in tone and noncommittal.

Not so, however, about the Chinese inhabitants of Nevada and California whose cause like that of the Negroes Clemens espoused very early. Unlike the Indians, the Chinese were quiet, peaceable, tractable, industrious — and a great convenience to everybody, even to the worst class of white men. "For the Chinaman bears the most of their sins, suffering fines for their petty thefts, imprisonment for their robberies, and death for their murders. Any white man can swear a Chinaman's life away in the courts, but no Chinaman can testify against a white man. Ours is the 'land of the free' — nobody denies that — nobody challenges it. (Maybe it is because we won't let other people testify.) As I write, news comes that in broad daylight in San Francisco, some boys have stoned an inoffensive Chinaman to death, and that, although a large crowd witnessed the shameful deed, no one interfered."

Making a modest fortune out of the silver mines at last, it was to California that the narrator of *Roughing It* moved in order to enjoy his wealth, his ease, his luxury. "After the sagebrush and alkali deserts of Washoe, San Francisco was Paradise to me. I lived at the best hotel, exhibited my clothes in the most conspicuous places, infested the opera, and learned to seem enraptured with music which oftener afflicted my ignorant ear than enchanted it, if I had had the vulgar honesty to confess it . . . I had longed to be a butterfly, and I was one at last. I attended private parties in sumptuous evening dress, simpered and aired my graces like a born beau, and polka'd and schottisched with a step peculiar to myself — and the kangaroo."

All, that is, until the silver-mine bubble exploded; the stocks which Clemens held were not worth the paper they were printed on. He went to work again on a newspaper, but lost heart, faltered, had the symptoms of a nervous breakdown. He became adept at "slinking" and suddenly found himself (as a correspondent for the Sacramento *Union*) on the Sandwich Islands. Typical of *Roughing It* is the abrupt alternation of mood and place and theme; the travelogue's form was simply the form which Sam Clemens' younger life had taken. And if the trip on the western Overland ended up on an enchanted tropical isle, what mattered after the surprise of the changing scene was what Mark Twain wrote about it. Just as in Herman Melville's case, the South Sea Islands left a lasting imprint on Sam Clemens. The hardened chronicler of a frontier civilization, overcome again by his "vagabond instinct," was entranced by the Polynesian natives.

"In place of roughs and rowdies staring and blackguarding on the corners, I saw long-haired, saddle-colored Sandwich Island maidens sitting on the ground in the shade of corner houses . . . instead of wretched cobblestone pavements I walked on a firm foundation of coral . . . instead of cramped and crowded street-cars, I met dusky native women, sweeping by, free as the wind, on fleet horses and astride, with gaudy riding-sashes, streaming like banners behind them; instead of the combined stenches of Chinadom and Brannan Street slaughter-houses, I breathed the balmy fragrance of jasmine, oleander, and the Pride of India; in place of the hurry and bustle and noisy confusion of San Francisco, I moved in the midst of a summer calm as tranquil as dawn in the Garden of Eden . . ." These natives, said Clemens, were almost as dark as Negroes in the main; and there were "women with comely features, fine black eyes, rounded forms inclining to the voluptuous, clad in a single bright red or white garment that fell free and unconfined from shoulders to heel, long black hair falling loose, gypsy hats, encircled with wreaths of natural flowers of a brilliant carmine tint; plenty of dark men in various costumes and some with nothing on but a battered stove-pipe hat tilted on the nose, and a very scant breech-clout; certain smoke-dried children were clothed in nothing but sunshine — a very neat-fitting and picturesque apparel indeed.

"It was trance luxury," he said, "to sit in the perfumed air and forget that there was any world but these enchanted islands" — and here indeed all the sensuous, pagan, and edenic elements in both *Innocents* and *Roughing It* found a natural climax. Just like Melville too, Clemens had some doubts as to the virtue of the Christianity which had been conferred upon these ignorant savages. "How sad it is to think of the multitudes who have gone to their graves in this beautiful island and never knew there was a hell." In the dark ages of Hawaii, that is, "long, long before the missionaries braved a thousand privations to come and make them permanently miserable . . ." And to show the poor native "what rapture it is to work all day long for fifty cents to buy food for next day with, as compared with fishing for a pastime and lolling in the shade through eternal summer, and eating of the bounty that nobody labored to provide but Nature." Working hand in hand indeed, Christianity and civilization had all but finished off this handsome playful race with our ameliorating and purifying influence.

"But doubtless this purifying is not far off, when we reflect that contact with civilization and the whites has reduced the native population from *four hundred thousand* (Captain Cook's estimate) to fifty-five thousand in something over eighty years!" This was the real price of the white man's "triumph" in the South Seas and of Hawaii's acquisition of American statehood almost a hundred years after *Roughing It;* and to the line of American writers from Melville and Twain and Eugene O'Neill the benefits were dubious. The conclusion of the western travelogue recorded Twain's fascination with primitive Hawaiian culture; while *The Gilded Age* (1873), written with Charles Dudley Warner, was a different and puzzling work.

It will be better to divide this book up into its two volumes, and for all its renown, the first volume of *The Gilded Age* is poor as literature and disappointing as a historical document. (The second volume is a very different story.) As Clemens himself noted, according to Justin Kaplan's *Mr. Clemens and Mark Twain,* while he and Warner were working together in the supposition that they were writing one coherent yarn, they were in fact writing "two *in*coherent ones." Nor is it very difficult, from Clemens' records and from the internal evidence of *The Gilded Age,* to separate the work of these two different writers — if it is worth it. The pre-Civil War opening in the east Tennessee town of "Squire Hawkins" is a crude parody of Twain's western material in *Roughing It* as well as a curious prelude to the mythical boyhood in Hannibal. This barren landscape and "these groping dumb creatures" constitute another view of that romantic western frontier which Sam Clemens had described. (Was he in such ambiguous conflict?) But the poverty, want, ignorance, the village types, and the language are overdone and unconvincing; just as the family slave of the Hawkinses, Uncle Dan'l, is a typically "comic" view of the ignorant and superstitious "darkie."

This was the first attempt at fiction proper by Clemens, and it marks the early Twain at his poorest. The passages on the river steamboats, intimations of *Life on the Mississippi,* are a relief since they are also bearing us away from the opening scenes of the book; and we notice here the "eager hands" and "warm Southern hearts" of the chronicle. Writing what was an obviously satirical survey of the most corrupt period in the national history, Clemens and Warner were not averse to using some patriotic ploys. With the advent of "Colonel" Beriah Sellers — his plan for a monopoly of the wildcat banks and his "Infallible, Imperial Oriental Optic Liniment" among a series of other such grandiose schemes — we come to the famous central figure in *The Gilded Age*. But Sellers, symbol of the get-rich-quick spirit of the time, is also, to this critic, something of a bore. In what seems to be Warner's part of the novel, we get two eastern heroes, Philip Sterling and Henry Brierly, a Quaker heroine, Ruth Bolton, and her financier father; and there are times in the course of this confused and uneasy narrative when we may think that Warner is writing another story altogether which the Twain shall never meet — but hold on. With the advent of the "Salt Lick Pacific Extension," as another example of congressional corruption, both in respect to the Reconstruction era in the South and the development of the western frontier, *The Gilded Age* begins to take on focus and form, and even more, a historical content. In the narrative, Washington Hawkins (based on Sam's hapless brother, Orion) takes on a fictional prominence, while his sister Laura emerges as a hard, glossy, cunning financial and political operator. She is the curious princess of this whole group of scoundrels, rascals, quacks, and dupes who are all obsessed by the vision of sudden and fraudulent wealth. What is interesting in Laura's portrait is the frank sexuality which she uses to gain power over the men who will further her own self-interest. Here *The Gilded Age* has created an American heroine who is far different from the whole line of "innocent maidens" and "nice girls" and all those sweet, passive ladies fainting (when not having the vapors), who generally dominated the literary scene of the Victorian epoch in the United States.

At the beginning of this sexual career, Harry Brierly, Laura's first victim, is completely destroyed by her. (She is just practic-

ing.) "She excited his hopes and denied him, inflamed his
passion and restrained it, and wound him in her toils day by
day. To what purpose? It was a keen delight to Laura to prove
that she had power over men" — and to use that power for financial gain. In Washington, in Congress, this scheming, plotting, and manipulative heroine, in the age of virtuous and spot-
less literary ladies, finds a natural field for her sexual wiles
and her acquisitive instincts.*

She takes up her role in Senator Dilworthy's life and affairs
very much in the style of Dreiser's Jennie Gerhardt, if for different reasons. She is the link between the Senator (based on the
notorious Samuel Pomeroy) and Sellers in their scheme for a
Negro college on the unsalable Tennessee lands. Both Dilworthy and Sellers are concerned about the condition of the
emancipated race, although the Colonel has certain reservations. "You can't do much with 'em . . . They are a speculating race, sir, disinclined to work for white folks without security, planning how to live by only working for themselves.
Idle, sir, there's my garden just a ruin of weeds. Nothing practical in 'em . . . You educate the niggro and you make him
more speculating than he was before. If he won't stick to any
industry except for himself now, what will he do then? He
would only have a wider scope to injure himself. A niggro has
no grasp, sir. Now a white man can conceive great operations,
and carry them out; a niggro can't." But when the Senator ar-
gues for multiplying the Negro's chances for the hereafter, Sellers promptly agrees. "I'd elevate his soul — that's just it;

* It is amusing to compare Laura with the charming and innocent young American maidens of Henry James, virgins all, who are also "making their way" in
the circles of James' Washington aristocracy, since their unspeakable, unrecog-
nized bourgeois families were useful only for their financial support. As in
"Pandora," James was still writing these stories more than a decade after *The
Gilded Age.*

you can't make his soul too immortal, but I wouldn't touch *him,*
himself. Yes, sir! make his soul immortal, but don't disturb
the niggro as he is." And beneath the satire of Twain's description of the "speculating race" that wants to work only for itself lies the grim truth of the white man's version of true Negro
religion.

Beneath his own clownishness indeed, Sellers has no heart
of gold; this "comic" figure is often brutally cruel, and just as
corrupt, in his idiocy, as is the successful Senator Dilworthy.
Now the grand scheme for improving the navigation on the
Columbus River begins to bear fruit. "An appropriation was a
tangible thing, if you could get hold of it, and it made little
difference what it was appropriated for, so long as you got hold
of it." The physical panorama of Washington itself, the raw,
cheap, and ugly capital of this sordid socio-economic system,
and the account of Washington's daily political life are described in brilliant pages of satire. Harry and Sellers become
"rich" with their Columbus River Slackwater Navigation Company; the appropriations come out of Congress nicely; the visionary western town of Napoleon starts to boom with land lots
and a newspaper — until the actual money is held up in the
New York brokers' office. "Beautiful credit! The foundation of
modern society. Who shall say that this is not the golden age
of mutual trust, of unlimited reliance upon human promises?
That is a peculiar condition of society which enables a whole
nation to instantly recognize point and meaning in the familiar
newspaper anecdote, which puts into the mouth of a distin-
guished speculator in lands and mines this remark: 'I wasn't
worth a cent two years ago, and now I owe two millions of dollars.'" Like Dreiser's odes to gold in the Cowperwood novels,
and his descriptions of money behaving like a hysterical
woman, *The Gilded Age* is very sharp on the cash nexus of a
morally distraught society.

The two hundred thousand dollars appropriated by Congress is divided about equally between Congress itself and the New York bankers. Both Sellers and Harry Brierly are duped, while being assured that the first congressional appropriation is simply to pave the way for future appropriations. And again Clemens used his familiar pagan comparison. "We send missionaries to lift up the benighted races of other lands. How much cheaper and better it would be if those people could come here and drink of our civilization at its fountainhead." Thus, if *The Gilded Age* is an inferior literary work, it is still, in these sections of the novel, a rough, tough, honest, and ironical source book of crucial areas of the American life of its time, from the vicious political corruption in Washington to the dreary, sordid, depressing frontier boomtowns. It is an ugly picture of the manners and habits of a supposedly great nation and a fortunate people; it describes the Washington mud literally, financially, politically, socially. It is a hardbitten view of the American frontier and the development of the west, and of the Robber Baron epoch and the politicos whom Matthew Josephson described. It shows the political treatment of "the emancipated race" directly after the high moral crusade of Abolitionism. It is a sharp, clear, ironical picture of a rich and powerful continent, an energetic people, all duped and corrupted by an obviously false, greedy, and dishonest social system of finance and politics. And it is an almost impossible book, *The Gilded Age,* to evaluate by ordinary critical standards.

For this is hardly a novel at all in technical terms, and yet it is a unique chronicle in the national letters; and without it our literature would be immeasurably impoverished. Laura, too, her heart filled with Christian piety, is willing to sacrifice her "landed estates" to the spiritual uplifting of the downtrodden Negro; and here we have the description of the parvenu Washington aristocracy which now wielded the real power in the nation. "Great wealth gave a man a still higher and nobler place . . . than did official position. If this wealth had been acquired by conspicuous ingenuity with just a pleasant little spice of illegality about it, all the better. This aristocracy was 'fast,' and not averse to ostentation." *The Gilded Age* is not kindly to any of the three circles of aristocracy which it describes, and one notices that long before Veblen the key words here are "conspicuous" and "ostentation."

It is not impossible that Veblen garnered some of his observations about American society from this early and original source book. "The Hon. Higgins had not come to serve his country in Washington for nothing. The appropriation which he had engineered through Congress for the maintenance of the Indians in his territory would have made all those savages rich if it had ever got to them." And here Twain's hatred of the noble savage was equaled only by his savage ridicule of American civilization. The Washington profiles in the second volume of *The Gilded Age* are brilliant, and no punches are pulled. "Petroleum was the agent that had suddenly transformed the Gashlys from modest hard-working country village folk into 'loud' aristocrats and ornaments of the city . . . The Hon. Patrique Oreille was a wealthy Frenchman from Cork. Not that he was wealthy when he first came from Cork, but just the reverse." And there follows the description of a typical Irish contractor-politician who is a friend of New York's Boss "William M. Weed" of Tammany Hall.

Just as in Lincoln Steffens' *The Shame of the Cities,* there is a certain grudging admiration in *The Gilded Age*'s portraits of these colorful and corrupt figures. In Clemens, at least, there was nothing of the self-righteous moralist. Crime, as a principle, attracted him more than conformity. What a panorama of "democracy," of capitalism at its peak of primitive power is here, down to the Lardnerian dialogues among the wives of these fantastic crooks. *"Hon. Mrs. Higgins* — 'Is François's health good now, Mrs. Oreille?' *Mrs. O. (Thankful for the intervention)* — 'Not very. A body couldn't expect it. He was always delicate — especially his lungs — and this odious climate tells on him strong, now, after Parry, which is so mild.' " It comes as small surprise that "François" is the Oreilles' canine pet, while the authors added: "As impossible and exasperating as this conversation may sound to a person who is not an idiot, it is scarcely in any respect an exaggeration of one which one of us actually listened to in an American drawing room."

The note of hypocritical moral virtue on the part of all these political knaves expands proportionately as the financial corruption increases. In this "wearing, sordid, heartless game" of American democracy at work, a chronicle of political improbabilities is made entirely plausible — and factual. And already, barely beyond the bloody wound of the Civil War, there is the smell of a new empire. " 'Don't you think we want Cuba, Mr. Hawkins?' 'I think we want it bad . . . And Santo Domingo. Senator Dilworthy says we are bound to extend our religion over the isles of the sea. We've got to round out our territory.' "

The atmosphere in Washington is almost identical with that of the silver boom in *Roughing It* as Sellers reaches the peak of his prominence. "He was now at the center of the manufacture of gigantic schemes, of speculations of all sorts, of political and social gossip. The atmosphere was full of little and big rumors and of vast, undefined expectations. Everybody was in haste, too, to push on his private plan, and feverish in his haste, as if in constant apprehension that to-morrow would be Judgment Day." But when Laura reaches the height of her own career as a congressional lobbyist, promoter, intrigante, sexual tease, and even blackmailer, and when, still consumed by her jealous passion for Colonel Selby, she kills him, *The Gilded Age* expires on the same note of melodrama upon which it started; or rather, the slow, aimless, confused opening of the book is resolved by a far-fetched ending.

Realizing what a wealth of marvelous social satire still resides in the almost unreadable ending of *The Gilded Age,* we see finally that Clemens, at least, used the improbable romance as a kind of native surrealism upon which to drape the brilliance of his artistic vision. He has not the least concern with the credibility of his "plot" — to the point of often not even having, or simply reversing the plot. He has immense concern with the credibility of his moral and social commentary — just as the absurd "trial" of Laura for an absurd murder presents, in the end, a beautiful panorama of "justice" in the democracy. Poorly written, tedious to read, false and artificial in both human and literary terms as is much of *The Gilded Age,* it still discloses hidden veins of satire in retrospect. Our early annoyance at the literary quality of the novel is replaced by a growing admiration for a large part of the novel's content. This was Sam Clemens' natural literary "form," or lack of form very often, which one must understand and accept in order to grasp the secret of his greatness.

*Sketches Old and New,* in 1875, followed *The Gilded Age* and preceded *Tom Sawyer.* This was the volume from which earlier I quoted the Jumping Frog's metamorphosis into the French and then back again into the English language, and perhaps this tour de force was the headiest item in the collection of Clemens' newspaper sketches and essays. Casual, minor pieces — but in Mark Twain's writing the golden nuggets of humor appear in the unlikeliest places; it was a matter of inspiration rather than intent. There was the fable of the good little boy who got punished for all his virtues and the bad little boy who was rewarded for his sins; a parody of the Sunday school morality and the exhortatory juvenile fiction of Clemens' time. In the line of Josh Billings, Petroleum V. Nasby, and other American humorists who all worked for James Redpath's Lecture Bureau in Boston along with Twain, he helped to initiate these inverted western fables and perverse "fairy tales" which, as we noticed elsewhere, later on, George Ade and Ring Lardner would develop even further. In the early *Sketches,* even more clearly, Sam Clemens was out to break all the Victorian taboos of his period, while the main thrust of his satire was directed against American puritanism and the developing middle-class ethos of materialism, mediocrity, conformity.

Very early, Clemens was in direct revolt against the salient features of his own society. His answer to the Moral Statistician, written as early as 1865, was clear.

Money can't save your infinitesimal soul. All the use that money can be put to is to purchase comfort and enjoyment in this life; therefore, as you are an enemy to comfort and enjoyment, where is the use of accumulating cash? It won't do for you to say that you can use it to better purpose in furnishing a good table, and in charities, and in supporting tract societies, because you know yourself that you people who have no petty vices are never known to give away a cent, and that you stint yourselves so in the matter of food that you are always feeble and hungry. And you never dare to laugh in the daytime for fear some poor wretch, seeing you in a good humor, will try to borrow a dollar of you; and in church you are always down on your knees, with your eyes buried in the cushion, when the contribution-box comes around; and you never give the revenue officers a full statement of your income. Now you know all these things yourself, don't you? Very well, then, what is the use of your stringing out your miserable lives to a lean and withered old age?

Now wasn't this a sort of prose variation on Whitman's description of those who, "smartly attired, countenance smiling, form upright," had still suffered a spiritual death under the breastbone:

> Under the broadcloth and gloves, under the ribbons and artificial
>   flowers,
> Keeping fair with the customs, speaking not a syllable of itself,
> Speaking of anything else but never of itself.

Speaking never of Clemens' joy and pleasure in this life, or later, of Henry Miller's love and laughter, while inside of the respectable dresses and ornaments, "Inside of those wash'd and trimm'd faces, behold a secret silent loathing and despair." Yes, surely, no major American writer has had much sympathy for the walking skeletons of broadcloth puritanism or the subsequent middle-class materialism. Following this essay, there is Clemens' even more vehement attack on Ben Franklin's abstemious morality. (Here D. H. Lawrence trod directly in Clemens' footsteps, in his *Studies in Classic American Literature*.) "The subject of this memoir was of a vicious disposition, and early prostituted his talents to the invention of maxims and aphorisms calculated to inflict suffering upon the rising generation of all subsequent ages. His simplest acts, also, were contrived with a view of their being held up for the emulation of boys forever — boys who might otherwise have been happy . . . With a malevolence which is without parallel in history, he would work all day, and then sit up nights, and let on to be studying algebra by the light of a smoldering fire, so that all other boys might have to do that also."

In this pernicious biography of Franklin, Clemens said, "his maxims were full of animosity toward boys. Nowadays a boy cannot follow out a single natural instinct without tumbling over some of those everlasting aphorisms and hearing from Franklin on the spot . . . If he does a virtuous action, he never gets anything for it, because 'Virtue is its own reward.' And that boy is hounded to death and robbed of his natural rest because Franklin said once, in one of his inspired flights of malignity: 'Early to bed and early to rise/Makes a man healthy, wealthy, and wise.' As if it were any object to a boy to be healthy and wealthy and wise on such terms. The sorrow that that maxim has cost me, through my parents, experimenting on me with it, tongue cannot tell. The legitimate result is my present state of general debility, indigence, and mental aberration."

One notices how Clemens stressed Franklin's malignity and malevolence — strong words used not altogether comically — and here, of course, we are back to that state of childhood freedom from which Mark Twain viewed caustically all modes of morality and "education," not to mention the repressions of civilization itself. This was an early and clear view of the born rebel against the duress of whatever code threatened the fullest expression of the natural life; one who affirmed all the pleasures of "this life" against all the penny-pinching reservations and restrictions of the living dead on earth. This was another early revolt of the flesh in American letters; of the instincts and of the dominant pleasure principle without which there was no full existence; and these western "boys" of Sam Clemens sprang from this deep source exactly as did the marvelous outbursts of the "reversed" — that is to say, natural — humor of a pagan vision. Clemens was of course in the whole tradition of wild western journalism and irreverent native humorists, but in this tradition, how divinely original he was!

*Sketches New and Old* has many other sections of trivia; casual, hasty little familiar essays as that on raising poultry: "When you wish to raise a fine, large, donkey-voiced Shanghai rooster, you do it with a lasso, just as you would a bull." Or on the raising of children: "Love, it is notorious that pine is the least nutritious food that a child can eat." Or on ladies' fashions: "She wore a pink satin dress, plain in front but with a good deal of rake to it — to the train, I mean; it was said to be two or three yards long. One could see it creeping along the floor some little time after the woman was gone. Mrs. C. wore also a white bodice, cut bias, with Pompadour sleeves, flounced with ruches; low neck, with the inside handkerchief not visible, with white kid gloves. She had on a pearl necklace, which glinted lonely, high up the midst of that barren waste of neck and shoulders. Her hair was frizzled into a tangled chaparral, forward of her ears, aft it was drawn together, and compactly bound and plaited into a stump like a pony's tail, and furthermore was canted upward at a sharp angle, and ingeniously supported by a red velvet crupper, whose forward extremity was made fast with a half-hitch around a hairpin on the top of her head. Her whole top hamper was neat and becoming."

This was Clemens writing in heat again; this was a kind of verbal pyrotechnics dazzling out of Clemens at any point when the genie seized him — this was another example of native Dada in the mid-seventies. Somewhat as in the "Jumping Frog," there were examples here of Clemens' trick of starting an open sentence, and letting free association take over the direction and the subordinate clauses until the prose reached the complexity of, say, *The Golden Bowl*.

Distressing Accident — Last evening, about six o'clock, as Mr. William Schuyler, an old and respectable citizen of South Park, was leaving his residence to go downtown, as has been his usual custom for many years with the exception only of a short interval in the spring of 1850, during which he was confined to his bed by injuries received in attempting to stop a runaway horse by thoughtlessly placing himself directly in its wake and throwing up his hands and shouting, which if he had done so even a single moment sooner, must inevitably have frightened the animal still more instead of checking its speed, although disastrous enough to himself as it was, and rendered more melancholy and distressing by reason of the presence of his wife's mother, who was there and saw the sad occurrence notwithstanding it is at least likely, though not necessarily so, that she should be reconnoitering in another direction when the incident occurred, not being vivacious and on the lookout, as a general thing, but even the reverse, as her own mother is said to have stated, who is no more, but died in the full hope of a glorious resurrection, upwards of three years ago, aged eighty-six, being a Christian woman and without guile, as it were, or property, in consequence of the fire of 1849, which destroyed every single thing she had in the world . . .

In the *Sketches* there was also a strange, dark tale of a grave-yard whose inhabitants decide to move one night (an early sample of Clemens' mortuary humor), and the famous item called "A True Story." This was the story, told in the Negro dialect of the period, of a black "mammy" whose son, sold off in a slave auction, returns to her in a Negro regiment during the Civil War. But despite Clemens' sympathy for his heroine, who anticipates the Roxanna of *Pudd'nhead Wilson,* and despite much praise through the years for this touching picture of slavery, the story is sentimental and the cadences of the Negro dialect, despite Clemens' usually accurate ear, are stylized here and questionable. There were other pieces in *Sketches New and Old* that went back to Clemens' mining experience as well as his early journalism, and back to his own youth, which was the setting for the first epic of boyhood, *The Adventures of Tom Sawyer,* a year later, in 1876.

Whether this was a children's book for adults, as Clemens first believed, or for children, as it turned out at the time, and not too successfully either, it is certain that when Mark Twain went back to his memories of childhood the deepest preoccupations of his temperament emerged more clearly. If Twain traced his own ancestry to the Garden of Eden in fact, this was an edenic vision of frontier life in which the young hero was both an orphan and a devil. "He's full of the Old Scratch," says Aunt Polly, "but laws-a-me! he is my own dead sister's boy, poor thing, and I ain't got the heart to lash him, somehow." And if there was one thing in the world that Tom Sawyer hated more than anything else, it was *work*. In its underlying satire, this paradise of playtime was also a travesty not merely of American society but of civilization's basic values. It was an outwitting, through art, of the adult world which all "mature" adults could approve of, just as it praised freely the variations of childhood's gangsters, thieves and crooks in its antisocial revolt. In Tom's first battle with the new boy "in the little shabby village of St. Petersburg," Clemens showed up the mixture of cowardice, bluffing, verbal bombast, and chicanery which all the animals indulge in, and only man deplores. In this heavenly arena, too, there were happy slaves and a racial intermingling.*

In the opening scene of the novel, the whitewashing of the fence, Tom remembers the company of children at the town pump. "White, mulatto, and Negro boys and girls were always there waiting their turns, resting, trading playthings, quarreling, fighting, skylarking . . ." And we are told that Work consists of whatever a body is *obliged* to do, and Play consists of whatever a body is not obliged to do. While Ben, forsaking

---

* Since the English critic, F. R. Leavis, uses the word "nigger" with almost obscene pleasure in his absurd introduction to *Pudd'nhead Wilson*, it is interesting to note that the first mention in *Tom Sawyer* is of "Negro boys and girls." The point here is that Clemens himself, with a few rare exceptions, used "Negro" this early when speaking in his own voice, and "nigger" when it is used as the common usage of the period. Both Mr. Leavis and the NAACP, for different reasons, do not seem to grasp this distinction.

his "Mississippi steamboat," takes over the coveted job of whitewashing, Tom, the "retired artist," sits in the shade, dangles his legs, munches his apple, and plans "the slaughter of more innocents." By the middle of the afternoon, Tom, a poverty-stricken boy in the morning, is literally "rolling in wealth" — having been given a kite in good repair, a dead rat on a string, twelve marbles, part of a jew's-harp, a piece of blue bottle-glass, a spool cannon, a key that wouldn't unlock anything, a tin soldier, a couple of tadpoles, six firecrackers, a kitten with only one eye . . . Just as Tom's infantine wickedness is cast in the comic mode, so is the parody of the "acquisitive society," or of capitalism's spurious wealth gained by such devilish manipulation and double-talk on the part of the novel's hero.

Tom Sawyer is certainly a boyhood entrepreneur of the highest order, and carries over his trickery (and vanity) into the field of adolescent love affairs. But the emotions of real love are centered in the relationship between him and Aunt Polly. And what is curious is the intensity and the *flow* of such affection under the mask of orphanhood and half-brothers (the suffering Sid of the novel) and mother surrogates and missing (dead) fathers. All of Tom's ostentatious moods of guilt, martyrdom, suffering, remorse are designed to attract Aunt Polly's eye and to solicit her attention; here the cunning mockery of love leads into the genuine article. In terms of Aunt Polly's "punishments" too, and of the harsh moral and religious tradition of the frontier, one is reminded of those cannibalistic savages in Melville's *Typee* who worshiped their savage deities — and beat them up when they were angry at them. The chapter on Sunday school is hilarious in *Tom Sawyer*. There is the boy of German parentage (Twain is careful not to say "German boy") who once recited three thousand verses from the Bible without stopping, "but the strain upon his mental faculties was too great, and he was little better than an idiot from that day forth."

What is apparent in the blissful atmosphere of frontier boyhood in *Tom Sawyer* is that the sense of evil is comic too. The "diabolism" of the hero, however deep this strain ran in Sam Clemens himself, and despite what might come of it later, is itself a form of playful parody; and life is basically innocent and loving.* If *Tom Sawyer* is, on one level, a parody of an adult society of power and manipulation, of property and place, of trading and acquisition — the parody itself is divine, is innocent, is wistful and comic. (That is the real secret of the book's lasting appeal.) Beneath all the humor is the deeper rhythm of Sam Clemens' affinity with animal life and a natural sense of pleasure. Monday mornings always found Tom Sawyer miserable "because it began another week's slow suffering in school," and school, like church, is human nature in fetters, in the prison of civilization. Just here we have the advent of Huckleberry Finn, son of the town drunkard, even more idle, lawless, vulgar; and culture hero that he is to all the "respectable children" who are envious of his gaudy outcast condition.

"Huckleberry came and went, at his own free will. He slept on doorsteps in fine weather and in empty hogsheads in wet; he did not have to go to school or to church, or call any being master or obey anybody; he could go fishing or swimming when and where he chose, and stay as long as it suited him; nobody

* In view of so much stress in contemporary thought (in a period of social and historical reaction) on the evil sources of life, or on evil itself as the life force, it is important to note this. And the related fact that — despite so much personal tragedy later on, and so much criticism which stressed this tragedy, and the "failure" or "frustration" of Twain's life and career — this edenic strain remained constant in Mark Twain's temperament to the end. Compare, for example, the amoral children of Richard Hughes' *The Innocent Voyage* or the evil ones in William Golding's *Lord of the Flies.*

forbade him to fight; he could sit up as late as he pleased; he was always the first boy that went barefoot in the spring and the last to resume leather in the fall; he never had to wash, nor put on clean clothes; he could swear wonderfully. In a word, everything that goes to make life precious that boy had. So thought every harassed, hampered, respectable boy in St. Petersburg . . . Tom hailed the romantic outcast." Thus, in this boyhood idyll of freedom from civilization in a frontier town, we come finally to the symbol of absolute freedom. In this radically democratic antisocial chronicle of youth, we have at the climax the outcast hero who is the antithesis of all ethical, moral, social, worldly, or financial patterns of "maturity," of human "betterment" or success. Even in the comic mode of childhood.

It is from the ignorant Huck also that we get the dominant use of "nigger" in this story, as though already in the reaches of his unconscious Clemens was evolving his parable of Huck's education. Through Huck also we get the sense of that darker stream of Negro superstitiousness, of African witchcraft, of voo-doo charms and cures and curses which runs, like a sub-merged Mississippi current, through the pages of *Tom Sawyer*. (I mean the worship of that ancient and primitive "White God-dess" of fertility and sexuality, in short, who is here quite ob-viously a Black Goddess.) Does this classical work of child-hood also hinge upon a ridiculous melodrama: the murder of Dr. Robinson by Injun Joe, who blames the murder on his partner in crime, Muff Potter? We realize again that Clem-ens was supremely careless about the plot structure of his narratives — or supremely confident that any improvised, twisted, shaky narrative structure could be used to convey his own vision of experience . . . and that what counted was not the improbable structure of his tale but what he could do with it. The episodes of calf love between Tom and Becky Thatcher take up more space in the story, too, than they are worth, and Clemens was slightly uneasy in this area of emotions.* And the subplot of the boys escaping to the island, while the whole town and their parents and relatives believe they are dead and prepare a mock funeral, has a sadistic undertone which the comedy of the trick barely obscures.

But then there is the description of the first raft scene in these frontier idylls. Clemens' evocation of the womb theme, or of the (lost!) plenary state of man, or of that childhood garden of innocence which is man's deepest myth, is done so naturally, surely, accurately. There is the water fighting of the naked boys, not altogether in accordance with the Victorian proprieties, and the sumptuous island breakfasts of fish and bacon while these social exiles loaf and contemplate their souls. There are the brilliant passages on frontier education and the "moral and religious mind" (partly reminiscent of Edward Eggleston's *The Hoosier Schoolmaster*, published some five years earlier). There are those pages in *Tom Sawyer* where Clemens indulged himself with some of his satire on school compositions, schoolchildren, and schoolmasters — and on provincial poetry:

> And cold must be mine eyes, and heart, and tete,
> When, dear Alabama! they turn cold on thee!

In these Twainish notes from an older world, recalling the vanished democracy of the raw western towns in the mid-

---

* It was William Dean Howells who made Clemens tone down the scene of Becky's discovering the schoolteacher's hidden book of anatomy and coming across "a handsomely engraved and colored frontispiece — a human figure, stark naked" which she Freudianly rips while trying to hide the book from Tom Sawyer.

nineteenth century, before the Civil War and before the establishment of the great American fortunes which changed the
whole texture of American life, we realize that the poor, the
idle, the vagrants are much more prominent in a village life
which has not yet been altogether converted to the rationale of
work, social respectability, and material success. The boys
pay a visit to the innocent Muff Potter at the town jail, where
he is lodged without guards, to bring him tobacco and matches.
And indeed, as in his attack on Ben Franklin in *Sketches New
and Old,* Clemens makes this point very specifically. "Huck
was willing. Huck was always willing to take a hand in any
enterprise that offered entertainment and required no capital,
for he had troublesome superabundance of that sort of time
which is *not* money." You might say that Clemens was the
spokesman for that central line of American writers who were
at variance from the outset with the materialistic hypocrisy of
Franklin.

The end of this childhood classic revolves upon the melodrama of the nightmare vigil of Tom and Becky lost in the island
cave — and the "happy ending" of Tom and Huck dividing up
the cash loot of twelve thousand dollars which they have discovered in the cave. A happy ending of easy money which is
apparently the complete antithesis of the central vision of *Tom
Sawyer,* until we realize that Mark Twain was just as adroit as
Henry James, say, in the use of literary decoys. For Huck was
now rich, and being "educated" into civilized ways by the
Widow Douglas.

"He had to go to church; he had to talk so properly
that speech was become insipid in his mouth; whither-
soever he turned, the bars and shackles of civilization shut him
in and bound him hand and foot." And he can't stand the
process and throws it all over. "Don't talk about it, Tom. I've

tried it, and it don't work, it don't work, Tom. It ain't for me; I ain't used to it. The widder's good to me, and friendly; but I can't stand them ways . . . Tom, I wouldn't ever got into all this trouble if it hadn't 'a' been for that money; now you just take my sheer of it along with your'n, and gimme a ten-center sometimes — not many times, becuz I don't give a dern for a thing 'thout it's tollable hard to git — and you go and beg off for me with the widder." Or at least Huck wants to throw it all over, since the novel ends on an ambiguous note, just as Clemens does later on in another childhood romance.

In the western speech rhythms of *Tom Sawyer,* we may notice that apparently casual, and yet very skillful use of repetition, and repetition with variation, which Twain brought into our national literary style, which later on, Sherwood Anderson, among others, would cultivate, and which Ernest Hemingway refined into a kind of fixed perfection that was almost too perfect, too fixed. Meanwhile, shortly after *Tom Sawyer* and while working on another children's tale, *The Prince and the Pauper,* and reading the diary of Samuel Pepys, Clemens tossed off a celebrated tour de force called *1601: or Conversation as It Was by the Social Fireside in the Time of the Tudors.* A few copies of this were privately printed in 1880, and reprinted in 1882, and then reprinted ever since. This pamphlet, hardly so much pornography as erotica, showed a remarkable virtuosity in Clemens' use of an earlier, franker English language; and, despite a stress on anal-erotic as well as genital humor, it is an entertaining satire.

Howells had already commented on Clemens' "Elizabethan breadth of parlance" in those letters which he could not bear to burn, yet, after the first reading, could not bear to look at again. The script of *1601* was written to Clemens' other close friend, the robust divine, Joseph Twichell of Hartford.

It was an afternoon's entertainment for Clemens; it was a private protest against Victorian censorship, as he said. At any rate Elizabeth the Queen, Ben Jonson, Lady Helen, Walter Raleigh, Lord Bacon, and "Shaxpur" — and "ye child Francis Beaumonte" and "ye Duchess of Bilgewater" among other court ladies — are the principal figures in this social conversation, and there was an opening reference to Twain's own epoch.

"Then spake ye damned windmill, Sir Walter, of a people in ye uttermost parts of America, ye copulate not until they be five and thirty yeres of age, ye women being eight and twenty, and do it then but once in seven years." While the little pamphlet was centered around the inciting of young or precocious sexuality, as the Queen verbally seduces the child Beaumonte — "With such a tongue as thine, lad, thou'lt spread the ivory thighs of many a willing maid in thy good time, an thy codpiece be as handy as thy speeche" — Clemens could not forbear a literary thrust at "that poor ass, Lille himself." He had little in common with the Euphuists of an older time or his own. And one notes the beautiful rhythmics, reminiscent of John Donne's love poetry, in the last line of *1601* which, like Howells, I cannot bear to ignore, yet cannot quite bring myself to quote here.

In our own period it hardly needed the Kinsey laboratory or a Steven Marcus, or a bulky and tedious "masterpiece" like *My Secret Life,* privately printed for a century, and first published in 1967, to remind us not only of *The Other Victorians* but that the great Victorians had other selves, since they were after all barely removed from the early nineteenth century verve for life. Yet *1601* does raise some interesting questions about the private and public personalities of Samuel Clemens that we will keep in mind. In 1877, "A True Story" was the Negro mammy tale reprinted as a separate item from *Sketches New and Old;* and *Punch, Brothers, Punch,* in 1878, contained some jingle verses which achieved popularity at the time. But the *True Story* volume contained a more interesting tale of Twain's which was called "The Recent Carnival of Crime."

Reprinted in Twain's collected works as "The Facts Concerning the Recent Carnival of Crime in Connecticut," this story was actually the prelude to a dark line of surrealistic parables which would include *Pudd'nhead Wilson,* "The Man That Corrupted Hadleyburg," and *The Mysterious Stranger,* in a different and more complex vein of Clemens' talent. Here we meet "the shriveled, shabby dwarf" who is about forty years old and no more than two feet high — this little person who is a deformity as a whole, "a vague, general, evenly blended, nicely adjusted deformity." And yet, "this vile bit of human rubbish seemed to bear a sort of remote and ill-defined resemblance to me!" He knows everything that goes on in the narrator's (Clemens') mind and spirit; he knows all his lies, vices, and sins, his arrogance, dishonesty, faithlessness, disloyalty, fits of violent anger, remorse. Clemens paints a very low view of himself here, and it is recognizable, until the narrator suddenly accuses his tormentor of being the devil, of being Satan himself. In this dubious shifting light, Clemens stresses his lifelong affinity with the fallen angel. But the odious and moldy dwarf turns out to be not the devil or Satan at all, but Twain's *conscience.*

And while the autobiographical narrator of the story is being roundly abused by his Conscience, he in turn abuses his Conscience and is intent upon capturing and killing the malignant dwarf. "Dwarf," as the dwarf explains, because while originally he started out precisely as tall as Clemens, his being neglected and abused through the years has steadily reduced his stature and power.

What abuse and self-abuse abounds in this curious parable; what violence of language in Clemens' charges and counter-charges. "My good slave, you are curiously witless — no, I mean characteristically so. In truth, you are always consistent, always yourself, always an ass," says Clemens' Conscience to Clemens, addressing him in his own "s-n-i-v-e-l-i-n-g d-r-a-w-l — baby!" while the outraged victim of this impudence is plotting the sudden demise of the insolent demon. "If I only had you shrunk down to a homeopathic pill, and could get my hands on you, would I put you in a glass case for a keepsake? No, sir. I would give you to a yellow dog! That is where *you* ought to be . . ." Now was the "aunt" of this story — always reproaching the Clemens narrator for his smoking, among other vices, rather like the Aunt Polly of *Tom Sawyer* — a mother surrogate or a wife surrogate? It is her intrusion, at any rate, which allows the dualistic and divided hero to achieve his deadly purpose. "My breath was coming in short, quick gasps now, and my excitement was almost uncontrollable. My aunt cried out: 'Oh, do not look so! You appal me! Oh, what can the matter be? What is it you see? Why do you stare so? Why do you work your fingers like that?'" While the aunt pleads hysterically with the hero to drop the vices which lead to such fits, Clemens' Conscience "began to reel drowsily and grope with his hands — enchanting spectacle!" and droops languidly to the floor "blinking toward me a last supplication for mercy, with heavy eyes," when

With an exultant shout I sprang past my aunt, and in an instant I had my lifelong foe by the throat. After so many years of waiting and longing, he was mine at last. I tore him to shreds and fragments. I rent the fragments into bits. I cast the bleeding rubbish into the fire, and drew into my nostrils the grateful incense of my burnt-offering. At last, and forever, my Conscience was dead!

This was the history of the narrator's "freedom" in "The Recent Carnival of Crime," as his aunt, with all her charities and mercies, flies from him in terror; and in "bliss, unalloyed bliss" he embarks upon a criminal career.

Now in orthodox Freudian terms this story is just what it sounds like, and orthodox Freudians can shake their heads sadly and commiserate ad nauseam over poor Sam Clemens' burden of sin and guilt. In Rankian cultural terms, however, what this story marks (as Clemens must have felt and known in his depths) is the hero's *liberation* from the repressive burden of civilizational discontents, his defiance of conventional morality, his determination to be himself at all costs (every artist's design) — and hence, the "bliss, unalloyed bliss," of Clemens' natural spirit, and the carnival of crime which is the organism's realization it is enjoying itself despite the dictates of society. — A kind of vestigial guilt, yes, which is laughing at itself. This curious parable, so much harped upon by conventional depth psychology, proves to be the exact opposite, or the true rationale of art and the artist. This was Sam Clemens exorcising his Puritan past.

And why not? Clemens was riding high in those days. And yet the mixed tone of the fable, and the curious confusion of Satan, who is the obvious symbol of pagan life, with his own conscience, rather than, as elsewhere, with his true temperament, indicated certain strains in Eden.

With the popular success of *The Innocents Abroad* and *Roughing It* — his first two books selling one hundred thousand copies each — Mark Twain became something of a phenomenon in American literature. In its purely worldly aspects, his career surpassed anything before it, and probably almost everything after it. His royalties were immense; his lecture tours and magazine articles brought in a large income besides — and he had

married an heiress. Their first house in Buffalo was presented
to them by Livy's father as a wedding gift; it included the cook
Ellen and the Irish coachman, Patrick McAleer, who became
their lifelong servant and Clemens' confidant. Even more successful in the middle of the seventies, the Clemenses planned
and built the great mansion in Hartford, adding a corps of new
domestics, and living in the grand style of millionaires — all of
which Clemens, so desperately poor, searching, unknown, a
working-class ruffian of sorts just a few years before, accepted
with the equanimity of genius.

Yet Hartford life was exhausting to them both; the early years
of their marriage were full of tension. There was the steady
presence of house guests, the parties and lunches and dinners,
all the elaborate trappings of wealth, and the large expenses.
They lost their first son, Langdon, named after Livy's father
(who had died shortly after their marriage), at the age of two,
and Clemens blamed himself for this death. Susy and Clara were
delicate children physically and precocious in spirit; Livy drove
herself into a series of physical and nervous ailments. The
European trip of the seventies was in reality a flight from their
grandiose American existence in a home they loved and a
social sphere they hated. Clemens was also worried about
money; toward the decade's end the sales of his books had de-
creased sharply. The Hartford mansion would become a monster to him; and the beginning of his career, so grand, so magnificent, so fortunate, had already changed sharply for the
worse in what was to be a lifelong pattern of ups and downs.

He was exhausted and depressed by a decade of glory and
feasting, and he hoped to find both solitude and freedom to work
in Europe — the peace of death as he said. But, struggling
with the manuscript of *A Tramp Abroad* in Heidelberg, Mu-
nich, and Paris, after having invited Twichell to join him on

his tour, after having "lost" one of the notebooks for his manuscript and then, unhappily, discovering it again, Clemens found
little zest either in his tramping abroad or in writing the book
itself. Although this was another travel book, returning to the
first success of *The Innocents Abroad,* Clemens' mood was dark.
"I *hate* travel, and I *hate* hotels, and I *hate* the opera, and I
*hate* the old masters," he wrote to Howells from Italy, as recorded by his first biographer, Albert Bigelow Paine. "In
truth I don't ever seem to be in a good enough humor with
anything to satirize it. No, I want to stand up before it and
curse it and foam at the mouth, or take a club and pound it to
rags and pulp. I have got in two or three chapters about Wagner's operas, and managed to do it without showing temper,
but the strain of another such effort would burst me."

Even this outrage and anger was not evident in the sluggish
prose of *A Tramp Abroad,* in 1880, while Howells himself was
just then publishing a dreadful novel called *The Lady of the
Aroostook,* which Clemens dutifully praised. (It was on the
same trip abroad, in London, just before returning home, that
Mrs. Clemens had her chat with Henry James; while Clemens
mentioned only his visit with the great Darwin.) In the travel
book itself there was, to be sure, the western tall tale of Jim
Baker's bluejays, another brilliant animistic legend. But this
piece of "padding" had little to do with Twain's torpid descriptions of student life in Heidelberg, say, and the dueling clubs of
the young German officers whom he found so gently bred and
kindly natured. There are still good lines, of course. "One
day we took the train and went down to Mannheim to see
'King Lear' played in German. It was a mistake." And there
is a section of hilarious farce on *Lohengrin* and the other Wag-
nerian operas.

There is a comic episode of Clemens' insomnia; there are his

brilliant drawings, and his reflections, always funny, on the
German language: "I can *understand* German as well as the
maniac that invented it, but I *talk* it best through an inter-
preter." There is a parody of the Lorelei legend as "translated"
by Twain from the German:

> I believe the turbulent waves
>   Swallow at last skipper and boat;
> She with her singing craves
>   All to visit her magic moat.

But still these are the exceptions to the prevailing sense of te-
diousness in *A Tramp Abroad*. It was one of the two Mark
Twain books not reprinted by the year 1970, and this publishing verdict was probably sound.

Yet even as I say this I come across another comic passage
on Baden-Baden, and let us record at least some other good
things in this generally subdued book. As art critic, Clemens
was hilarious about Turner's *Slave Ship,* in his "vulgar" western lowbrow mask. What a red rag is to a bull, said he, Turner's
painting was to him before he studied art. "Mr. Ruskin is educated in art up to a point where that picture throws him into as
mad an ecstasy of pleasure as it used to throw me into one of
rage last year, when I was ignorant. His cultivation enables
him — and me, now — to see water in that glaring yellow
mud, and natural effects in those lurid explosions of mixed
smoke and flame, and crimson sunset glories; it reconciles him
— and me, now — to the floating of iron cable-chains and
other unfloatable things; it reconciles us to fishes swimming
around on top of the mud — I mean of the water. The most
of the picture is a manifest impossibility — that is to say, a lie;
and only rigid cultivation can enable a man to find truth in a
lie. But it enables Mr. Ruskin to do it, and it has enabled me

to do it, and I am thankful for it. A Boston newspaper reporter went and took a look at the Slave Ship floundering about
in that fierce conflagration of reds and yellows, and said it reminded him of a tortoise-shell cat having a fit in a platter of
tomatoes. In my then uneducated state, that went home to my
non-cultivation, and I thought here is a man with an unobstructed eye. Mr. Ruskin would have said: This person is an
ass. That is what I would say, now."

It was the "unobstructed eye" which Clemens brought to so
many shams of life beyond those of European travel and the
fashionable taste of the time. This remarkable writer looked at
everything with the candid, unblinking and clear gaze of the
"innocent." Even though he may have sometimes clowned up
the frontier spirit, though he was full of notions and obsessions
which he did not try to hide, the source of everything good in
Mark Twain lies in this transparently honest, open, and full
human vision, so rare, even in art, as to be priceless. And what
is interesting in the development of *A Tramp Abroad* itself, is
that the second volume, as Clemens overcame his initial resistance to the writing of the book, is so much better than the
first. As in the case of *The Gilded Age,* the mediocre esthetic
entity is saved by the brilliance of the parts. If *A Tramp Abroad*
is a poor narrative, it still contains some of the best items of
classical Clemens humor, nonsense and Dada; and it reminds
us that very rarely can a Mark Twain book be wholly written
off. Take the example of the clothing of the Swiss waitresses.
(Though this was a familiar gambit of Twain's comedy.)

"The table d'hote was served by waitresses dressed in the
quaint and comely costume of the Swiss peasants. This consists of a simple gros de laine, trimmed with ashes of roses, with
overskirt of sacre bleu ventre saint gris, cut bias on the off-side,
with facings of petit polonaise and narrow insertions of pâté de

foie gras backstitched to the mise en scène in the form of a jeu
d'esprit. It gives to the wearer a singularly piquant and al-
luring aspect . . ." One of these waitresses, a woman of forty,
"had side-whiskers reaching half-way down her jaw," but
nevertheless Clemens is one of the few American writers with
an eye for women's clothes (and for women). And there is the
later episode when the hotel laundry returns the wrong under-
clothing. "I did not get back the same drawers I sent down,
when our things came up at six-fifteen. They were merely a pair
of white ruffle-cuffed absurdities, hitched together at the top
with a narrow band, and they did not come quite down to my
knees. They were pretty enough, but they made me feel like
two people, and disconnected at that. The man must have
been an idiot that got himself up like that to rough it in the
Swiss mountains."

He was almost savage about a young American maiden
(and her young American boy) whom he encountered on this
trip; just as he was the only writer of his time to question the
cultural dominance of the innocent virgin, which Howells
grumbled at but accepted; which led to the fatal flaw in
all the Henry Jamesian ladies. (Though he appeared to
relent about the American youth by saying that you could not
keep a grudge against a vacuum.) In Venice, Clemens found he
had more pleasure in contemplating the Old Masters than on his
previous trips. "But still it was a calm pleasure; there was nothing overheated about it." And yet, describing Tintoretto's three-
acre picture in the Doge's palace, he could write:

> The movement of this great work is very fine. There are ten
> thousand figures, and they are all doing something. There is a
> wonderful "go" to the whole composition. Some of the figures are
> diving headlong downward, with clasped hands, other are swim-
> ming through the cloud-shoals — some on their faces, some on

their backs — great processions of bishops, martyrs, and angels are pouring swiftly centerward from various outlying directions — everywhere is enthusiastic joy, there is rushing movement everywhere. There are fifteen or twenty figures scattered here and there, with books, but they cannot keep their attention on their reading — they offer the books to others, but no one wishes to read, now. The Lion of St. Mark is there with his book; St. Mark is there with his pen uplifted; he and the Lion are looking each other earnestly in the face, disputing about the way to spell a word — the Lion looks up in rapt admiration while St. Mark spells . . .

When it came to painting he liked, this so-called frontier ignoramus was writing art criticism of a high order. He came also to feel pleasure in the completely perfect and soothing ugliness of Saint Mark's Cathedral. Too many famous buildings were comprised of both ugliness and beauty, Clemens said, and left you confused and uneasy. "But one is calm before St. Mark's; one is calm within it, one would be calm on top of it, calm in the cellars; for its details are masterfully ugly, no misplaced and impertinent beauties are intruded anywhere; and the consequent result is a grand harmonious whole of soothing, entrancing, tranquilizing, soul-satisfying ugliness. One's admiration of a perfect thing always grows, never declines; and this is the surest evidence to him that it *is* perfect. St. Mark's is perfect. To me it soon grew to be so nobly, so augustly ugly, that it was difficult to stay away from it, even for a little while. Every time its squat domes disappeared from my view, I had a despondent feeling; when they reappeared, I felt an honest rapture — I have not known any happier hours than those I daily spent in front of Florian's, looking across the Great Square at it. Propped on its long row of low thick-legged columns, its back knobbed with domes, it seemed like a vast warty bug taking a meditative walk."

For prose passages like this, the whole ordeal of reading the central narrative of *A Tramp Abroad* is justified; and indeed one must read the book just to discover passages like this. But then there are those sections, also on Italian art, which reveal such curious ambiguities in this "Puritan in Paradise." Twain noticed with indignation the advent of the fig leaf on ancient statuary. "It makes a body ooze sarcasm at every pore, to go about Rome and Florence and see what this last generation has been doing with the statues. These works, which had stood in innocent nakedness for ages, are all fig-leaved now. Yes, every one of them. Nobody noticed their nakedness before, perhaps; nobody can help noticing it now, the fig-leaf makes it so conspicuous. But the comical thing about it all, is that the fig-leaf is confined to cold and pallid marble, which would be still cold and unsuggestive without this sham and ostentatious symbol of modesty, whereas warm-blooded paintings which do really need it have in no case been furnished with it." There was an odd turning in Clemens' thoughts within a single passage here; a curious sensitivity to the nature of the medium. And of these "warm-blooded paintings" which could use a touch of censorship, there was no doubt that Titian's Venus was among the worst (or best?).

"At the door of the Uffizzi, in Florence, one is confronted by statues of a man and a woman, noseless, battered, black with accumulated grime — they hardly suggest human beings — yet these ridiculous creatures have been thoughtfully and conscientiously fig-leaved by this fastidious generation. You enter and proceed to the most-visited little gallery that exists in the world — the Tribune — and there, against the wall, without obstructing rag or leaf, you may look your fill upon the foulest, the vilest, the obscenest picture the world possesses — Titian's Venus. It isn't that she is naked and stretched out on a bed —

no, it is the attitude of one of her arms and hand. If I ventured
to describe that attitude, there would be a fine howl — but there
the Venus lies, for anybody to gloat over that wants to — and
there she has a right to lie, for she is a work of art, and Art
has its privileges. I saw young girls stealing furtive glances at
her; I saw young men gaze long and absorbedly at her; I saw
aged, infirm men hang upon her charms with a pathetic interest. How I should like to describe her — just to see what a holy
indignation I could stir up in the world — just to hear the
unreflecting average man deliver himself about my grossness
and coarseness, and all that . . ."

Clemens continued these animadversions on "Titian's beast,"
just as he had already pointed out that Fielding and Smollett
"could portray the beastliness of their day in the beastliest language," when compared with modern propriety. "Art retains
her privileges, Literature has lost hers." But what was the meaning of all this hocus-pocus where Clemens was (apparently)
wavering between censorship and obscenity, between pleasure
and puritanism? Was it put on, with a straight face, for the edi-
fication of his audience, or did it reflect the contradictions in his
own temperament? Was he honestly shocked by Titian's Venus
or secretly enjoying it; defending or attacking the principle of
censorship and fig-leafing? Was his writing, marked at the outset with such frankness and openness about so many Victorian
taboos, already coming under the prudish sway of his period; or
did these passages reflect deeper contradictions in Clemens'
own temperament? Or was he "putting on" the whole show of
mock-virtue? Written so directly after *1601,* moreover, these
sections of *A Tramp Abroad* create a curious impression of ambiguity — or of suppressed irony. And these later sections of
the book conclude with the first of Clemens' descriptions of "The
Awful German Language." There is, for example, the paren-

thesis disease and the separable verb. "The trunks being now ready, he DE —— after kissing his mother and sisters, and once more pressing to his bosom his adored Gretchen, who, dressed in simple white muslin, with a single tuberose in the ample folds of her rich brown hair, had tottered feebly down the stairs, still pale from the terror and excitement of the past evening, but longing to lay her poor aching head yet once again upon the breast of him whom she loved more dearly than life itself, PARTED."

There are the different declensions and cases in the German language. "For instance, if one is casually referring to a house, *Haus,* or a horse, *Pferd,* or a dog, *Hund,* he spells these words as I have indicated; but if he is referring to them in the Dative case, he sticks on a foolish and unnecessary *e* and spells them *Hause, Pferde, Hunde.* So, as an added *e* often signifies the plural, as the *s* does with us, the new student is likely to go on for a month making twins out of a Dative dog before he discovers his mistake; and on the other hand, many a new student who could ill afford loss, has bought and paid for two dogs and only got one of them, because he ignorantly bought that dog in the Dative singular when he really supposed he was talking plural — which left the law on the seller's side, of course, by the strict rules of grammar, and therefore a suit for recovery could not lie."

This was grammar as never before taught on land and sea; and what a student of languages was this maker of the plainest and homeliest native American prose. In the closing pages of *A Tramp Abroad,* in the "Appendix" in which Clemens poured such handsome "asides," there followed the "reduction" from German into English of the fable called "Tale of the Fishwife and its Sad Fate." "It is a bleak Day. Hear the Rain, how he pours, and the Hail, how he rattles; and see the Snow, how he drifts along, and oh the Mud, how deep he is! Ah the poor Fishwife, it is stuck fast in the Mire . . ." (He was capitalizing the nouns, Clemens added, in the German and ancient English fashion.) "It has dropped its Basket of Fishes; and its Hands have been cut by the Scales as it seized some of the falling Creatures; and one Scale has even got into its Eye, and it cannot get her out. It opens its Mouth to cry for Help; but if any Sound comes out of him, alas he is drowned by the raging of the Storm. And now a Tomcat has got one of the Fishes and she will surely escape with him. No, she bites off a Fin, she holds her in her Mouth — will she swallow her? No, the Fishwife's brave Mother-dog deserts his Puppies and rescues the Fin — which he eats, himself, as his Reward. O, horror, the Lightning has struck the Fish-basket; he sets him on Fire; see the Flame, how he licks the doomed Utensil with her red and angry Tongue; she attacks the Fishwife's Leg and destroys *it;* she attacks its Hand and destroys *her;* she attacks its poor worn Garment and destroys *her* also; she attacks its Body and consumes *him;* she wreathes herself about its Heart and *it* is consumed; next about its Breast, and in a Moment *she* is a Cinder; now she reaches its Neck — *he* goes; now its Chin — *it* goes; now its Nose — *she* goes . . ."

In this discourse on the shifting sexuality of the German language, Clemens also caught all the latent sadism of a whole tradition of German "fairy tales" for children. And so we see it is almost impossible to ignore any book of Mark Twain's without the risk of missing some remarkable prose episodes. Yes, the decade of the seventies foreshadowed the alternation of Sam Clemens' life between peaks of splendor and depths of despair, failure, and frustration — financial, domestic, personal. But he loved two things: his wife Livy and their home life, and his own literary work. Beneath all his comic poses he knew deep in his heart he was destined to be a great writer. Life would betray him as it betrays all things except death; but his art, his writing, would sustain him to the last. He would survive; he would survive and flourish and throw off his splendor until the end of his days.

# THREE

# THE RIVER
# AND THE RAFT

THE PRINCE AND THE PAUPER, in 1882, was a blessed relief
for Clemens to write, as Paine tells us, after the nightmare of
composing *A Tramp Abroad.* "I am as soary (and flighty) as
a rocket to-day, with the unutterable joy of getting that Old
Man of the Sea off my back where he has been roosting more
than a year and a half," Clemens wrote to Howells. He took a
jubilant delight in writing this children's book, even if it never
sold, and Mrs. Clemens pursued him to continue it like a
"horse-leech's daughter."

The point was, of course, that Clemens was momentarily
abandoning his "comedy," or his rebellious satire, and writing
a typical romance melodrama of sixteenth-century England for
that audience of "good little children" (and good parents)
which he had previously mocked. Escaping from his status as
a mere "humorist," thinking not even to publish the book under
his own name, he had become a juvenile moralist. No wonder
Livy admired and pressed him; or that his own children reported
this was his finest work, a new and more elevated stage of literary development. Clemens had come to terms, apparently,

with his own society, and Howells, too, was delighted, as were the Hartford clergy, the critics of the time, and Harriet Beecher Stowe. The New York *Herald,* the Boston *Transcript,* the *Atlantic,* the *Century* used such words as pure, noble, subdued, delicate, and "refined."

The fit of repentance was not for long, however, since directly after the publication of *The Prince and the Pauper,* Clemens began work on his "demonic" biography of the villainous Whitelaw Reid. But meanwhile the damage had been done. In the parable of Edward Tudor, the young Prince of Wales, and Tom Canty, outcast child of a thief and a beggar, it is difficult to know whether Tom is more tedious as the false king of England, or Edward more affected as the real one. The Prince of Poverty meets the Prince of Plenty in a dreamworld of artificial romance and, for Clemens, quite execrable language. As he would again toward the close of the century, in *Joan of Arc,* Clemens apparently lost his head when encountering these adolescent figureheads of antique royalty. This is silly stuff, this is Twain at his worst, as we realize when we meet Lady Elizabeth, or Mary Stuart "with her gloomy mien," or when the Prince's eyes begin to flash — and we rather yearn for *1601.*

In the scenes of London poverty and crime, there is a kind of Dickensian pathos, but even Clemens' central view of the "good king Edward VI," based mainly on Hume's history, was contrived and inadequate.* The central plot was hokum, the im-

---

* Beset by internecine wars and religious persecution, by the rivalry among the children of Henry VIII, by court intrigues of the most terrible and obscene nature in this period of Elizabeth and Mary of Scotland, the brief reign of young Edward VI was really not distinguishable from the bloody nightmare of English history which surrounded it. This panorama of "noble" savagery, crime, passion, the use of raw power, evil, cunning, of debauchery and bloodshed, easily matched that of the Russian Czars (the only difference was one of historical time) and was sufficient, as Clemens came to realize, to make the English, the French, and the Russian revolutions appear as benevolent interludes of social progress.

plausible narrative proceeded by a sequence of improbable scenes related in a fancy, stilted, and "noble" manner. When the young Edward is thrown out of the palace because he had unwittingly allowed Tom Canty to try on his clothes — "There followed such a thing as England had never seen before," Clemens said, "the sacred person of the heir to the throne rudely buffeted by plebian hands, and set upon and torn by dogs." And "plebian hands" is very un-Twainish Twain. When Tom Canty assumes the royal place for which he has been unwittingly training himself in his earlier fantasies of nobility, it is Lady Jane Grey, all innocent grace and goodness, who notices his discomfort. "Oh, what aileth thee, my lord?" When the dying Henry wants Norfolk's head to take with him — "Warn my parliament to bring me Norfolk's doom before the sun rise again, else shall they answer for it grievously!" he cries in ringing tones. This is the feudal age in feudal prose, in a very dreamy dream of the past.

The central fantasy of the barefoot boy become proxy king was Sam Clemens' own dream, no doubt, and in his case a fact. But it was also a racial myth from the time of Moses — the illegitimate origins of the great prophet — as well as, in America, a national materialistic obsession. In *The Prince and the Pauper* we notice also the converse of this proposition: the young king who *loses* his royal status, power, and prerogatives. This double and conjoined fantasy embraced both Clemens' youth and his maturity, his dream of success and his fear of losing it which was indeed prophetic, and the loss imminent. This fantasy was in a sense two sides of the same coin, and here we are back to the double personality intrinsic in Sam Clemens' nature . . . But a double personality which has been, for his juvenile audiences, purged of the demonic and satanic elements. Which indeed was the "dream self" in Mark Twain, or which the impostor, in this continuously shifting psychic dualism of such intertwined and interchanging phases of his personality? The ambitious dream of the pauper prince became the horrid nightmare of the outcast and persecuted king. But make no mistake — despite the literary failure of *The Prince and the Pauper,* the inadequate form, the surrender to the conventions, the whole pious fraud which Clemens was attempting to put over, even on himself — the central vision of the book was one of royalty.

For the orphan and pauper, Tom Canty, took on his newly assumed nobility with remarkable ease, just as though he had been indeed "rehearsing" for it. And Childe Edward is definitely still a king when unacknowledged and in rags. What we have here is *two* kings; and what we have been discussing is only the narrow Freudian concept of the early Mark Twain's fears and anxieties, from which in a sense he was also purging himself in this oblique parable. The true issue of Twain's "Double" can be understood only on a larger scale more closely identified with the Rankian *cultural* psychology, where ego is entwined with the social process, and the history of evolutionary development. And when young Edward is kidnapped by John Canty and meets up with a gang of dispossessed yeomanry in the book, Clemens begins to hit his stride again. Made poor, shiftless, and violent by the land enclosures, these outcast English farmers are "controlled" by the barbaric criminal code of sixteenth-century England. "They begged, and were whipped at the cart's tail . . . till the blood ran, then set in the stocks to be pelted; they begged again, and were whipped again, and deprived of an ear; they begged a third time — poor devils, what else could they do? — and were branded on the cheek with a red hot iron, and then sold for slaves; they ran away, were hunted down, and hanged." * And set against these dark

* There were as many as sixty thousand convicts at one time in Henry VIII's prisons, and over seventy thousand thieves and robbers were executed, according to Hume's *History of England,* quoted by Clemens.

scenes of social victims, outcasts, criminals, with the accompanying undertones of witchcraft and the devil-cult, there is the scene where the suffering Edward, released from these customs of "civilization," sleeps with a calf. After these horrible glimpses of English life under the Tudors, the innocent child and the innocent animal find a brief happiness together. "He was free of the bonds of servitude and crime, free of the companionship of base and brutal outlaws; he was warm, he was sheltered . . . He merely snuggled the closer to his friend, in a luxury of warm contentment, and drifted blissfully out of consciousness into a deep and dreamless sleep that was full of serenity and peace. The distant dogs howled, the melancholy kine complained, and the winds went on raging, whilst furious sheets of rain drove along the roof; but the majesty of England slept on undisturbed, and the calf did the same, it being a simple creature and not easily troubled by storms nor embarrassed by sleeping with a king."

Even the rats are innocent in this familiar evocation of the plenary state, the womb feeling, the Garden of Man, and the Twainian raft — and do not bother to bite the peacefully sleeping child-prince. There are elements in the juvenile novel which may remind us in part of the Mark Twain who wrote *Tom Sawyer* and *Huck Finn,* though the ending of *The Prince and the Pauper* is as ridiculous as the beginning, and most of the middle is also. Perhaps it need only be added that Albert Bigelow Paine, Clemens' first and official biographer, considered this book as having an "imperishable charm" and the two heroes, twins in spirit, ranking "with the purest and loveliest creations of child life in the realm of fiction." And that the pauper theme had not only a mythic and biopsychic origin in Samuel Clemens' life, but, living as he was at a scale of one hundred thousand dollars a year, almost half of this being invested in mystical patents and inventions which never paid him back a cent, the other half of his income, very large for that time, expended on the Hartford mansion — the pauper theme was also to be encountered in fact and lived and realized in the flesh.

"The Stolen White Elephant," published in the same year as *The Prince and the Pauper*, was an elaborate parody, in a vein repeated later in "A Double-Barreled Detective Story," both of the conventional mystery tale of the time and of police graft, inefficiency, and stupidity. But now Clemens was on the edge of his two great (and related) works of the 1880s, and perhaps the two best books of his early, though not of his mature and late career. He had in fact been brooding over *Life on the Mississippi,* in 1883, for seven years, ever since he had published the series of sketches in the *Atlantic* called "Old Times on the Mississippi," which formed the core of the first half of the book. In 1882 he took a trip back to the river to refresh his memories, and this account forms the disappointing last half of *Life on the Mississippi*. For all practical purposes it is better to divide the book into two volumes, the first one, ending with that famous twentieth chapter, a great imaginative work;* the second volume another one of Twain's lesser travelogues.

At this period of his life he was already revealing dark speculations about the future in his letters to Joe Twichell. Delighted

* Thomas Hardy believed that *Life on the Mississippi* was the best of Clemens' books, and added, "Why don't people understand that Mark Twain is not merely a great humorist. He is a very remarkable fellow in a very different way." Clemens was already an international figure, celebrated in Germany as well as England, and yet at the *Atlantic* dinners he was not seated on the dais with Emerson, Longfellow, Holmes, Whittier, Howells, and Aldrich — all of these writers, except Emerson, and in some respects Howells, being of the second rank. Perhaps this explains Clemens' particular admiration for and gratitude to Howells, who, after all, did understand his talent and was Clemens' link to New England's decaying pantheon. Both Emerson and Longfellow died while Clemens was writing the Mississippi book.

with the birth of his daughter Jean, he was beset by anxious visions of failure, pain, illness, and death. But who could guess this when he swung into the introduction to *Life on the Mississippi* which gave the background of the great river itself: its age, size, grandeur, and the early history of that mighty stream which the ignorant Captain Marryat had called "the great sewer."

Typically, Clemens almost forgot his own prejudice against the American Indians in the account of their persecution. "For more than a hundred and fifty years there had been white settlements on our Atlantic coasts. These people were in intimate communication with the Indians: in the south the Spaniards were robbing, slaughtering, enslaving, and converting them; higher up, the English were trading beads and blankets to them for a consideration, and throwing in civilization and whisky, for lagniappe . . ." Indeed, as Clemens drew freely from Parkman's history, while making this material his own, the Mississippi River Indians are described almost uniformly as gracious, dignified, hospitable; peaceful victims of the white man's conquest. "Then, to the admiration of the savages, La Salle set up a cross with the arms of France on it, and took possession of the whole country for the king — the cool fashion of the time — while the priest piously consecrated the robbery with a hymn. The priest explained the mysteries of the faith 'by signs,' for the saving of the savages; thus compensating them with possible possessions in heaven for the certain ones on earth which they had just been robbed of. Nobody smiles at these colossal ironies."

Very early, Clemens viewed the whole process of empire building and colonialism with a savage irony of his own. "France stole that vast country on that spot . . . and by and by Napoleon himself was to give the country back again —

make restitution, not to the owners, but to their white American heirs." (It is interesting, incidentally, to notice Clemens' contempt for the Sultan of Versailles — "Louis the Putrid" said this vulgar democrat — and his early admiration for the French Revolution.) The history of the Mississippi moves into the period of commercial great barges and keelboats. "Hordes of rough and hardy men; rude, uneducated, brave, suffering terrific hardships with sailor-like stoicism; heavy drinkers, coarse frolickers in moral sties like the Natchez-under-the-hill of that day, heavy fighters, reckless fellows, everyone, elephantinely jolly, foul-witted, profane, prodigal of their money, bankrupt at the end of the trip, fond of barbaric finery, prodigious braggarts; yet in the main, honest, trustworthy, faithful to promises and duty, and often picturesquely magnanimous." And wasn't this a passage straight out of the Democratic Vistas of that fellow bard whose work Mark Twain never mentions?

Clemens was often, in fact, a prose Whitman; or Whitman a poetical Clemens. These two writers often say the same things in almost identical language, just as the dark endings of their entwined visions of democracy were curiously similar. The river steamboats marked the end of keelboating, while *Life on the Mississippi* describes the annual procession of mighty rafts that used to glide by Hannibal when Clemens was a boy. And he threw in here a chapter of a book he had been working on for the past five or six years, the story of an outcast village boy named Huck Finn. Clemens' literary "form" was that of pure association, or inspiration, or of simple padding when inspiration was lacking. The value of the form, at polar opposites from the cunning and calculated Jamesian esthetics of "effects," was determined by the value of the content — never forgetting the beautiful natural form of Clemens' mind and his prose alike.

This chapter was the famous raft episode from *The Adven-*

*tures of Huckleberry Finn* where, en route to Cairo, Huck
sneaks aboard a river barge and is captured by the boisterous
but good-natured crew. The two boys are heading to where
"the negro will seek freedom in the heart of the free states," as
Clemens said in his own voice. "Jim had a wonderful level head
for a nigger," says Huck in his natural dialect.

These pages in *Life on the Mississippi* are unusual in that one
great book in American letters makes the first historical mention of another great book. Sam Clemens himself tipped us off
about the imminent arrival of Huck Finn. And then in what
was poetry the young hero of the present chronicle announced
his own determination to become a river pilot. "So, by and by/
I ran away./ I said I never would come home again/till I was
a pilot/and could come in glory." The opening description of
the frontier town of Hannibal, Missouri, would also echo
through American literature; but upon his leaving it, the river
has already given the hero a special eminence. "I was in such
a glorified condition that all ignoble feelings departed out of me,
and I was able to look down and pity the untraveled with a
compassion that had hardly a trace of contempt in it." As a
youth Clemens was never great on details, and he had had a
vague plan of sailing to explore the mouth of the Amazon. But
he was instantly smitten by the mate of the river steamer. "It
was not in (young) human nature not to admire him. He was
huge and muscular, his face was bearded and whiskered all
over; he had a red woman and a blue woman tattooed on his
right arm . . . and in the matter of profanity he was sublime."

Since *Life on the Mississippi* is ostensibly another of Mark
Twain's travel books, it has not been sufficiently realized that it
is also a work of literary imagination. The young hero of the
chronicle — who is the autobiographical Clemens looking back
on the early Clemens with such wistful and nostalgic humor —

is surely an older brother of Huck Finn, and a more complex figure. But the mate rebukes young Clemens' advances and the night watchman, the humblest personage on the boat, is the only one who will talk to him. "What was it to me that he was soiled and seedy and fragrant with gin?" Or what to Clemens that, as he would discover, he was "a low, vulgar, ignorant, sentimental, half-witted humbug"? The point is precisely that *Life on the Mississippi* presents all the lower depths of river life with unflinching truth, and yet, through the worshipful eyes of its young apprentice, with a glowing and even heroic glamor. It is social realism, yes, to the utmost; but it is also, definitely, epic realism.

It is as though the great river itself, in the days of Mark Twain's youth, cast an extra dimension upon everything around it. Just as in Clemens' world of childhood the sordid is not quite sordid, in these glowing pages drunks are not drunk, dirt is not dirty, lies are romantic illusions — though there will be horrors and nightmares to come. It was just then that the ambitious and wily Clemens persuaded Horace Bixby to teach him piloting in return for five hundred dollars payable later on — and we reach the central relationship in the book. Bixby is a hard master who will "learn" his apprentice the river or kill him. But the river is a hard master too. There is the chapter on Clemens' first experiences as a cub pilot, and what is remarkable again is not merely the total recall of this artist, but the complete candor, the entertaining honesty in the self-confessions and self-descriptions of this temperament — this altogether Open Ego. Clemens' personality is totally unarmored, as may be seen by now, and the direct opposite of his contemporary, the autistic Henry James, who was in turn close to Bruno Bettelheim's concept of "the empty fortress," in the book by that name.

The youthful Clemens, in all his naive presumptuousness, was subjected to the worst forms of ridicule and abuse by the implacable Mr. Bixby; and there is Clemens' rage at his master, and his fantasy of revenge when the great pilot is landing at Jones' plantation on a dark night. "My exultation began to cool and my wonder to come up. Here was a man who not only proposed to find this plantation on such a night, but to find either end of it you preferred. I dreadfully wanted to ask a question, but I was carrying about as many short answers as my cargo-room would admit of, so I held my peace. All I desired to ask Mr. Bixby was the simple question whether he was ass enough to really imagine he was going to find that plantation on a night when all plantations were exactly alike and all of the same color. But I held in. I used to have fine inspirations of prudence in those days."

Notice Twain's classic answer to Bixby's catechism on the "points" in the river. "I was gratified to be able to answer promptly, and I did. I said I didn't know." There are Bixby's rages at Clemens, since the young hero of *Life on the Mississippi* had something of Tom Sawyer's verbal insouciance. "Oh, but his wrath was up! He was a nervous man, and he shuffled from one side of his wheel to the other as if the floor was hot. He would boil awhile to himself, and then overflow and scald me again." And there is the grand episode in *Life on the Mississippi* when a whole group of visiting pilots attend upon Mr. Bixby's feat of running Hat Island by night:

Now the engines were stopped altogether and we drifted with the current. Not that I could see the boat drift, for I could not, the stars being all gone by this time. The drifting was the dismalest work; it held one's heart still. Presently I discovered a blacker gloom than that which surrounded us. It was the head of the island. We were closing right down upon it. We entered its deeper shadow, and so imminent seemed the peril that I was likely to suffocate; and I had the strongest impulse to do *something,* anything, to save the vessel. But still Mr. Bixby stood by his wheel, silent, intent as a cat, and all the pilots stood shoulder to shoulder at his back.

A remarkable, almost mythic scene of the Freudian "son-horde," grouped behind the parental figure. Only not in a cunning death struggle and parricide, but in admiration and support of individual daring and collective survival.

There is Pilot Bixby teaching the young Clemens the different kinds of darkness on the river, and the changing shape of the river — and the "exact spot and the exact marks the boat lay in when we had the shoalest water in every one of the five hundred shoal places between St. Louis and New Orleans." To which the young apprentice rejoins: "When I get so that I can do that, I'll be able to raise the dead, and then I won't have to pilot a steamboat to make a living. I want to retire from this business. I want a slush-bucket and a brush; I'm only fit for a roustabout. I haven't got brains enough to be a pilot; and if I had I wouldn't have strength enough to carry them around, unless I went on crutches." To which Bixby replies: "Now drop that! When I say I'll learn a man the river, I mean it. And you can depend on it, I'll learn him or kill him." And there is Bixby teaching Clemens a lesson on water-reading and boat-reading.

Now watch her; watch her like a cat, or she'll get away from you. When she fights strong and the tiller slips a little, in a jerky, greasy sort of way, let up on her a trifle; it is the way she tells you at night that the water is too shoal; but keep edging her up, little by little, toward the point. You are well up on the bar now; there is a bar under every point, because the water that comes down around it forms an eddy and allows the sediment to sink. Do you see those fine lines on the face of the water that branch out like the ribs of a fan? Well, those are little reefs; you want to just miss the ends of them, but run them pretty close. Now look out — look out! Don't you crowd that slick, greasy-looking place; there ain't nine feet there; she won't stand it. She begins to smell it; look sharp, I tell you! Oh, blazes, there you go! Stop the starboard wheel! Quick! Ship up to back! Set her back!

Here of course the ship has become a living creature in this prevailing animism of Clemens, or a pantheism where the pilot of the watery universe projects his spirit into every faintest surface ripple, slick, and point. Then there is that nightmarish sequence when Clemens, piloting at night, encounters a wind reef. "Once I inspected rather long, and when I faced to the front again my heart flew into my mouth so suddenly that if I hadn't clapped my teeth together I should have lost it. One of those frightful bluff reefs was stretching its deadly length right across our bows! My head was gone in a moment; I did not know which end I stood on; I gasped and could not get my breath; I spun the wheel down with such rapidity that it wove itself together like a spider's web; the boat answered and turned square away from the reef, but the reef followed her! I fled, but still it followed, still it kept — right across my bows! I never looked to see where I was going, I only fled." And there is Bixby's serenity as he rescues the steamer from crashing into the forest woods. "Just then Mr. Bixby stepped calmly into view on the hurricane-deck. My soul went out to him in gratitude. My distress vanished; I would have felt safe on the brink of Niagara with Mr. Bixby on the hurricane-deck. He blandly and sweetly took his tooth pick out of his mouth between his fingers, as if it were a cigar — we were just in the act of climbing an overhanging big tree, and the passengers were scudding astern like rats — and lifted up these commands to me ever so gently . . ."

And Bixby asks Clemens just why he had brought the ship

into the forest woods because of a rippling wind on the water, the water whose face Clemens does get to know so intimately. "It turned out to be true. The face of the water, in time, became a wonderful book — a book that was a dead language to the uneducated passenger, but which told its mind to me without reserve, delivering its most cherished secrets as clearly as if it uttered them with a voice . . . There never was so wonderful a book written by man, never one whose interest was so absorbing, so unflagging, so sparklingly renewed with every reperusal." And that "knowledge" of the water, as Mark Twain realized, also meant that he could never more enjoy the river so purely for its own sake, since all the river's beauties now held the hint of treachery. "Since those days, I have pitied doctors from my heart. What does the lovely flush in a beauty's cheek mean to a doctor but a 'break' that ripples above some deadly disease? Are not all her visible charms sown thick with what are to him the signs and symbols of hidden decay? Does he ever see her beauty at all, or doesn't he simply view her professionally, and comment upon her unwholesome condition all to himself? And doesn't he sometimes wonder whether he has gained most or lost most by learning his trade?"

On the river, too, "reason" and knowledge replace, and suppress the original state of innocent pleasure and enjoyment — though of course it is just that state of feeling which sets off *Life on the Mississippi* as a primitive epic, and those primary emotions of pleasure, admiration, awe, worship, and affection which pervade its pages. This work of art records the inevitable suppression of feeling by the intellect while it simultaneously evokes the suppressed emotions that reason or civilization must deny.*

---

* For these insights and indeed for the whole view of Mark Twain, in terms of Rankian cultural psychology rather than the much narrower concepts of Freudian psychological blockage and trauma — an ideology of personal neurosis

In the close study of the *trade* of piloting, *Life on the Missis-sippi* reminds us of the hard economics of whaling in *Moby Dick,* and both these great works of the watery domain, soaring up to the heights of art, still rest securely on a firm basis of material factuality. And just here occurs another fine section of Twain's epic — that which describes the big rise in the river, the river life at floodtime, when all the farmers and merchants who live along the banks take to their keelboats and barges in an enormous flotilla of nautical riffraff. "During this big rise these small-fry craft were an intolerable nuisance" — and these pages of *Life on the Mississippi* are a gaudy pageant of American lowlife casually afloat on the great southern river.

The flooding river has changed its shape again.

We were shaving stumpy shores, like that at the foot of Madrid Bend, which I had always seen avoided before; we were clattering through chutes like that of 82, where the opening at the foot was an unbroken wall of timber till our nose was almost at the very spot. Some of these chutes were utter solitudes. The dense, untouched forest overhung both banks of the crooked little creek, and one could believe that human creatures had never intruded there before. The swinging grape-vines, the grassy nooks and vistas glimpsed as we swept by, the flowering creepers waving their red blossoms from the tops of dead trunks, and all the spendthrift richness of the forest foliage, were wasted and thrown away there.

Slipping through these newly formed chutes, they came across families of poverty-stricken poor-white farmers huddled

---

which hardly can encompass Samuel Clemens' outgoing soul and his cosmic empathies — I am greatly in debt to a massive and illuminating, though as yet unpublished, study of modern depth psychology by the brilliant American cultural historian Jack Jones . . . For the reader who may be puzzled by a certain inversion, or subversion, of commonly accepted psychological notions, I can only beg patience until the development of the present book makes them clearer with reference to Mark Twain himself.

together on improvised rafts and boats, waiting for days or weeks until the floodwater would subside — or crazy fences with "one or two jeans-clad, chills-racked, yellow-faced male miserables roosting on the top rail, elbows on knees, jaws in hands, grinding tobacco and discharging the result at floating chips through crevices left by lost teeth." In such flood changes the monster river, like the great white whale, was a triumphant and irresistible force of nature, beyond good and evil, unchecked and untamed except by those bold pilots who rode its back with such human grace and skill and style. And here we reach another crucial statement in *Life on the Mississippi* when Clemens adds: "If I have seemed to love my subject, it is no surprising thing, for I loved the profession far better than any I have followed since, and I took a measureless pride in it. The reason is plain: a pilot, in those days, was the only unfettered and entirely independent human being that lived in the earth. Kings are but the pampered servants of parliament and people; parliaments sit in chains forged by their constituency; the editor of a newspaper cannot be independent, but must work with one hand tied behind him by party and patrons, and be content to utter only half or two-thirds of his mind; no clergyman is a free man and may speak the whole truth, regardless of his parish's opinions; writers of all kinds are manacled servants of the public. We write frankly and fearlessly, but then we 'modify' before we print. In truth, every man and woman and child has a master, and worries and frets in servitude; but in the day I write of, the Mississippi pilot had *none*."

He had seen a boy of eighteen, "taking a great steamer serenely into what seemed almost certain destruction," while the aged captain stood by powerless to interfere. And: "I think pilots were about the only people I ever knew who failed to show, in some degree, embarrassment in the presence of traveling foreign princes. But then, people in one's own grade of life are not usually embarrassing objects . . . By long habit, pilots came to put all their wishes in the form of commands. It 'gravels' me, to this day, to put my will in the weak shape of a request, instead of launching it in the crisp language of an order." Thus the freedom of primitive nature along the banks of the Mississippi River and the freedom of the natural life are matched by the sense of human freedom in the spirit of the Mississippi pilots. Then the book adds further portraits of these sublime beings, of whom Bixby was the supreme example, and following is the account of the pilots' guild — "perhaps the compactest, the completest, and the strongest commercial organization ever formed among men."

The formation of this guild becomes another folk epic in these pages. After so many early failures and disasters, and so much patient cunning on the part of the guild organizers, in the moment of its success "the organization seemed indestructible. It was the tightest monopoly in the world" — until, with the Civil War and the advent of the railroads, and then the development of the Mississippi River tugboats, the whole steamboat industry collapsed in a few brief years. In the closing pages of the first part of *Life on the Mississippi*, Clemens described the famous river races which were in fact less dangerous than an ordinary run with a careless engineer; he listed the names of the famous steamers and their record trips — and he introduced the nemesis of his story, a certain Captain Brown of the steamer *Pennsylvania*. "He was a middle-aged, long, slim, bony, smooth-shaven, horse-faced, ignorant, stingy, malicious, snarling, fault-hunting, mote-magnifying tyrant." There was obviously no love lost between the evil pilot, who concludes this triumphant chronicle of innocence in life, and Horace Bixby's cub. Indeed all of young Clemens' pleasure in his newly acquired craft seems to crash upon the rock of Brown's conniving sadism and ridicule; and he spent his spare time inventing ways of killing his new master.

"That was the thing I used always to do the moment I was abed. Instead of going over my river in my mind, as was my duty, I threw business aside for pleasure, and killed Brown. I killed Brown every night for months; not in old, stale, commonplace ways, but in new and picturesque ones — ways that were sometimes surprising for freshness of design and ghastliness of situation and environment." Was the demonic element in Mark Twain, so long repressed, absent and wanting in the chronicle of youth and the great river, rising to the surface at the book's conclusion? It was unthinkable in the river code to strike a pilot in the performance of his duty, and Clemens believed there was a penitentiary law against it. It was only when Captain Brown physically attacked Sam's brother Henry that his rage erupted. "The boy started out, and even had his foot on the upper step outside the door, when Brown, with a sudden access of fury, picked up a ten-pound lump of coal and sprang after him; but I was between, with a heavy stool, and I hit Brown a good honest blow which stretched him out." Once Clemens had committed the crime of crimes, he concluded there was nothing to stop him from continuing, and he added to his blows a long-delayed tongue-lashing of Brown's character. And this episode, which did not turn out so fatally in itself, was the prelude to the final tragedy in the book. For Clemens was forced to leave the *Pennsylvania,* while Henry remained on it, and the *Pennsylvania* blew up, and Henry was fatally wounded. If Clemens, who always blamed himself for the twist of fate which led so ironically to his brother's death, showed little concern for conventional literary form as such, he had a deeper sense of organic form. For here the epic chronicle of innocence and goodness and the wondrous natural life, these blessed notes from an older world, still ends on the tragic theme of guilt, death, and a blighted career. After chapter twenty, the second half of *Life on the Mississippi* describes the western trip of Mark Twain to see Hannibal and the great river once more; it is an inferior travelogue which really forms the prelude to *The Adventures of Huckleberry Finn,* published a year later, in 1884.

This was Clemens' most celebrated book, although not by any means, as so often claimed, his single great book; nor was this redoubtable genius of our native literature confined, in my view, to the world of childhood, or to the "natural boy" of a Rousseauism which Mark Twain had never heard of. Indeed it was most clearly Clemens' deep sense of the early world of childhood and of natural pleasure which made his view of maturity and of society so penetrating, so caustic, so comic, and so wise.

It was around this famous juvenile that the issue of censorship — what was proper fare for young American children — came out most sharply both within the bosom of the Clemens family and in the outraged reviews and editorials which first greeted a classic of world literature. "Ever since papa and mama were married papa has written his books and then taken them to mama in manuscript and she has expurgated them," so Susy Clemens declared in her autobiography. "Papa read *Huckleberry Finn* to us in manuscript, just before it came out, and then he would leave parts of it with mama to expurgate, while he went off to the study to work, and sometimes Clara and I would be sitting with mama while she was looking the manuscript over, and I remember so well, with what pangs of regret we used to see her turn down the leaves of the pages, which meant that some delightfully terrible part must be scratched out. And I remember one part pertickularly which was perfectly fascinating it was so terrible, that Clara and I used to delight in and oh, with what despair we saw mama turn down the leaf on which it was written, we thought the book would almost be ruined without it . . ."

But in this account (Paine's) the censorial process itself carries the note of childhood delight. This was a nice moment in the Clemens family idyll of domestic bliss. Livy was hardly as severe on her husband as were Howells and other literary friends; Sam used to put in the "offensive words" deliberately in order for them to be scratched out. Olivia Langdon's notorious censorship of Mark Twain's writings was not really very serious. It was not in what his family condemned about his work, but in what they approved of, that his trouble lay. During this period Clemens was also in a frenzy of playwriting; within weeks he had done dramatizations of *The Prince and the Pauper* and *Tom Sawyer* which never reached the stage; with Howells he was writing *The American Claimant,* as a sequel to *The Gilded Age.* On a lecture tour, which he had originally envisaged as including Howells, Thomas Bailey Aldrich, George Cable, and himself traveling over the country in their private railroad car, he was paying Cable $450 a week and expenses, plus the commission for his agent J. B. Pond. Perhaps the humorless and prissy English writer Matthew Arnold was "the only literary Englishman left," as Paine adds, "who had not accepted Mark Twain at his larger value." *

But did *The Adventures of Huckleberry Finn* actually mark the climax of his career, and a decline in his creative powers as suggested by his most recent biographer, Justin Kaplan? Was Twain caught up in his idyll of western adolescence to the point

---

* "And is he *never* serious?" so Howells quotes Arnold as asking about Clemens, while "his hand laxly held mine in greeting." In this connection, it is interesting to remember that Matthew Arnold was Lionel Trilling's early "master" and influence, and to a large degree it was Arnold's respectability, conventionality, "good taste," and all-around esthetic mediocrity that the young Trilling brought over to his criticism of the modern American writers whom he found so vulgar and tasteless (and radical).

of retreating from all contemporary reality, or even, let us say, from artistic maturity itself? This curious vein of Mark Twain criticism was also propounded in various ways by such critics as Van Wyck Brooks in the twenties, Bernard DeVoto in the forties, Mr. Kaplan and Charles Neider in the fifties and sixties. What nonsense, really! *Huck Finn* did indeed take eight years and seven other books before it was finished; but was this a mark of deep inner conflict or perhaps of Clemens' deep intuitive sense of craftsmanship — or of both, as occurs usually with such great books? Was the publication of the book "jinxed from the start," and accompanied by more than usual of Clemens' emotional tantrums and rages, as we are told? — though it is a classic work which finally sold over ten million copies in almost every language, as Mr. Kaplan does finally concede. The reviewers' silence at the time of publication, and then the abuse, the attacks, the attempted censorship of this masterpiece of "vernacular naturalism," this most revolutionary children's book for that time which was described as "gutter realism," as degrading, immoral, improper, irreverent, flat, coarse, trash that was "suitable only for the slums" — all this which redounds so clearly to the credit of an original work of art, of a great and original artist, hardly serves to lift Mr. Kaplan's Freudian gloom.*

* In *Mr. Clemens and Mark Twain* (New York, 1966). Mr. Kaplan's biography is an essential supplement to Albert Bigelow Paine's standard three-volume work published in 1912. I have used both biographies throughout this book, but Paine's, despite its obvious Victorianism and omissions, with an increasing admiration, and Mr. Kaplan's with an increasing reserve. To use, as Kaplan continually does, orthodox Freudianism on Twain's talent and work alike is simply to reduce all that was original, bold, and best in him to some kind of trivial personal maladjustment. We have already seen that Twain can hardly be comprehended within such a narrow framework; that a better illumination comes from Rankian cultural psychology. It is unfortunate, moreover, that Mr. Kaplan, working within the Cold War period of our literary scholarship, either ignores or detracts from just those aspects of Twain's writing which have made him universally admired and beloved.

Maybe Mark Twain's joy in the book was beclouded by its initial reception, but still there must have been some pleasure in the writing of the book, and, in his own lifetime, its growing acclaim.

There was. There were times in the writing of it when Clemens went soaring away on the wings of his tale, when he could hardly stop writing it. The narrative carries this imprint of a special pleasure and delight, from the beautiful, lyrical opening of Huck's discontent with even the civilization of the frontier towns. "I felt so lonesome I most wished I was dead." There are the undertones of primitive superstition (the black slave folklore) which surround this chronicle of native boyhood. Miss Watson has attempted to "convert" Huck, the town's bad boy, to respectability and culture and religion. "She told me to pray every day, and whatever I asked for I would get it. But it wasn't so. I tried it. Once I got a fish line but no hooks. It warn't any good to me without hooks . . . I set down one time back in the woods and had a long think about it. I says to myself, if a body can get anything they pray for, why don't Deacon Winn get back the money he lost on pork? Why can't the widow get back her silver snuff-box that was stole? Why can't Miss Watson fat up? No, say I to myself, there ain't anything in it."

*Tom Sawyer* had satirized, as we know, all the conventional values of "maturity," social success and social power and place. But from the very outset Huckleberry Finn *defied* all the proprieties, including also wealth, success, social position, and conventional religion of the time. It was outrageous what Clemens got away with. It is curious, too, that Twain's Freudian biographer did not stress the opening fantasy of Huck's horrid father (as projected by the outcast prince, Huck-Sam) who was the evil guardian, in Clemens' mind, of the natural child. Like any good primitive myth, the opening of *Huck Finn* is heavy with dubious and shifting oedipal imagery; it is through this drunken, outcast, scheming, cruel — also impotent, pathetic, and helpless — father figure that Huck achieves his escape from the Widow and "sivilization." (First, Huck gives up his inheritance to Judge Thatcher for a consideration of one dollar; no more cash nexus.) And Huck appeals to "Nigger Jim" in his urgent need for charms and witchcraft to help him against the villainous parent. "So the hair-ball talked to Jim, and Jim told it to me. He says: 'Yo' ole father doan' know yit what he's a-gwyne to do. Sometimes he spec he'll go 'way, en den ag'in he spec he'll stay. De bes' way is to res' easy en let de ole man take his own way. Dey's two angels hoverin' roun' 'bout him. One uv 'em is white en shiny, en t'other one is black . . .'"

These two angels, these contraries, these doubles give Jim an easy out, of course, just as he foresees two girls playing contrary parts in Huck's own future. "Dey's two gals flyin' 'bout you in yo' life. One uv 'em's light en t'other one is dark. One is rich en t'other is po'. You's gwyne to marry de po' one fust en de rich one by en by. You wants to keep 'way fum de water as much as you kin, en don't run no resk, 'kase it's down in de bills dat you's gwyne to git hung." And after the fantasies (and plots) of murdering the father, Huck escapes to the woods by feigning his own murder. After this mock-primitive hero has his mock-primitive ritual of death and resurrection, we enter the primeval world of the great river and the western wilderness. Time stops; there is the immense black water at night, the first gray of dawn; the fleeing boy takes a nap before daylight. "I was powerful lazy and comfortable — didn't want to get up and cook breakfast." And there is the haunting refrain of this primitive return. "I wanted to put in the time," which is the pure spending of time, the "waste" of time according to society and civilization, the time which is not money;

but the passing of time which is "merely" living for pleasure —
according to Twain — or *living*. Huck gets the "lonesome"
feeling at night, he goes to the river again, and then he goes to
bed. "There ain't no better way to put in time when you are
lonesome; you can't stay so, you soon get over it."

But Huck discovers that Nigger Jim has run away and is also
on the island — thinking that Huck is dead. "He bounced up
and stared at me wild. Then he drops down on his knees, and
puts his hands together and says: 'Doan' hurt me — don't!
I hain't ever done no harm to a ghos'. I awluz liked dead people, en done all I could for 'em. You go en git in de river ag'in,
whah you b'longs, en doan' do nuffn to Ole Jim, 'at 'uz awluz
yo' fren'.' " They feed up together, Jim stops calling Huck
"sah," and tells him how Miss Watson has planned to sell him
down to Orleans, and how he has managed to escape.*

"She didn' want to, but she could git eight hund'd dollars
for me, en it 'uz sich a big stack o' money she couldn' resis'. De
widder she try to git her to say she wouldn' do it, but I never
waited to hear de res'. I lit out mighty quick, I tell you." Thus,
as in Thomas Wentworth Higginson's classic account of Negro
troops in the Civil War, *Army Life in a Black Regiment,* once
again these "lazy," no-account, improvident and incompetent

---

* "Nigger Jim," one of the heroic figures in American fiction against whom the
NAACP has recently been raising some academic objections, is to some degree
a stereotype of the Negro slave or even an Uncle Tom in name, behavior,
language perhaps — but he is a very ambiguous stereotype indeed. First of all,
Huck is obviously the "innocent" hero, the story is his education, and it is told
through the classical double vision of all such stories. Twain always knows more
than Huck seems to know, and very often he deliberately contrives Huck as a
deadpan comic figure in the process of his education. The double vision is
thus almost a triple vision. Moreover this "Nigger Jim" — and again "Nigger"
is Huck's natural and ignorant usage, while Twain uses "Negro" — is also
playing *his* role, as a typical slave and Uncle Tom. It is only gradually that
Huck begins to realize — and that Twain lets him realize — and that Jim lets
him realize — the true nature and temperament of the runaway Negro slave
who is the book's alternate or double hero.

African slaves could be very decisive, quick, energetic and remarkably capable when they had to be, or wanted to be. Jim's
account of his own escape testifies to this. And so much, in these
three brief sentences of Jim's, for the "good" slaveholders of
family-type slaves whom Sam Clemens himself sometimes tried
to contrast with the "evil" deep-south cotton plantation owners. Now comes Jim's plaintive and "capitalistic" comment.
"Yes, en I's rich now, come to look at it. I owns mysef, en I's
wuth eight hund'd dollars. I wisht I had de money, I wouldn'
want no mo'." And then, as these two rebels bid farewell to
the inequities of civilization, the story is suddenly saturated by
the signs and portents of primitive man and nature. When the
birds are flying low, as a sign of rain, and Huck is about to kill
them, Jim invokes all the ritualistic taboos about the sacred-
ness of animal life.

There is the episode of the snake bite where Jim again suf-
fers from Huck's practical jokes; the snake evil is overcome
but not exorcised from the story, as Jim knows. We get the
first of a recurrent series of "visits," or revisits to the civilizational restraints of the frontier towns, where Huck attempts to
personify a girl — and then the swift escape back to the raft:
the first of these great plenary-pagan womb episodes of "drifting" down the limitless void of the great river. "This second
night we run between seven and eight hours, with a current that
was making over four mile an hour. We catched fish and talked,
and we took a swim now and then to keep off sleepiness. It was
kind of solemn, drifting down the big, still river, laying on our
backs, looking up at the stars, and we didn't ever feel like talking loud, and it warn't often that we laughed — only a
little kind of low chuckle. We had mighty good weather as a
general thing, and nothing ever happened to us at all — that
night, nor the next, nor the next." The silence, the solemnity,

the grandeur, the peace of this dark, rocking infinitude are set off by Twain's wry humor. They pass a series of river towns, "nothing but just a shiny bed of lights," at night, and Huck seizes upon these occasions to slip ashore at times to "borrow" a watermelon or a muskmelon or a chicken "that warn't roosting comfortable." To "liberate" them.

In this watery Eden the "crimes" of society are indulged in with all the impunity of childhood play, and "Take it all around, we lived pretty high." Civilization comes back to them briefly, and anticipatorily, in the lurid episode of the floating river boat, the three robbers, and their own hasty, terrified escape — the ominous hint of violence in Eden — while Huck gradually comes to a truer realization of Jim's "black soul." Their conversations are grand affairs where Huck is "teaching" Jim. When Jim doesn't accept the lesson or the moral and wins the argument, Huck takes refuge in the white man's superiority. "I see it warn't no use wasting words — you can't learn a nigger to argue. So I quit." But Jim of course is teaching Huck much more about nature, life, and human beings, as Huck has the grace to admit. "Well, he was right; he was most always right; he had an uncommon level head for a nigger."

But the story's subtlety lies in the fact that Huck does not yet know how much more Jim still has to teach him. Are some of these scenes and episodes and passages to be considered "paternalistic" in the hard light of the race conflict in modern times? Perhaps; and some of them are obviously sentimental, too. Yet this narrative was remarkably open and bold for its own time and place; and it is still very fresh and touching in its fundamental human terms. Sometimes Jim's natural heroic splendor makes Huck feel so ordinary and mean that he humbles himself before the Negro — and "warn't very sorry for it afterward, neither." This is another stage in the developing relationship between what you might call the poor-white-trash boy and the runaway slave: these mutual outcasts who fashion their own world of affection, pleasure, and "underground" trust and responsibility. And the language? Clemens was very proud, technically, of the "four dialects" — or actually six, counting his modifications of the Missouri Negro and ordinary Pike County speech — in which *Huck Finn* was composed; and while it is questionable if any white writer has ever recorded black southern talk accurately, Clemens had perhaps the best "ear" of his time. The different dialects in his book are convincing and consistent within themselves as a literary achievement "based on" southern Negro language, if one can't quite attest to their social and historical verisimilitude. Despite the fact that Clemens had become, by the first decade of his mature career, the most "desouthernized" of southern writers — and would become infinitely more so — there were still lingering prejudices perhaps never, in the case of any southerner or even any white man, to be completely eliminated; and he had a curious weakness for the stylized Negro dialect of Joel Chandler Harris' Uncle Remus.

But still, accepting these modern strictures, it was a lovely language that Mark Twain fashioned to carry along the exuberant, lyrical, touching, entertaining, and deceptively "simple" narrative line in this parable of a southwestern boyhood.* Yes, there was still a false "innocence" about the whole question of slavery which Huck's mind could not be expected to entertain; and there are the familiar "fillers" of romance melodrama in this

---

* It was from this book, of course, that both Sherwood Anderson and Ernest Hemingway, among others such as Gertrude Stein, got their "plain Western rhythms" in the fiction of our own day. Hemingway even claimed, mentioning Thoreau, that American literature started with *Huck Finn*, while Anderson used the Twainian word "fan-tods" in a variety of midwestern tales of adolescence.

book of Mark Twain's, too. Clemens plays cat's-paw with his audience as the raft fluctuates around that Mississippi River "Cairo" where Jim is to find his freedom, and when Huck begins those remarkable reveries as to his own "guilt" in aiding a runaway slave. "Jim said it made him all over trembly and feverish to be so close to freedom. Well, I can tell you it made me all over trembly and feverish, too, to hear him, because I begun to get it through my head that he *was* most free — and who was to blame for it? Why, *me*. I couldn't get that out of my conscience, no how nor no way . . ." And moreover, when Jim comes close to freedom's line he begins to act (and talk) quite differently from his behavior as a black slave — he even plans to buy back or to steal back his wife and children. He begins to act like a free man, a human being. In that double view of Clemens' craft we realize, while it is quite *natural* for Huck to go through those agonized reveries about Jim's freedom, what illuminating and ironical effects Twain achieved through his "innocent" hero. For the "conscience" which so torments Huck is the Freudian superego, the voice of parents, the community, of habit and conformity, which Sam Clemens himself had already seen through.

This is a deadpan, double-edged social satire which is brilliantly entertaining and acute. For Clemens was describing the Freudian "false conscience" — or pseudo-conscience — which, alas, so many practitioners of psychotherapy still value as the only true conscience, not knowing what the human will is. And with what simplicity, irony, and grandeur prevailing over deep social taboos, does Huck finally resolve that he might as well do evil and *not* betray his friend. "Then I thought a minute, and says to myself, hold on; s'pose you'd 'a' done right and give Jim up, would you felt better than what you do now? No, say I, I'd feel bad — I'd feel just the same way I do now. Well, then, says I, what's the use you learning to do right when it's troublesome to do right and ain't no trouble to do wrong, and the wages is just the same? I was stuck. I couldn't answer that. So I reckoned I wouldn't bother no more about it, but after this always do whichever come handiest at the time." Mark Twain was on his most familiar and penetrating ethical grounds: not only attacking human morality for its general hypocrisy, but attacking a specific social "virtue" based on the deepest social crime of slavery. In the caricature of Huck resolving to do "good or bad" depending on which was most convenient, wasn't Twain reaching for a still deeper human impulse: namely, a basic indifference to morality for its own sake and a simple deference to those habits and customs, whether moral or not, which are socially acceptable — convenient — at any given historical moment.

Where was morality now? But we are projecting certain implications of Clemens' thought which were developed later on in his career, and perhaps were not even conscious in *Huck Finn* itself. In the midst of Huck's conflict, he is stricken by Jim's trust in him. "Dah you goes, de ole true Huck; de on'y white genlman dat ever kep' his promise to ole Jim." And there was still here a profound note of natural virtue in contrast with social "ethics" or civilized repression — and a sly pagan laughter. "The place to buy canoes is off of rafts laying up at shore." Now the narrative begins a long disquisition on the frontier culture of the Grangerford and Shepherdson families: on the frontier southern "nobility," on their family feuds, systems of slavery, their household furnishings, their "culture" and art — including the brilliant set piece of Clemens on the interior decoration of the Grangerford house, and the commentary on the mortuary paintings of young Emmeline Grangerford. "These was all nice pictures, I reckon," Huck says, "but I didn't somehow seem to take to them, because if ever I was down a little they always give me the fan-tods. Everybody was sorry she died, because she had laid out a lot more of these pictures to do, and a body could see by what she had done what they had lost. But I reckoned that with her disposition she was having a better time in the graveyard."

Emmeline wrote poetry, too —

### Ode to Stephen Dowling Bots, Dec'd

And did young Stephen sicken,
And did young Stephen die?
And did the sad hearts thicken,
And did the mourners cry?

But despite a few saving passages, this is a laborious and dreary episode in *Huck Finn*. It is with some relief that we escape from these horrible southern "gentry" and their farcical codes of gentlemanly behavior; their "loyal niggers," their squalor, prejudices, and violence; the continuous and senseless family feuding — to return to the fullness and peace of the raft again.

This is a sordid and depressing picture of the southwestern country "gentry" which will be useful to remember when we come to a similar problem of interpretation in *The Tragedy of Pudd'nhead Wilson*. "The boys jumped for the river," Huck says, describing a frontier killing, "both of them hurt — and as they swum down the current the men run along the bank shooting at them and singing out, 'Kill them, kill them!' It made me so sick I most fell out of the tree. I ain't a-going to tell *all* that happened — it would make me sick again if I was to do that. I wished I hadn't ever come ashore that night to see such things. I ain't ever going to get shut of them — lots of times I dream about them." And for contrast there is Jim's affectionate delight at Huck's return to the raft.

"Good lan'! is dat you, honey? Doan' make no noise." It was Jim's voice — nothing ever sounded so good before. I run along the bank a piece and got aboard, and Jim he grabbed me and hugged me, he was so glad to see me. He says: "Laws bless you, chile, I 'us right down sho' you's dead ag'in . . . Lawsy, I's mighty glad to git you back ag'in, honey."

Now it was from such passages of physical affection between Jim and Huck — scandalous for their time; and there is more — and from such direct emotional tenderness that the critic Leslie Fiedler found his inspiration for the charge of "homosexuality" in *Huck Finn* — one of the most absurd statements in contemporary criticism. Mr. Fiedler, however, in hot pursuit of love-and-death in American literature, is guilty so often of an utterly misleading and purely sensational use of Freudian symbolism that one wonders if he is even trying to be a responsible critic. (The article on the homosexuality in *Huck Finn* was run by the *Partisan Review* as a hoax; only later did they discover that Mr. Fiedler was serious.) Here this critic has missed not only the whole point of the central relationship in the novel, but the meaning of the raft itself in terms of frontier "civilization." * Get off the raft, Leslie! — and return it to the natives.

While Huck and Jim eat supper they talk again. "We said there warn't no home like a raft, after all. Other places do seem so cramped up and smothery, but a raft don't. You feel mighty free and easy and comfortable on a raft." There is a description of a sunrise on the Mississippi, after two or three days and

---

* It should be obvious that the present writer also uses Freudian insights when they are relevant, and not when they are *not* relevant. In Mark Twain's case, within the Rankian cultural psychology, the Freudian symbols have a sometimes interesting but usually minor significance. They cannot define a culture hero such as Twain; while Rank pointed out that the Artist is not a cured or sublimated neurotic — but an artist. The difference is qualitative; it is a different kind of animal. Though it is chic for contemporary Freudians to pursue the mystery of "Art," they will never, I believe, be able to understand it within the limits of their methodology.

nights went by, timelessly, sliding along "so quiet and smooth and lovely." And we suddenly realize that *this* is the real form of *The Adventures of Huckleberry Finn*: a series of long, overdone, brutal and otherwise unpleasant forays into "civilization" (so-called), or forays of civilization onto the raft. And then the return into natural and altogether pleasurable existence, a natural existence on the blessed raft, with the "uncivilized" black slave and the delinquent and "uneducable" juvenile dropout.

Here indeed the tone of the narrative grows more overtly and sensuously pagan, as Huck rejects even the clothing prepared for him by the frontier gentry. "So we would put in the day, lazying around, listening to the stillness." There is the smell of Eden, the silence yes, the stillness, the timelessness. "We was always naked, day and night, whenever the mosquitoes would let us — the new clothes Buck's folks made for me was too good to be comfortable, and besides I didn't go much on clothes, nohow." (Another passage to offend the more tender or repressed sensibilities on the race question perhaps, just as Melville opened another great epic of the water by having Ishmael share his bed with similar heathens and pagans.) There is the tremendous lyrical ode to the great river, defying description, in these pages of *Huck Finn*; and the necessary obeisance to the darker spirits of nature — just before the advent of the Duke and the Dauphin. Alas! The serenity and satisfaction of infancy and the more primitive stages of man alike, existing before the cumulative repressions of societal sacrifice; the fullness of a presocial and more organic functioning (in the memories and dreams of man at least) — all is shattered again by the "comic" dregs of civilization, two coarse, cruel, and commercial scoundrels, attired with all the false trappings of English "nobility."

How can Jim and Huck be taken in by these crude and vulgar practitioners of such farcical pretensions? Such, Mark Twain implied, laying it on heavy and thick, is the fate of all innocents caught in the web of civilization. But one notices another aspect of Twinship even in these raucous parodies of the Jamesian "Dream of Europe." If Clemens reversed the cultural myth quite deliberately here, he was not altogether immune to its appeal, or that of the larger racial, or biopsychic, myth which it rehearsed — the theme of the Noble Pretender (the American Claimant) — or of the ancient folk hero of disguised royalty who is here being satirized. Through these implausible frauds of the "Duke" and the "Dauphin" (as though Clemens, half realizing his own vulnerability to the concept, were even more savagely and brutally exorcising it), we are treated to another dose of southwestern pioneer culture. The terrible "theatrical performances" in the ugly halls of the hideous river towns which are at the center of *Huck Finn*'s narrative are the worst things yet. Here as in *The Gilded Age,* Clemens became the crude satirist of a crude frontier, and he anticipated the "Menckenian" tone of disgust for the boobs of the hinterland. There is the cruel trick played by the Duke who ties Jim up in the daytime to exhibit him as a captured slave, and Jim's weary reaction. "I doan' mine one or two kings, but dat's enough."

Yet Clemens rescues some of this overdone farce and heavy tedium by flashes of brilliant sophistication which, as in the "Shakespearian" reverie, predates a similar episode in an English musical satire, *Beyond the Fringe,* by over half a century:

To be, or not to be; that is the bare bodkin
That makes calamity of so long life;
For who would fardels bear, till Birnam Wood do come to Dunsinane,
But that the fear of something after death

Murders the innocent sleep,
Great nature's second course,
And makes us rather sling the arrows of outrageous fortune
Than fly to others we know not of.
There's the respect must give us pause . . .

There is another famous episode made familiar to modern audiences by Hal Holbrook's theatrical presentations, where a southern gentleman, Colonel Sherburn, routs a mob and indulges in some famous reflections about lynchings — even though we may not remember that this same southern colonel has just wantonly shot down a helpless drunkard.

After the failure of their "Shakespearian" revival with the "Arkansaw lunkheads," the Duke and Dauphin arrange an obscene "comedy" for the river towns where the Duke prances on all fours, nude. This is an obvious comparison with the idyllic nakedness of the raft, and Jim says mournfully, "But, Huck, dese kings o' ourn is reglar rapscallions; dat's jist what dey is; dey's reglar rapscallions." "All kings is mostly rapscallions, as fur as I can make out," says Huck. "Take them all around, they're a mighty ornery lot. It's the way they're raised." "But dis one do *smell* so like de nation, Huck." "Well, they all do, Jim. *We* can't help the way a king smells; history don't tell no way." And Huck adds: "What was the use to tell Jim these warn't real kings and dukes? It wouldn't 'a' done no good; and, besides, it was just as I said; you couldn't tell them from the real kind." And then Jim is miserable again at the memory of his wife and children. "I knowed what it was about. He was thinking about his wife and his children, away up yonder, and he was low and homesick . . . and I do believe he cared just as much for his people as white folks does for their'n. It don't seem natural, but I reckon it's so."

It was the whole concept of the Negro as subhuman, as animal

— a concept assiduously cultivated by the slave-owning classes, and then the post Civil War south, and still insidiously established in the white man's psyche in the latter half of the twentieth century — that Huck's great innocent "discoveries" were being directed at in the mid 1880s.* And just as Twain's double-barreled use of the word "conscience" means with Huck only a tribal custom at first; so his hero's original use of the word "natural" meant cultural and societal. What the book reveals is Huck's discovery of both a true conscience, his own, and a true use of "natural" as being often *anti*social: a defiance of stale (or evil) customs.

The whole episode of the bewildered frontier village where the Duke and the King try to steal the fortune of the deceased Peter Wilks is poor and heavy again; but an interesting prelude to *The Man That Corrupted Hadleyburg.* Now in the alternating sequence of a beneficent nature and repressive civilization which forms the true plot structure of *Huck Finn,* and in the up-and-down sequence of a beautiful lyrical prose narrative and heavy romance-melodrama blocks of action — just here come the final reveries of that boyhood hero who chooses pagan damnation in preference to Christian virtue.

Huck does indeed write to Miss Watson that "your runaway nigger Jim is down here two mile below Pikesville, and Mr. Phelps has got him and he will give him up for the reward if you send." And he feels good "and all washed clean of sin for the

---

* See for example William Styron's *Confessions of Nat Turner* in 1968, where the author ignores the very solid possibility of Turner's black wife and children being sold away from him as another cause of his anger and revolutionary passion — and makes Turner into the kind of black sexual pervert, one who lusts for and murders a beautiful white southern lady, that a middle-class white audience would recognize with pleasure. But then, Styron's novel ignores or reverses many of the known facts about both Nat Turner and the long history of slave revolts in the South which have been recognized in Abolitionist and Negro history alike. It does express beautifully the typical fantasy life of a southern liberal — so to speak.

first time I had ever felt so in my life, and I knowed I could pray now. But I didn't do it straight off, but laid the paper down and set there thinking — thinking how good it was all this happened so, and how near I come to being lost and going to hell. And went on thinking . . ." So Clemens wrote in a burst of inspired irony, eloquence, insight:

And got to thinking over our trip down the river; and I see Jim before me all the time: in the day and in the night-time, sometimes moonlight, sometimes storms, and we a-floating along, talking and singing and laughing. But somehow I couldn't seem to strike no places to harden me against him, but only the other kind. I'd see him standing my watch on top of his'n, 'stead of calling me, so I could go on sleeping; and see him how glad he was when I come back out of the fog; and when I come to him again in the swamp, up there where the feud was; and such-like times; and would always call me honey, and pet me, and do everything he could think of for me, and how good he always was; and at last I struck the time I saved him by telling the men we had smallpox aboard, and he was so grateful, and said I was the best friend old Jim ever had in the world, and the *only* one he's got now; and then I happened to look around and see that paper.

It was a close place. I took it up, and held it in my hand. I was a-trembling, because I'd got to decide, forever, betwixt two things, and I knowed it. I studied a minute, sort of holding my breath, and then says to myself:

"All right, then, I'll *go* to hell" — and tore it up.

It was awful thoughts and awful words, but they was said. And I let them stay said; and never thought no more about reforming. I shoved the whole thing out of my head, and said I would take up wickedness again, which was in my line, being brung up to it, and the other warn't. And for a starter I would go to work and steal Jim out of slavery again; and if I could think up anything worse, I would do that, too; because as long as I was in, and in for good, I might as well go the whole hog.

This was the real ending of *The Adventures of Huckleberry Finn,* although the narrative, as usual, ran through another hundred pages of inferior plot sequence until Huck lighted out for the territory before Aunt Sally could adopt and civilize him again. "I can't stand it. I been there before." And this was also the conclusion of Mark Twain's first great burst of creative fiction in the 1870s and 1880s, including *The Innocents Abroad, Roughing It,* parts of *The Gilded Age, Tom Sawyer, Life on the Mississippi,* and *Huckleberry Finn* itself. And let us note now that "the river and the raft," the true theme of this period of Mark Twain's work, is by no means to be interpreted as the Freudian "return to the womb." It is indeed a "floating" — but a *floating through life,* unencumbered by society or civilization, just for the sake of living each moment, hour and day. It is that familiar dashing and floating so joyously and freely that Clemens invoked in the western stage coaches of *Roughing It,* as he unconsciously continued to use similar or the same symbolism throughout his work.

The common denominator of these early books is, of course, that idyll of "innocent" childhood and youth. Twain's accounts of the primitive yearnings of the frontier town boys for fame and glory, pleasure and excitement, may remind you of Jelly Roll Morton's descriptions of the gamblers, pimps, and musicians in the early days of New Orleans' jazz — the accent is the same, the accent of great art in its first flush of joy. Depicting the garden of boyhood in these books, the carry-over of this mood, so central to Mark Twain, was in the rest of the early works too and would remain constant during the rest of his career. And reducing all the "mature" values of ambition, competition, possession, material wealth, fame, and success to these boyhood fits of admiration, envy, rage, jealousy, yearning and emulation, scorn, trickery, revenge, Clemens displayed his deepest and central vein of edenic-satanic feeling. Life here was a cosmic kind of merriment — and this theme, this tone, this concept had never appeared before in the national letters so clearly and purely all its own.

Our adult strivings appear to be as ludicrous as they really are: mature achievement is a satiric joke. And here all the low, base, and sordid — or even evil — emotions can be openly described for what they are, since in this childhood context they are at the same time not "serious." This is Satan playing in the garden of innocence. And this "make-believe" world of infancy and childhood, of the primitive emotions, even of the animal life that Clemens described so intimately, is in fact, as in the parallel cases of William Blake and Henry Miller, to cite only two examples, a classic source of man's dreams, his psychology, his deep nostalgia, his myths, his art. Before the Fall, in this world of boyhood yearning, while "adventure," "glory," "fame" are primary things, sin is not sin, evil is not evil, cupidity is not cupidity nor is corruption corruption, and death is not yet death. The heroics and villainies of human nature are revealed more clearly just because their whole context and weight has been shifted in the "comedy" scene of childhood innocence; while all of human pretense could be stripped away by the un-blinking gaze of childhood candor. This is mock heroics, mock villainy, mock passion, mock pride, and mock despair, in a world of poetic mockery — just as Clemens told us, in the Mississippi book, how his own youthful ambition was formed.

Or notice Mark Twain's letter to Horace Bixby, the pi-lot-teacher of his youth whom he had met once more in his later trip to the river. "I didn't see half enough of you. It was a sore disappointment. Osgood could have told you, if he would — discreet old dog — I expected to have you with me *all* the time. Altogether the most pleasant part of my visit with

you was after we arrived in St. Louis, and you were your old natural self again. Twenty years have not added a month to your
age or taken a fraction of your loveliness . . ." In this touching
epistle to the old river friend whom he had made the hero of a
classic book was revealed all of Clemens' own sense of venera-
tion, respect, awe, affection, an outgoing sense of love and concern for all human beings which is rare in our literature, which
was perhaps even more "un-American" in Mark Twain's more
inhibited period than in our own. This was simply another example of Sam Clemens' unique core of primary emotion, not to
be subjected to any kind of niggardly Freudian "analysis."

Now obviously this is not to say that Clemens was a saint —
since the range of human affection in his temperament would
be matched by an equal range of anger, wrath, jealousy, vanity, or plain pique, yes and delicious malice, in what was simply
a natural, open, organic, and notably unrepressed and "uncivilized" human being. In much of his later work Clemens
would indeed appear, consciously and "rationally," to stress
the baser human motives almost exclusively and dwell upon
them in his central literary vision, and in his rages, polemics,
and furious parodies of the "damned human race." He was
obviously more sensitive to, and more affected by the baseness
of humanity than humanity was. A good man is hurt more by
badness; a loving man is more vulnerable to hatred; an innocent man (like almost all great artists in a special sense of
"innocence") is more betrayed by evil. Right here was one
element of Clemens' later periods of blackness, bitterness, and
despairing cynicism, so puzzling to describe at times, but perhaps very simple to locate in the extent and degree of his basic
human trust.

He was presently at the early peak, the golden day of his career. Paine's biography of Twain gives us the whole story of

Clemens' rescue of the bankrupt, disgraced, and dying General Ulysses S. Grant; of the publication of Grant's *Memoirs* by Mark Twain, and the book's huge success; of the royalty check of two hundred thousand dollars which Clemens delivered, after the general's death, to Grant's family. The characters of both Grant and Twain are illuminated in this extraordinary relationship; it was actually again a touching friendship, with a great admiration and respect on the part of both men. And whether Grant (like Horace Bixby?) was a "surrogate-father" figure, or not, according to the Freudians, is of singularly little importance. This was a meeting of two immortals in American history; and what really matters about Sam Clemens is that he extended his affection to the unknown river pilot just as fully as to the famous warrior.

His publishing house had a vista of immense success, including the memoirs of the other Civil War generals like McClellan, Sheridan, Wylie Crawford, and culminating with an "Authorized Life" of Pope Leo XIII, which had been contracted for in what amounted to a papal mission to Rome, in April, 1886. The fabulous Paige typesetting machine, in which he was investing half his annual income, was on the verge of success, it seemed; and Clemens — how like Balzac this native genius was — had involved himself in a dozen other deals to secure his fame and fortune as inventor, promoter, businessman, tycoon. Or was he closer to Dostoevski's "Gambler"?

His home life was never happier; his social life never more full and gay; even when he was not writing his days were bounteously full, and Clemens, like Huck, was never more fulfilled than when just "putting in the time." But he was ironic and superstitious and prophetic about his own good fortune. "I am frightened at the proportions of my prosperity. It seems to

me that whatever I touch turns to gold." Or, as it would turn
out, to false gold; but meanwhile Livy, too, was the best
mother in the world, as Sam said, and one whose children
adored her. Much as she never contented herself "with anything short of a perfect obedience," he wrote in the *Christian
Union,* "they know her, and I know her, for the best and dear-
est mother that lives." The Clemens household was another
kind of untouched nest of domestic fun and games for Jean
and Clara; while Susy, the prodigy, embarked upon her celebrated biography which was kept under her pillow so conven-
iently for the infatuated parents to read it. Her father, she
said, was a perfect figure of a man except for his teeth and his
temper. In turn, Sam wrote a Lardnerian love song to Jean's
donkey Cadichon —

> O du lieb' Kiditchin
> Du bist ganz bewitchin,
>   Waw- - - -he!
>
> In summer days Kiditchin
> Thou'rt dear from nose to britchin
>   War-- -- -- -he!

Life at Quarry Farm, in Elmira, included eleven cats, while
Clemens rose at seven-thirty, according to Clara's diary, break-
fasted at eight, wrote, played tennis with his daughters, and
"tried to make the donkey go." Mrs. Clemens meanwhile had
a strictly arranged day with her children in the study of languages, reading, history until after dinner when she played
whist with Sam until bedtime. Clemens was nearing fifty; gray-
haired, he was still a funny-looking and tiny-bodied smallish
man, full of adoring worship for his beautiful and cultivated
and wealthy wife. (Later his features became handsome, his

own face beautiful to look at.) At his birthday there were verses by Oliver Wendell Holmes; Richard Watson Gilder made much of the affair in *The Critic;* Frank Stockton, Charles Dudley Warner, Joel Chandler Harris sent letters; Andrew Lang sent a poem. As with Howells and the New Englanders, Clemens welcomed the approval of all these fashionable literary figures of the time, among whom, in fact, he was the only first-rate talent.

His business agent, F. G. Whitmore, lived near the Hartford mansion; even their housekeeper for thirty years, Katie Leary, would eventually set down her reminiscences of this famous family . . . Years later, after Susy's early death, and the tragic deterioration of this whole so happily self-enclosed, talented, and mutually adoring family group, Clemens would brood over the broken sentence which ended Susy's diary of that period. "When I look at the arrested sentence that ends the little book it seems as if the hand that traced it cannot be far — it is gone for a moment only, and will come again and finish it. But that is a dream; a creature of the heart, not of the mind — a feeling, a longing, not a mental product; the same that lured Aaron Burr, old, gray, forlorn, forsaken, to the pier day after day, week after week, there to stand in the gloom and the chill of the dawn, gazing seaward through veiling mists and sleet and snow for the ship which he knew was gone down, the ship that bore all his treasure — his daughter." But that was to be another world of Mark Twain's, imminent but unsuspected in the eighties — when Clemens was still taken up in their Browning readings if he could not quite cotton to the Meredith cult. "It doesn't seem to me that Diana lives up to her reputation," he told Livy. "The author keeps telling us how smart she is, how brilliant, but I never seem to hear her say anything smart or brilliant. Read me some of Diana's smart utterances."

Here was Clemens' statement to Howells, paralleling and confirming the sections on the French Revolution he would write for *A Connecticut Yankee,* on the "catalytic influence" — in reverse — of Carlyle's *French Revolution* upon his own thinking. "How stunning are the changes which age makes in man while he sleeps! When I finished Carlyle's *French Revolution* in 1871 I was a Girondin; every time I have read it since I have read it differently — being influenced & changed, little by little, by life & environment (& Taine & St. Simon); & now I lay the book down once more, & recognize that I am a Sansculotte! — And not a pale, characterless Sansculotte, but a Marat. Carlyle teaches no such gospel, so the change is in *me* — in my vision of the evidence." Carlyle taught no such gospel indeed, and what is fascinating in this letter, to confound Mark Twain's critics and apologists alike, is the simple fact that this statement of radical conviction was written — as we see — just at the height and peak of Sam Clemens' worldly fame and success. Proclaiming himself a Marat Sansculotte, via the reactionary Carlyle, at this golden noon of Clemens' career — why, then, what becomes of the critical orthodoxy which holds that Mark Twain's "black despair" came out of his depths of frustration, financial loss, family pain, and suffering? That it was simply a "bitter old man," perhaps even a drunkard, who penned those brilliant, flaming, sardonic, pulsing revolutionary papers of his later period, and toward the very close of his life? What was most curious, indeed, was the exact opposite of this thesis — that Clemens' spirit was virtually untouched by his own fame, wealth, and popular success, or by his showy and extravagant way of life, or his friendships with men of great status in life, or even with the robber barons of the time who courted him so assiduously. By what remarkable and untoward streak of genius, what innate perversity of feeling, so to say, or originality of vision was it that the more successful Samuel Clemens was, the more rebellious, radical, or revolutionary in essence his inner spirit became!

It was actually the "river and the raft" — that sweet spirit of the garden, infancy, and childhood untouched by the temptations and corruptions of civilization — which saved him. Like Huck, he could not seem to abide conventional American civilization. He had no use for this kind of schooling and "learning," and would rather put in his time loafing and playing, searching his soul, and thinking his own private thoughts. Social fame, success, respectability were all right in their place. But he had been there.

# FOUR

# FAILURE AND TRIUMPH

THERE IS NO question that the decade of the nineties was one of trauma and disaster in Mark Twain's life, financially and domestically. It did indeed *appear* to split his life in two; and life for him would never be the same again. Yet he emerged on the other side of the chasm bloody and beaten in spirit, but unconquered — unconquerable. He had added a dimension of tragic experience to his unique sense of the general comedy of living. The memory of the Garden entails the knowledge of the Fall.

The life of his imagination would take on more complex, darker hues of emotion; his own judgment of his social period and country became sharper and brilliantly prophetic; in the first decade of the twentieth century he wrote one of his greatest books, *The Autobiography of Mark Twain* — one of the great books of our literature. In the last half of his life, indeed, Sam Clemens produced some of his best writing — much of it newly released to the public eye — and the whole thesis of his being a childhood writer destroyed by the pressures of maturity falls to the ground. In terms of a broad cultural psychology, rather, he was a writer who carried his edenic vision of life to the very end; and it was precisely that vision, embedded in his deepest spirit, untouchable, uncorruptible, which *created* his whole remarkable description of our human pilgrimage undertaken amidst so much laughter and so many tears.

But meanwhile the mounting financial crisis of the late eighties was reflected in the uneven writing of *A Connecticut Yankee in King Arthur's Court,* in 1889, and in its divided or even contradictory theme. Was it written as a justification of "the living, tearing, booming Nineteenth, the mightiest of all centuries"? Clemens' description of his own period was not without equivocation, as the book itself was full of ambivalence. It was interesting that he invoked his memories of the Sandwich Isles, "that peaceful land, that beautiful land" as an earthly haven and paradise which he remembered so vividly from a visit of twenty-three years ago.

> That far-off home of solitude, and soft idleness, and repose and dreams, where life is one long slumberous Sabbath, the climate one long summer day, and the good that die experience no change, for they but fall asleep in one heaven and wake up in another . . . No alien land in all the earth has any deep, strong charm for me but that one; no other land could so longingly and so beseechingly haunt me, sleeping and waking, through half a lifetime as that one has done . . .

But was it an "alien land," or was it more likely Sam Clemens' true home? — as the natural genius of the latter nineteenth century would find himself increasingly alienated from his own pushing, tearing, booming, materialistic American society.

That was the hidden conflict in the *Connecticut Yankee,* and the main reason for the book's confused structure. It is true that just before it, enraged by what he felt to be a hostile and unperceptive critical reception of his work, and increasingly torn between the glittering diversions and the mounting anxieties of his lavish career, Clemens had *said* he wanted to retire permanently from literature — and pass "to the cemetery unclodded." But that was the anger of genius, the mask of a prophet; in his heart he had known from the start that he would be a writer, and a writer he was until the last day of his life. He had written the *Yankee* in great bursts of savage energy between his other affairs at the time, and the story also showed its hasty and careless composition. Cast in the Arthurian landscape of sixth-century England, the novel was a curious hodgepodge of juvenile romance (a sort of sequel to *The Prince and the Pauper*), of a burlesque plot line often exaggerated and tedious, of heavy satire — and of great, eloquent passages of social and historical commentary which are still remarkably fresh today.

The hero was a New England mechanic-superman who had returned to the year 528 in the Arthurian court. Clemens did not bother to make this hero any more credible or sympathetic — it is a question of whether he wanted to — than the primitive feudal nobility he satirized here, and who reflected so coarsely his readings in Sir Thomas Malory's "enchanting book." "You soon saw that brains were not needed in a society like that," says the Yankee — but since when had Sam Clemens, the poet of human feeling, cared so much for the rational power of science? In real life, of course, he was in a state of momentary intoxication with his fabulous typesetter — and increasing hatred of it.

The book's opening makes much of the "childlike" nature of the Arthurian court, the dirt and coarseness of life there, the open and frank bawdiness of the conversation, while the

Yankee struggles with the magician Merlin for the supreme power in the kingdom through a series of "scientific" miracles. What is curious, of course, is that Clemens, always so much at home with primitive life and people, did not bring over this insight to Arthurian legend; he was probably too obsessed by his message of radical democracy in the *Yankee* and the evils of monarchy.

In a satanic fantasy of Twain's, his hero becomes the "Boss" of early or prefeudal England. How this artist varied between dreams of omnipotence and visions, satirical and terrifying, of total impotence, failure, and destruction! But just as we almost lose patience with the opening sections of the book, we meet those great passages of personal utterance which do indeed, in the pages of the *Connecticut Yankee,* redeem everything else in the story. The middle Mark Twain, still believing in his vision of ideal democracy, and using his radical democratic critique — far from the "socialism" that Albert Bigelow Paine deplores in hushed tones — on the feudal nobility and the church, on monarchy and the whole European social structure, was very eloquent. In a curious way he reminds us, nostalgic, heartwarming, and lyrical as he sounds today, of *our* past. Our national past.

It was pitiful for a person born in a wholesome free atmosphere to listen to their humble and hearty outpourings of loyalty toward their king and Church and nobility; as if they had any more occasion to love and honor king and Church and noble than a slave has to love and honor the lash, or a dog has to love and honor the stranger that kicks him! Why, dear me, *any* kind of royalty, howsoever modified, *any* kind of aristocracy, howsoever pruned, is rightly an insult . . . It is enough to make a body ashamed of his race to think of the sort of froth that has always occupied its thrones without a shadow of right or reason, and the seventh-rate people that have always figured as its aristocracies — a company of monarchs and nobles who, as a rule, would have achieved only poverty and obscurity if left, like their betters, to their own exertions.

Nor is it any reflection on these sentiments to add that Sam Clemens himself basked, like any provincial westerner, in the glow of the European nobility who happened to admire his work. It is imperative to realize about this special spirit, as we have just noticed, that Clemens' personal life, for good or bad, his personal fame, success, glory, or failure, his grand virtues and his flamboyant faults, hardly seemed to affect the secret, inner core of his genius living its own private, sheltered, wayward, and inspired existence. "The most of King Arthur's British nation," he added here, "were slaves, pure and simple, and bore that name, and wore the iron collar on their necks; and the rest were slaves in fact, but without the name; they imagined themselves men and freemen, and called themselves so. The truth was, the nation as a body was in the world for one object, and one only: to grovel before king and Church and noble; to slave for them, sweat blood for them, starve that they might be fed, work that they might play, drink misery to the dregs that they might be happy, go naked that they might wear silks and jewels, pay taxes that they might be spared from paying them, be familiar all their lives with the degrading language and postures of adulation that they might walk in pride and think themselves the gods of this world . . ."

Despite the uneasy narrative line in the book, the broad and often flat farce, the somewhat paranoid fantasy of the superman mechanic in a world of feudal oafs, the improbable characters who were fashioned out of the Arthurian legends, and the cheap humor of their depiction — Sam Clemens was beginning to wake up in *A Connecticut Yankee,* was gradually

rousing his talent and his temper. Just as he had intuitively
sensed the restrictive and exploitative purpose of the Christian
missionaries in the South Sea Islands (and how much more so,
he would discover, in Africa, Asia, China, where the figure of
Jesus became the sign of racial oppression), so now he knew
the historical role of the medieval Church.

In two or three centuries it had converted a nation of men to a
nation of worms. Before the day of the Church's supremacy in
the world, men were men and held their heads up, and had a man's
pride and spirit and independence; and what of greatness and
position a person got, he got mainly by achievement, not by birth.
But then the Church came to the front with an ax to grind; and
she was wise, subtle, and knew more than one way to skin a cat —
or a nation; she invented "divine right of things," and propped it
all around, brick by brick, with the Beatitudes — wrenching them
from their good purpose to make them fortify an evil one; she
preached (to the commoner) meakness under insult; preached
(still to the commoner, always to the commoner) patience, meanness of spirit, non-resistance under oppression; and she introduced
heritable ranks and aristocracies, and taught all the Christian
populations of the earth to bow down to them and worship them.

Was this poison still in the blood of Christendom right down
to the days of Mark Twain's own birth, as he said? Was the
taint of that reverence for rank and title in the American blood
too? — even more in the age of a new and brazen financial
"aristocracy" seeking patents of Old World nobility for its
primitive and barbarous use of social power. And pawning and
manipulating its "innocent young maidens," of the Jamesian
fantasy, in order to inveigle and trap and bind securely a deca-
dent and bankrupt European nobility in a kind of international con game whose final victors and victims were difficult to
tell apart.

Well, as he added, it just seemed to show "that there isn't

anything you can't stand, if you are only born and bred to it"
— and he continued his discussion of the so-called English
"freeman."

"By a sarcasm of law and phrase they were freemen. Seven-
tenths of the free-population of the country were of just their
class and degree; small 'independent' farmers, artisans, etc.;
which is to say they were the nation, the actual Nation; they
were about all of it that was useful, or worth saving, or really
respectworthy, and to subtract them would have been to subtract the Nation and leave behind some dregs, some refuse, in
the shape of a king, nobility and gentry, idle, unproductive, acquainted mainly with the arts of wasting and destroying . . ."
And then there came the famous passages on the French Revolution, so reviled and misinterpreted in Clemens' day and even
more in our own period. "Why, it was like reading about France
and the French before the ever memorable and blessed Revolution, which swept a thousand years of such villainy away in one
swift tidal wave of blood — one: a settlement of that hoary
debt in the proportion of half a drop of blood for each hogshead
of it that had been pressed by slow tortures out of that people in
the weary stretch of ten centuries of wrong and shame and misery the like of which was not to be mated but in hell. There
were two 'Reigns of Terror,' if we would but remember it and
consider it; the one wrought murder in hot passion, the other
in heartless cold blood; the one lasted mere months, the other
had lasted a thousand years; the one inflicted death upon ten
thousand persons, the other upon a hundred millions; but our
shudders are all for the 'horrors' of the minor Terror, the momentary Terror, so to speak; whereas, what is the horror of
swift death by the ax compared with lifelong death from hunger,
cold, insult, cruelty, and heartbreak? What is swift death by
lightning compared with death by slow fire at the stake? A city

cemetery could contain the coffins filled by that brief Terror which we have all been so diligently taught to shiver at and mourn over; but all France could hardly contain the coffins filled by that older and real Terror — that unspeakable bitter and awful Terror which none of us has been taught to see in its vastness or pity as it deserves."

A cogent indictment of history both past and present in these passages of fiery eloquence on the ever memorable and "blessed Revolution"; passages which enliven and make bearable the tedious plot narrative which Clemens strung out to contain such reflections on history, society, and the sacred institutions of civilization. No wonder that the English nation did not receive the *Yankee* with great plaudits. Or that the United States itself, just then turning away from its own republican heritage of the American Revolution and turning back, as I say, to all the trappings and perquisites of a foundering European nobility — that those privileged and "cultivated" circles of American society also looked with disdain and fear upon such subversive principles and such incendiary talk!

To compound this injury, Clemens insisted upon bringing over his lesson directly to his own period. "You see my kind of loyalty was loyalty to one's country, not to its institutions or its office-holders. The country is the real thing, the substantial thing, the eternal thing; it is the thing to watch over, and care for, and be loyal to; institutions are extraneous, they are its mere clothing, and clothing can wear out, become ragged, cease to be comfortable, cease to protect the body from winter, disease, and death. To be loyal to rags, to shout for rags, to worship rags, to die for rags — that is a loyalty of unreason; it is pure animal; it belongs to monarchy; let monarchy keep it." Were Samuel Clemens' republican impulses still perhaps local, partial, and restricted to an ideal country or democratic nation, a fortunate

and cultivated part of humanity as a whole; while the family of
man is superior to any particular and usually prejudicial patriotism? He was only midway in his process of artistic self-
education; and he shared Whitman's optimistic illusions of
America, which were not at base invidious, or partisan in essence; and Clemens was approaching a larger and grander vista
of history as a whole. "I was from Connecticut, whose Consti-
tution declares 'that all political power is inherent in the people, and all free governments are founded on their authority
and instituted for their benefit; and that they have *at all times*
an undeniable and indefeasible right to *alter their form of government* in such a manner as they may think expedient.' "

He was turning Carlyle's doctrine of "clothes" upon its head.
What impudence and bad taste to recall these revolutionary origins to an established nation embarked upon a new course of
commercialism which had no other concern with democratic
principles than to exploit, corrupt, and control them for its own
profit and privilege. And already sensing this new condition of
affairs, Mark Twain went on to espouse the duty of the rebellious minority *to* rebel. "Under that gospel, the citizen who
thinks he sees that the commonwealth's political clothes are
worn out, and yet holds his peace and does not agitate for a new
suit, is disloyal; he is a traitor. That he may be the only one
who thinks he sees this decay, does not excuse him; it is his
duty to agitate anyway." Harkening back to the inner voice
of the Transcendentalists and their political heirs, the Abolitionists of the earlier nineteenth century, and the revolutionary
activists of the pre-Civil War period, thus Mark Twain spoke
to the burgeoning epoch of the Robber Barons and the Politicos;
thus he spoke to a later age of the Cold War demagoguery and
various modes of McCarthyism. Invigorating words! while the
Yankee went on to declare that his Sandy was a "daisy," and to

describe as "cowboys" such illustrious knights as Sir Launcelot, Sir Pellinore, Sir Carados, and others. These cowboys later became sandwich men to advertise the Yankee's nineteenth-century miracles; and there is another not very entertaining episode about the half sister of King Arthur, Morgan le Fay, who was a medieval sorceress. In the uneven texture of the *Connecticut Yankee* this peculiar plot line contained other brilliant passages on the hypocrisy of man's spirit in those far-off days.

> I will say this for the nobility: that, tyrannical, murderous, rapacious and morally rotten as they were, they were deeply and enthusiastically religious. Nothing could divert them from the regular and faithful performance of the pieties enjoined by the Church. More than once I had seen a noble who had gotten his enemy at a disadvantage, stop to pray before cutting his throat; more than once I had seen a noble, after ambushing and despatching his enemy, retire to the nearest wayside shrine and humbly give thanks, without even waiting to rob the body.

Clemens was not much more helpful on the feudal ladies who all needed a bath, he claimed, who were foul-mouthed, intoxicated, and cruel, and reminded him of nothing so much as a bunch of Comanche squaws. The Twainian panorama of feudal society moved on to the law, as well as religion, to medieval forms of torture and slavery, while the heroic Yankee was developing the toothbrush and stove polish, if, alas, there had been any stoves, and again reflected upon the hopeless passivity of the sixth-century masses. "To wit, that this dreadful matter brought from these downtrodden people no outburst of rage against these oppressors. They had been heritors and subjects of cruelty and outrage so long that nothing could have startled them but a kindness."

Like Clemens, the Yankee abhors cruelty and is bothered by

his conscience, even while he realizes that compassion does not create revolutions. "For it could not help bringing up the un-get-aroundable fact that, all gentle cant and philosophizing to the contrary notwithstanding, no people in the world ever did achieve their freedom by goody-goody talk and moral suasion: it being immutable law that all revolutions that will succeed must *begin* in blood, whatever may answer afterward. If history teaches anything, it teaches that. What this folk needed, then, was a Reign of Terror and a guillotine, and I was the wrong man for them." This was again the objectivity of Clemens, the self-knowledge; in this case the separation of his own temperament from what his mind and heart knew as truth, and the acceptance of that truth — and what more can you really demand from an artist than this open vision of history and his own temperament alike? If Mark Twain still derived from that epoch of an earlier bourgeois society which did not scorn revolution and bloodshed for gaining its purposes — which did not yet fear all social change as a loss of its own power and property — he did not also, in such radical propensities, falsify his own nature, nor overmuch credit his own capacities. "You can't reason with your heart; it has its own laws, and thumps about things which the intellect scorns."

Yet, for an ignorant youth of the southwestern frontier, he had somehow become a self-made Abolitionist.* The middle and later sections of *A Connecticut Yankee* are almost obsessively concerned with a feudal slavery which was certainly not without reference to Twain's own historical period — and the postbellum slavery apologists and newly militant racists who were just then about to reimpose the yoke of white suprem-

* Of course Livy's family, the Langdons, were Abolitionists and had been active in the Underground Railway of Civil War days. But even here, Sam Clemens had apparently worked out his own conclusions about slavery very early in his career.

acy upon the "reconstructed South." A far-fetched analogy? Well, listen to Sam Clemens confirming it. "This was depressing — to a man with the dream of a republic in his head," he said about the apathy of the feudal slaves.

> It reminded me of a time thirteen centuries away when the "poor whites" of our South who were always despised and frequently insulted by the slave-lords around them, and who owed their base conditions simply to the presence of slavery in their midst, were yet pusillanimously ready to side with the slave-lords in all political moves for the upholding and perpetuating of slavery, and did also finally shoulder their muskets and pour out lives in an effort to prevent the destruction of that very institution which degraded them.

Many or most poor-whites, yes; but Clemens had not yet heard of, and would certainly have applauded the martial virtue of those black slaves — unmasked at last from their Uncle Tomism — who actually turned the tide of battle in the Civil War. But now let us note that if *A Connecticut Yankee in King Arthur's Court* opened in defense of the busy, bustling, scientific, commercial, and industrialized nineteenth century as the last, best hope in man's history, there was also a curious kind of underground conflict in both the book and Mark Twain's view of the book. This was a conflict between the public Twain and the private Clemens; and the concluding section of this literary satire on feudal ignorance and superstition is curiously ambiguous, dark-hued, contradictory and destructive. If the basic vision of the middle Mark Twain was that of a bold, open, tough, and radical republicanism, of an older American democracy, as we have seen, this book marked a turning point not merely in his personal fortunes and personal temperament, as Mr. Kaplan et al. would have it, but in something much larger: In Mark Twain's increasing disenchantment with his own American society — that

society, in short, which was already rejecting all his own agrarian democratic and libertarian beliefs. Intended as a lesson about feudalism and monarchy for the democracy, the *Yankee* ended as a lesson about democracy to Mark Twain himself.

Moreover, even at the start of this mixed chronicle, Sam Clemens was far more sympathetic than he appeared to be with the pagan-plenary mind of the sixth century which he was satirizing — and he was far less sympathetic at base with that nineteenth-century materialistic money society which he was ostensibly defending.

There are, at any rate, very curious episodes and passages in the last sections of *A Connecticut Yankee*. Were such figures as Gutenberg, Watt, Arkwright, Whitney, Morse, Stephenson, Bell the true creators of this world — after God — to the Yankee mechanic? It was a curious listing for Mark Twain, including God. The Yankee himself, this scientific superman with his monomaniacal and paranoidal visions of a "Bossism" based on the magic of nineteenth-century inventions, is a particularly tedious hero for the creator of Tom Sawyer and Huck Finn; or for the central narrator of *Roughing It* and *Life on the Mississippi*. During the disguised king's voyages with the Yankee guide, savage mobs of ignorant peasants become just as distasteful as the slave-masters who burn up women and children for their own warmth and comfort. A young mother and her babe are killed for stealing because of their hunger, while, in a holiday of hellions, a mob of men, women, and children rejoice in the spectacle of her suffering. This whole vista of antique injustice and social barbarism becomes a curious panorama of horrors.

There is civil war in Camelot; the nobility is destroyed; the Church declares a Holy Crusade against the Yankee, who, along with his trusted Clarence and fifty-two loyal boys, is then

besieged and imprisoned in a "fortress" which resembles a primitive kind of concentration camp. They have constructed electrical fences which will destroy the feudal knights on their horses at contact. In the fort's inner circle they group a battery of thirteen Gatling guns, protected by the "prettiest garden that was ever planted" — that is, planted with torpedo bombs which explode upon contact.

It was a haunting bit of unconsciousness that made Sam Clemens fall back upon the familiar garden image at the end of a civilization. Nor is Twain's prophetic gift to be altogether scorned in even the poorest flights of his fancy. The last chapters of this lurid chronicle may still remind us today of some harried "preparation" for a nuclear attack. The Yankee orders all factories and homes abandoned, all life removed to "some safe place," since everything is going to be destroyed by his secret bombs. There is a scene in the book where the massed feudal armies attacking the fortress are destroyed. And then as the next step — "I touched a button and shook the bones of England loose from her spine! In that explosion all our noble civilization-factories went up in the air and disappeared from the earth. It was a pity, but it was necessary . . ."

But necessary for whom, or what? This was in fact a horrid ending for Mark Twain's comic satire on feudal civilization. It was a curious conclusion for all the "miracles" of modern civilization: miracles which here, just as they would in later history, culminated in horrifying scenes of mass destruction. The dark fantasy of civilizational collapse was the nightmarish finale to all the nineteenth century's hopes for material achievement, prosperity, and "progress." If *A Connecticut Yankee in King Arthur's Court* is highly uneven, a deeply ambiguous, and often a tedious and haphazard literary production, we must still notice those penetrating and ebullient statements of radical democracy which have been quoted here; and after them, those deeply destructive and pessimistic visions of a purely commercial and material "success" society. The total obliteration of the factories, or the nation's economy, this was a desolate ending for Sam Clemens' mechanical superman. The fantasy of mass killing by scientific machines, of instantaneous destruction had superseded the earlier dream of mass education, physical and material prosperity, intellectual liberation, and spiritual freedom in Arthurian England.

If the *Connecticut Yankee* was partly intended as a juvenile adventure tale with a high moral purpose, in Clemens' uneasy focus on the book, this was hardly an edifying conclusion for eager young minds. The literary establishment of Mark Twain's time which had viewed with distaste the idyllic splendor of *Huck Finn* had here perhaps a better object of protest. At the book's close, the modern hero and his small band of confederates are surrounded by walls upon walls of dead bodies — and by a desolate countryside where the garden of feudal England had flourished.

There is no doubt, of course, that those visions and fantasies of horrible destruction had come partly from Clemens' personal life, as reflected also in the dream life which he used so openly and fully in his work. And indeed the thought of his own destruction translated into the terms of mass destruction and social suicide was only the opposite side of that coin whereby Clemens also identified his own joys and pleasures with nature itself: his primary narcissism in the mythic sense. The state of his personal ego, as a true folk bard, was hardly distinct from the world around him, transmuted into both nature and society. The whole secret of Sam Clemens is right here again in the natural (or "animal") fusion of his own identity with the landscape he occupied; as distinct from a later race of "artists" who deliberately set themselves apart from their society and culture, to become "alienated," "thinking," and "superior" individuals. (But it is safe to say that American literature as a whole until 1910, say, was a folk art when compared with the work of the modern group of expatriated individuals whether at home or abroad.) If the nineties were a crisis period for Mark Twain, and there were dry years and bad books, what was remarkable was not the sorrow and silence but the swiftness of his recovery; and in the midst of the later domestic tragedies, his refuge, as with all writers, was in the solace of writing itself. What is curious is how the critics of his collapse — his breakdown, his split career, his return to childhood, and his escape, above all, from contemporary American society into the past (!) — all following in each other's footsteps, mouthing the same truisms, have managed to ignore or distort Clemens' mature and later works in order to follow their fashionable and herdlike theory.

\* \* \* \*

In 1889 Clemens became the sole owner of the Paige typesetter, in return for paying the glossy inventor $160,000, and $25,000 a year for seventeen years; and he had already paid out $150,000 for the machine since 1885 — sheer phobic obsession and insanity. He was caught; he was hooked in that steel cage which he later envisioned Paige as dying in, while he watched. By 1890, Clemens was borrowing money from Livy's mother, and other members of the family, as Kaplan tells us. He was trying desperately — and sometimes almost on the brink of succeeding, when the machine went wrong again — to raise money from such old friends and acquaintances as another mining millionaire, Senator John P. Jones of Nevada; he invoked visions of Andrew Carnegie and the Standard Oil trust coming in on the world exploitation of the fabulous and diseased machine. In 1891, nearing the end, the Hartford mansion was closed up, the furniture sold, and the servants, after seventeen years, dismissed.* The Clemens family went on a European visit of eight years in order to economize; both Sam's and Livy's health began to break down. They were facing the claims of creditors and threats of bankruptcy. Clemens was making a series of hasty and harried Atlantic crossings between Europe and the United States in order to avoid this — when the stock-market crash, and a succession of railroad and business failures, brought about the great depression of 1893–94.

By the time of the final blow, Sam Clemens had lost almost two hundred thousand dollars on the never-to-be-finished Paige typesetter, and he had sunk over one hundred thousand dollars in the publishing firm, which owed Livy $60,000, and other investors over $80,000. This harrowing speculative and financial experience of the nineties, so highly personal with Clemens and so typical of his age, was part of the emotional ambiguity in *A Connecticut Yankee,* yes, but even more so in *The Tragedy of Pudd'nhead Wilson,* in 1894.

This was the first of those dark parables of the later Mark Twain which included some of his best work; and which, though not only because of financial and family reasons, marked a dividing line in Mark Twain's career. (Though not in half, say, but in thirds.) And at first sight, the drowsing river town of Dawson's Landing, in 1830, was simply another Hannibal of Huck Finn's enchanted youth. The opening descriptions pro-

---

* Clemens had originally built the Hartford house (for over one hundred thousand dollars) in the "Nook Farm" community of artists and intellectuals with an Abolitionist heritage, a bristling women's rights movement, and a radical hue — until the community was gradually taken over by more respectable and mediocre figures like Charles Dudley Warner . . . Toward the end, Harriet Beecher Stowe, symbol of the original colony along with her free-thinking sister, Isabella Beecher Hooker, could be seen wandering among the handsome houses like a mad ghost.

ject an idyllic image of comfort, grace, and cultivation — the outward signs of "an inward grace," according to the eminent English critic, Professor F. R. Leavis. "Provincial as Dawson's Landing may be, it represents a society that has kept its full heritage of civilisation," we are told. And, not unaware of its provinciality, it is far from having lost the desire to keep in touch "with the remoter centres of its civilisation and with its past" — and as evidence of this, Professor Leavis cites the piano-playing of the Italian twins in the story. In its whole attitude toward distinction, we are told, Dawson's Landing appeals "to standards other than the 'democratic,'" and "represents a subtler civilisation than accounts of 'the pioneer community' might suggest," and now Professor Leavis cites Judge Driscoll (York Leicester Driscoll, that is) as a Virginia gentleman without peer. As being fine and just and generous and respected, esteemed and beloved by the community. "It is quite unequivocal," adds the British arbiter, just because "he is a 'gentleman' — representing an ideal above that of material success and beyond the reach of the ordinary members of the community . . ."

Enough, I am tempted to add, of this nonsense, which forms the critical introduction to a standard textbook edition of a Mark Twain book which is compounded of equivocality; or which is devoted precisely to showing up *both* the aristocratic and the democratic codes of behavior in a slave-owning Missouri town. Professor Leavis is solemnly applying the standard (and procrustean) procedures of the "aristocratic" sensibility to a writer who had no use for such subtleties, other than upon occasion to deride them with hilarious parody. But Professor Leavis insists upon compounding his series of manifest absurdities. His Introduction — besides providing a startling example of the nature of contemporary "esthetic" criticism when it strays off its narrow and prim boundaries — is useful to us as describing precisely what Mark Twain was *not* doing in *Pudd'nhead Wilson*. The central point in the Leavis analysis of *Pudd'nhead Wilson* is an almost euphoric exaltation of that code of the Southern Christian Gentleman which Mark Twain consistently and continually satirized from the start to the finish of his career; and which, in this particular novel of slavery, he was subjecting to its most arduous and ironical moral judgment.

What could be more obtuse or perverse in the theory and practice of Formalist criticism? And who but Mark Twain could better illuminate the limits and failures of such a critical methodology, not only in relation to Twain's work, where its results are fatal, and laughable; but even in its own area, where its results can only be sterile and mediocre. What a bad day it was for the esteemed F. R. Leavis, whose critical opinions colored a whole sector of academic criticism around the mid-twentieth century, when he came to grips (as he thought) with the primary American genius of the late nineteenth century. "Mark Twain unmistakably admires Judge Driscoll and Pembroke Howard," Leavis adds — "they are the two most sympathetic characters in the drama"(!) and "they give the 'code' itself their active endorsement" — as though this 'code' was not precisely what Sam Clemens was crucifying in his somber allegory. Thus too, Pudd'nhead Wilson himself, who finally succumbs to the call of race, blood, and prejudice in the story, becomes "the poised pre-eminently civilised moral centre of the drama." And this kind of critical dogma ends by debasing even its own language in such a repetitive and incantative use of words like "moral centre" and "civilisation."

The real center of *Pudd'nhead Wilson* is not as easy to reach as Professor Leavis' peculiar analysis might suggest. For after all both Judge Driscoll and Pembroke Howard, who are the sympathetic, noble aristocratic heroes of the gentlemanly code in this culturally aspiring frontier village — according to our British cousin's view, that is — are the central slave owners of the story, and therefore responsible for all the social misery, suffering, and hatred of the novel. And one of the story's mysteries is precisely why "Pudd'nhead" himself, an ostensible outcast hero, surrenders his own humanity and dignity in order to support Twain's acerbic version of southern chivalry and honor.*

But all this hardly explains Professor Leavis' propensity for crying "nigger" — "nigger, nigger, nigger!" — in the preface to *Pudd'nhead Wilson,* with a kind of perverse delight in using a word which, as we have noticed, Sam Clemens was extraordinarily punctilious about for his period, and hardly ever used in his own auctorial voice. And finally — "The attitude of *Pudd'nhead Wilson* is remote from cynicism or pessimism," and here Mark Twain "has achieved a mature, balanced and impersonal view of humanity" — while in fact, if this book reveals anything, it is the depths of anger, sorrow, and despair from which Clemens wrote this curious fable of southern slavery and miscegenation.

It is refreshing after all this high-toned, morally righteous, noble Christian esthetic cant, to come upon the salty tang of the book's first aphorism selected from Pudd'nhead Wilson's Calendar. "There is no character, howsoever good and fine, but it

---

* To anybody who is acquainted with the body of Mark Twain's work, the Leavis analysis of *Pudd'nhead Wilson* is so aberrant as to illustrate the folly of a whole school of conservative academic literary criticism, which, rising to power during the moral and psychological decline of western European democracy, found an esthetic refuge, a supposedly esthetic haven, in devising the peculiar mode of "Christian" tradition and culture which has been described above. Denying the plain meaning of their own epoch of revolutionary history, these critics have deprived *all* history of any valid meaning; while their notions of Christianity, Culture, and Tradition, when applied to a writer like Mark Twain, are suddenly revealed in all their absurdity.

can be destroyed by ridicule . . . Observe the ass, for instance; his character is about perfect, he is the choicest spirit among all the humbler animals, and yet see what ridicule has brought him to. Instead of feeling complimented when we are called an ass, we are left in doubt." The first whiff of Clemens' acrid heresy disperses all the sanctimonious spiritual nobility of Dr. Leavis' academe; though we can never quite see any real connection between the Calendar's aphorisms and the novel's action, beyond the fact that Pudd'nhead's "Calendar" was probably taken from Clemens' own notebook. There is no doubt that this curiously gifted failure as a lawyer, and this superior social outcast in the town, Pudd'nhead Wilson himself — ruined by his humor, and represented as the tale's "observer" — is a projection of Clemens' own derogatory self-vision of the period. For the opening of *Pudd'nhead Wilson* presents almost a deliberately, even artificially, contrived effect of the familiar beauty and bliss of Huck Finn's youth — only here it is the *appearance* of paradise in the Mississippi River setting of Dawson's Landing which Clemens is deliberately invoking. It is a conspicuously false paradise.

It is obvious, similarly, that the glowing phrases of admiration for Judge York Leicester Driscoll, as the highest type of old-fashioned southern grandee, an FFV incarnate, is as ironical, ambiguous, and deceptive as is the whole "happy opening" of this Mississippi River anti-idyll. For the first time in his work, in a major sense, Clemens was deliberately adopting the sardonic and tragic mask which, say, Melville — another innocent native spirit who had felt himself similarly wounded and betrayed by life — used in the *Piazza Tales*. It is the Judge's brother, Percy Northumberland Driscoll (the ornate and aristocratic names are significant) who is Roxy's owner and who threatens to sell his slaves "down the river" — a nightmare vision for any Missouri Negro, as Clemens says — because of petty thievery in his house. It is this threat which forces Roxy to replace the "white" Driscoll baby with her own "black" Driscoll baby. The opening pages of the novel contain a remarkable discourse on "negritude" (and by implication on miscegenation) which immediately casts an ambiguous shadow over the high-flown admiration for the old southern slave-owning gentry. This is also a kind of super stage-setting, a deliberately conceived fictional illusion; or, to anybody but a Professor Leavis, it is pure hogwash.

Percy Driscoll gets all his Negro slaves to confess their guilt (true or not); does not carry through his threat to sell them to the cotton plantations; and makes a notation in his diary about his own magnanimity and humanity before his night's sleep; while the terrified Roxy carries through her fatal deed of duplicity — or revenge, or justice? What could be clearer than this in the novel's opening if one has but eyes to read? "To all intents and purposes Roxy was as white as anybody, but the one sixteenth of her which was black out-voted the other fifteen parts and made her a Negro. She was a slave and saleable as such. Her child was thirty-one parts white, and he, too, was a slave and, by a fiction of law and custom, a Negro." * It is this fiction of law and custom, which Clemens had suggested in *Huckleberry Finn,* that, much more savagely and ironically, *Pudd'nhead Wilson* would deal with. It is also interesting to recall that almost fifty years later, another southern writer, Ellen Glasgow, would state the same theme in almost the same words, in the novel called *In This Our Life,* in 1941.

In the basic structure of *Pudd'nhead Wilson,* too, let us note that when the white Driscoll baby is substituted for the "black"

---

* This of course became Nazi doctrine about any taint of Jewish blood in any remote ancestor. As we shall notice again in Mark Twain's work, the white man's treatment of the black man became a historical precedent and source for the white man's treatment of the white man.

Driscoll baby by Roxy (we are not yet told the real father of Roxy's child), we are to all effects and purposes dealing with another set of twins in Mark Twain's work — and to complicate things further there will be a "real" set of twins later on in the narrative. And the names of the two interchanged infants — "Thomas à Becket" Driscoll and "Valet de Chambre" (Driscoll, though not yet said) carry their own mocking irony, since Roxy's ignorant pretense of grandeur in naming her child also reflected on the false pretenses of the heroic English names in this southwestern frontier society. A "classical" English name that Clemens deliberately exaggerated in his text, for after all which given name was more pretentious or more ridiculous?

Dawson's Landing is halfway between the idyllic Hannibal of Huck Finn and the corrupted town of Hadleyburg in Mark Twain's fiction; and every soul in *Pudd'nhead Wilson,* including the noble slave Roxy herself, is subjected, if not to a cynical reduction of moral stature, at least to curious levels of behavior in Sam Clemens' darkening vision of experience. Irony and tragedy have taken over the center stage in Clemens' comic proscenium of life. What depths of ambiguity are expressed in the history of the transposed Tom — the falsely "Negro" Tom, who is also a later and darker cousin of Tom Sawyer in Mark Twain's genealogy of childhood — the falsely "Negro" Tom who then becomes a false white aristocrat. It is his undoing. He becomes spoiled, arrogant, deceitful, vicious-tempered, nasty (though verbally "clever" in the mode of Tom Sawyer); even while the history of the transposed white "aristocrat" now turned into the black Chambers reveals how easily a slave is made. The transposed "black child" takes on the worst aspects of the white master race, while Chambers Driscoll becomes so versed in human servility, obedience, docility that even when he regains his true personality and social position, he cannot unlearn the slave idiom — the slave ideology — of his youth. If Mark Twain is making a case here for human malleability, as was his wont, this time it is an ironic and rather horrifying case for mobility downward — in both the "highest" and the lowest levels of southwestern frontier society.

After a few severe canings by his father, the generous, humane, and aristocratic Percy Driscoll, Chambers becomes Tom's protector, guardian, and servant; the relationship is ruinous for both of them. So, too, Roxy surrenders all her human pleasures for the sake of her child's security.

> Tom had long ago taught Roxy "her place." It had been many a day now since she had ventured a caress or a fondling epithet in his quarter. Such things, from a "nigger," were repulsive to him, and she had been warned to keep her distance and remember who she was. She saw her darling gradually cease from being her son, she saw *that* detail perish utterly; all that was left was master — master, pure and simple, and it was not a gentle mastership either. She saw herself sink from the sublime height of motherhood to somber deeps of unmodified slavery. The abyss of separation between her and her boy was complete. She was merely his chattel, now, his convenience, his dog, his cringing and helpless slave, the humble and unresisting victim of his capricious temper and vicious nature.

Was Roxy's sublime sacrifice really worth it in the end — in the confines of a social system which by its nature corrupted both master and slave, or perhaps even in the larger confines of human nature itself? Clemens' answer is corrosive. Roxy is not only ruined — she is sold down the river — by the son she has protected and elevated in the world. In the process of deception her own character is ruined, rather than elevated, by her suffering; and in the end, when the true nature of her relationship with Tom is revealed, there is no hint, but rather the opposite, of any kind of mother-son affectional bond.

But right here is the flaw of Twain's enigmatic fable. If the *concept* of Roxy as a handsome, brilliant, passionate, and highly emotional mulatto slave heroine is admirable, the literary execution of this idea is uneven and sometimes quite false. Emancipated as Sam Clemens was for his period and place, there is still a kind of southern white paternalism in this portrait of the Negro woman. Her development in *Pudd'nhead Wilson* is not always consistent and sometimes quite erratic, and her character is often manipulated for the purposes of Clemens' plot line.* Similarly with Tom, the hero-villain of the story; while his white "twin," Chambers, becomes a kind of typical shuffling darkie, and the Italian twins of the story are little more than romantic images of European culture, never fully realized as people. The best that can be said for all the characters of *Pudd'nhead Wilson* as characters is that they are social or literary types whom Clemens is manipulating for the sake of his moral. What we really have here, as in the whole series of these later dark parables of Mark Twain, is a kind of literary surrealism, where the meaning of the artist's message is more important to him than the depiction of human character for the sake of human character.

* Compare Leslie Fiedler's commendation of Roxy as "a creature of passion and despair rare among the wooden images of virtue or bitchery that pass for females in American literature." But the plain fact is that Mark Twain, who loved women deeply (despite Mr. Fiedler's alternate charge of homosexuality in *Huck Finn*), did not create an effective heroine in the whole body of his work — except perhaps Livy, his Eve, and Mary Baker Eddy, his female Satan. Mr. Fiedler's study of love and death in the American novel is replete with similar misjudgments and shows a curious kind of ignorance and bad taste. For one thing, some admirable heroines — in Fiedler's depiction of women — are ignored; while the effective feminine portraits of Willa Cather, Ellen Glasgow, and Edith Wharton are misinterpreted. These are no wooden images of virtue or bitchery that pass for females in American literature — only Mr. Fiedler doesn't seem to know it. One reaches the conclusion that this critic, while he has picked up some obvious shortcomings in our culture and art, has not himself a perfect understanding of love or women, or of American literature. Dreiser, whose portraits of women are perhaps the best in American literature, is negated or ignored because Mr. Fiedler accepted the Cold War Culture platform that Dreiser was to be negated or ignored.

But still that ambiguous moral or "message" continues to haunt us in the pages of *Pudd'nhead*, and these curious characters, acting out a kind of modern morality play, do have their moments of eloquence or verisimilitude when they emerge as more than fictional props. We are caught by the power of Mark Twain's meaning here even when we are annoyed or uneasy at his use of his literary material. For all that, Roxy is often an angry, bitter, and brilliant mulatto woman, at her core both radical and rebellious. She is a big step forward in Clemens' own conceptualizing of American Negro slave types, and her perfectly natural wariness of the fingerprinting system (which eventually leads to Tom's ruin) even deceives Wilson himself into reflecting upon her black ignorance and "superstitiousness." And what shall we say of this "Pudd'nhead," the brightest man in the town who is yet condemned to a kind of provincial limbo through one careless and ironical remark — who spends all his spare time tinkering with new scientific and mechanical "miracles" like the fingerprinting system itself, and who yet does reach the central truth in the complex plot structure of the novel?

"Pudd'nhead" is of course another obvious projection of Sam Clemens' wounded and increasingly bitter self-image during the period of his mechanical and financial experiments with the printing press and the publishing house. Mark Twain, in his moment of desperation and dark despair, threw out a series of ambiguous and ironical and fractured literary projections of his own wounded and betrayed consciousness. Which character in *Pudd'nhead Wilson* is *not,* indeed, part of this process of psychic projection and catharsis — but a projection and catharsis, in turn, which created great literature?

The twin fantasy is again dominant, and here the true son and heir, the "white" Tom Driscoll, is condemned to a lifelong existence of black servitude from which he cannot free himself even after his actual liberation. (It is interesting to remember that Melville also used the ironical masks of black "slaves" and white "masters" in "Benito Cereno," where again the "black furies" have reduced the ship's master to a complete nervous breakdown and physical collapse.) And similarly, Tom Driscoll, the "black imposter," when raised to a position of white power, becomes heartless, cruel, vicious — his fall from grace when Roxy tells him that he is her son only increases the depth of his depravity. There is no doubt of Clemens' identification with Roxy's role also: the powerful spirit, rebellious and raging at a hard fate, which goes through life in a false state of servitude, and is destroyed, as it were, by its own act of generosity.

*Pudd'nhead Wilson* is full of these reverberations and reflections of Clemens' psychic state at the time, and if he hardly bothered to embody his characters in their human complexity, the power of the narrative comes from his own direct emotional involvement with the literary projection. The maxims of Pudd'n- head at the start of each chapter, in most cases having no apparent connection with the literary action, are even more directly Clemens' own mordant reflections about the bitterness of life, the folly, the tragedy here, much more than any sense of comedy. What is curiously absent from the description of Dawson's Landing in the years just before the Civil War is any theoretical or ideological discussion of the slavery issue itself. But the total picture of frontier life is really so negative and destructive in this reversed idyll of a southwestern river town that the social institution of slavery might appear to be only a minor sin, after all, in the sorry conditions of man's total existence. Since Pudd'nhead Wilson is the ostensible hero of the book, the bright and thinking man, the social outcast, it comes as a surprise and disappointment to us that he, too, subscribes without reflection to the southern code of honor in the book.

The subplot of the Italian twins, intended originally as a comic tale, was reworked into Roxy's story to demonstrate the same sense of tragedy and cruel irony pervading the novel. Their treatment as "foreigners" similarly reflects the inner flaw of that aristocratic southern "code" which in these pages condemned Roxy and the son she had sacrificed her life to save to such a hateful and treacherous bond of self-protection against all the destroying artifices of the white man's culture. "It was wonderful to find America," we are told in Pudd'nhead Wilson's Calendar, "but it would have been more wonderful to miss it."

But twins again; two sets of twins in this enigmatic fable that yet provides a key insight into Mark Twain's life and art: his Twinish nature. The irrelevant Italian twins (who do suggest, despite Mr. Leavis, how swiftly frontier society turned upon "foreign" royalty or European culture) lead us back to the original set of "white" and "black" twins who are interchanged — and hence interchangeable, despite all rigid racial taboos — and who constitute one of Mark Twain's most profound intuitions about not merely "the race problem" and the nature of slavery — but the nature of man himself. This shifting, enigmatic relationship of master and slave where the black child becomes the white child, and the white the black; where the seed of the "master race" becomes a perfect serf — and the scion of the submerged black race becomes a noxious, evil and degraded white "master": what a brilliantly disturbing central concept was Pudd'nhead Wilson based on! What contradictions, incongruities, contrarieties, hidden affinities, and polar oppositions does this mysterious fable suggest.

We have already noticed and will elaborate further the cultural concept of the double soul which Mark Twain embodied so purely; his embodiment of the pagan-plenary and primitive man conjoined with the moral-historical-social vision which is so clearly the result of civilizational repression. But just consider how accurately Sam Clemens' early identification with the black slave (versus the white masters) supports this thesis, while it echoes and reverberates through his art. The black slave who educates the white "master" in *Huck Finn*; the vagabond king and the king turned vagabond in *The Prince and the Pauper*; the central relationship of master-pilot and impudent cub in *Life on the Mississippi* — these are three obvious variations on this theme. It is quite true that these early meditations on black and white, master and slave, royalty and serfdom — and Twain's natural affinity with the black slave — were at the base of his later thinking, his mature role as America's conscience before the face of the world. This was the true emotional source of that whole later period of penetrating and prophetic social commentary; of that remarkable repudiation of a white Anglo-Saxon culture which was based on colonial conquest and oppression; and of that final identification with the darker-skinned races of the world which has made Mark Twain such a revered figure, not merely in revolutionary Russia, but in India, China, Asia, and South America today.

But the issue is still deeper. We also remember how those American writers of an earlier period, like Hawthorne and Melville, were disturbed by darkness as the symbol of sex, sin, and evil, despite their uneasy animadversions on the duplicity of "whiteness" in such novels as *Moby Dick* and *The Marble Faun*. Later on there was Sherwood Anderson's *Dark Laughter* as the mark of human pleasure and joy — but do you begin to see the matter now? For blackness was pagan freedom and splendor to the early Sam Clemens and the later Mark Twain alike. And whiteness was the "master race" of social repression, imperial power, and the exploitation of human innocence. Law and Order indeed. That fascination with darkness run-

ning through all American literature reflects our major writers' unconscious or half-conscious awareness of this problem;
but Sam Clemens was the first and only writer, among all the
earlier ones, to rush into the "ambush" of blackness and dusky
nature, to embrace it with all his soul, and hence to enrich his
whole life and art. That is the real fascination of *Pudd'nhead
Wilson,* its true meaning which was perhaps even unknown to
the artist who wrote it, and which will be verified by — even
while it helps to focus and explain — his later career and his
last, best enigmatic fable, *The Mysterious Stranger* itself.

Lurid, sentimental, melodramatic, highly uneven as the central scenes in *Pudd'nhead Wilson* are, they are yet rough gold
in a literary sense. And here Clemens anticipated many of the
racial insights of Richard Wright, for example, just as the
heavily detailed trial scene which concludes the book pointed
toward the literary form of both Dreiser's *An American Tragedy* and Wright's *Native Son.* If *Pudd'nhead* was a psychic projection of Clemens' growing sense of despair in the mid-nineties, both a literary configuration of his changing state of mind
and a partial catharsis for it, what is always relevant is how
completely he was able to project an almost purely personal
sense of failure and defeat into the social and historical issue of
slavery and miscegenation in a frontier river town. How he
merged and fused the personal and the communal again; and
after all, it is not with the human sources and origins of
*Pudd'nhead* we are finally concerned, but with the literary and
artistic result. What matters is not the fact that *Pudd'nhead,*
the first of a series of such dark fables by Mark Twain, was the
literary projection of a personal mood — but the *kind* of
psychological catharsis and literary achievement it was. And
just as *Pudd'nhead* was one of the most interesting precursors
of the best later work of Mark Twain in this uneasy, uneven,
obsessed, and irregular literary career which still remains one

of the major achievements of the national letters — so *Personal Recollections of Joan of Arc,* in 1896, was Sam Clemens' worst book.

This was perhaps the single exception to the Mark Twain rule that there is always something of value in even his worst work. It is difficult to find *anything* of interest in *Joan of Arc* — except its badness.

During the years of its composition, of course, Sam Clemens was still undergoing pangs and throes and horrid nightmare fantasies of the financial bankruptcy which threatened to leave him a broken and disgraced man. His finances had been in a critical condition since 1891. Begging and borrowing not only from Livy and her family, but from his friends and literary and artistic acquaintances, selling off his own securities, Sam Clemens was in an anguished state of mind.*

"I am terribly tired of business," he wrote to Fred Hall, the new manager of the Webster publishing house during those years. "I am by nature and disposition unfit for it, and I want to get out of it . . . Get me out of business!" A realization, rather like that of the Hemingway hero in *To Have and Have Not,* which had taken him all his life to reach — and which would never be quite fulfilled. "Great Scott, but it's a long year — for you & for me!" he wrote Hall again during those hectic days. "I never knew the almanac to drag so." And: "I am very glad indeed if you and Mr. Langdon (Livy's brother)

---

* Although Justin Kaplan's study of Mark Twain has corrected the facts and figures in Albert Bigelow Paine's standard three-volume earlier biography and added much new material, it is still Paine's work that we go to in order to find out the intimate, day-by-day account of the Clemens family and Clemens himself. I am drawing upon this earlier work here for the account of Clemens' alternating and conflicting emotions in his statements at that time. In some respects, indeed, despite Paine's obvious Victorianism (far easier to spot than our imbedded contemporary prejudices), despite his sentimentality, hero-worship, and generally bad literary judgments — all of which are overcorrected, so to speak, by Kaplan's astringent and reductive Freudism — Paine is perhaps closer to the essential truth about Sam Clemens' life, not to mention the complete and intimate documentation which he offers, and which can be evaluated from a modern point of view.

are able to see any daylight ahead. To me none is visible . . ."
But in the curious alternation of the American dream and
nightmare which Sam Clemens personified to the hilt — those
dramatic sequences of pleasure and despair; of fame and success and abysmal, heartsick failure; of gaiety and laughter, and
of utter, tragic depths — it would be the laughter that would
still prevail; and already in September, 1893, he had met his
Fairy Prince. Henry Huttleston Rogers, one of the most ruthless and arrogant and cunning directors of the Standard Oil
complex, and yet one of the most charming, cultivated and
generous of all the Robber Baron tribe, had become Clemens'
close friend, his patron and business manager. In the grand
manner of American finance capitalism at its peak, not unlike
the medieval Medicis who fascinated Theodore Dreiser, Rogers
simply liquidated all of Clemens' failing business enterprises
and took over the control of his finances. The publishing house
went first, although both Sam and Livy, and perhaps Livy
more, could hardly bear the disgrace of bankruptcy, and they
set themselves the hard task of repaying their creditors in full.

# FIVE

# THE ENRAGED RADICAL

Though there were moments in Mark Twain's life when you wonder if this amiable genius, all embedded in his rocking cradles, his floating rafts, his majestic sleeping couch, meandering and laughing his way through man's brief and essentially comic existence, was nevertheless — quite apart from and beyond the matter of civilizational discontents — pursued by some deeper, eternally vengeful and avenging furies, such as those imagined by man from the dawn of existence, and just as Clemens himself described Nature's perverted malice.

Directly after the return of Sam, Livy, and Clara to England, at the end of the worldwide lecture tour,* they heard that Susy, who had been left in America with Jean under Kate Leary's charge, was ill. This was August 15, 1896, and Livy and Clara took passage back home. Three days later, when they were about halfway across the ocean, Clemens received the news that Susy had died of meningitis. Nothing was spared the Clemenses in the terrible end of their favorite child. Three days before her death, Susy had become blind; before that she

*In 1896, bankrupt, in poor health and apparently hopelessly in debt at the age of 60, Sam Clemens had the inspiration of making a worldwide lecture tour—on which he spoke to huge audiences, earning as much as a thousand dollars a week, and discovering he was world-famous as the epitome of the American conscience, and our primary literary figure. Visiting Hawaii, New Zealand, Australia, India and South Africa on this trip, Sam Clemens also discovered the meaning of the white man's imperialism upon the darker peoples of the earth, and this became a central concern of his later writing.

had wandered through the rooms of the Hartford mansion in delirium and pain, calling for her mother.

After her death nothing was ever quite the same between Sam and Livy and the children, or with the whole domestic scene of affection and gaiety which had made the Clemenses' marriage and homelife so unique in literary history. Despite all the stress and strain, their Hartford house had been "not unsentient matter," as Clemens wrote to Twichell. "It had a heart & a soul & eyes to see us with, & approvals & solicitudes & deep sympathies; it was of us, & we were in its confidence, & lived in its grace & in the peace of its benediction. We never came home from an absence that its face did not light up & speak out its eloquent welcome — & we could not enter it unmoved." But now they knew they were not welcome in the Hartford house, and their temporary home in Chelsea (England) became a dismal place.

Clemens' notes and letters were full of anguished references to Susy, according to Paine's account; he accepted Livy's black despair on top of his own. They saw nobody and wished to see nobody; they concealed their address except for their closest friends. They refused to celebrate Thanksgiving and Christmas that year, and sat alone, nursing their sorrow. Clemens became superstitious about their bad luck and said that it was risky for people to have anything to do with them. He wrote desperate letters to Howells. "Will healing ever come, or life have value again? And shall we see Susy? Without doubt. Without a *shadow* of doubt if it can furnish opportunity to break our hearts again." He took, moreover, the full blame for Susy's death upon himself, as he had, so many years ago, for his brother's. The guilt for his own financial manipulations, for driving his family into the shame of bankruptcy, the ordeal of poverty and of scrimping afterwards — all this was blended with and exacerbated by the final agony of believing that Susy might not have died if they had not been away from her.

If Sam Clemens had a curious identification with Satan at the core of his psychic being, this was a sorrowing and sinful Satan now who took responsibility for all of God's doings, for the moral universe which indeed he had willfully defied. "To Mrs. Clemens," Paine writes, "he poured himself out in a letter in which he charged himself categorically as being wholly and solely responsible for the tragedy, detailing step by step with fearful reality his mistakes and weaknesses which had led to their downfall, the separation from Susy, and this final incredible disaster. Only a human being, he said, could have done these things." Very similarly, later on, in Mark Twain's *Autobiography,* we learn that Clemens blamed himself completely for the death of their first child, their baby son; a guilty "secret" he had contained within himself for almost his entire life. Did Livy also believe this in her secret heart; or did she allow Sam to believe it without relieving his burden? There is no doubt, at least, that after Susy's death the domestic life of the Clemenses turned upon itself. From this point started Livy's psychic and physical decline which also affected Clara's uneasy temperament, while Jean's health had already been failing.

After a long and full career of such extraordinary fame and wealth and pleasure and affection, surviving even the worst blows of harsh adversity with remarkable fortitude, tenacity, and courage; for almost a full decade of their later life facing a penurious and disgraceful old age, as it seemed, and suddenly liberated only to meet with a last deep blow, a fatal domestic tragedy, the once blessed and exceptionally fortunate and graceful spiritual union of the Clemenses finally cracked.

Yet Sam Clemens himself remained forever faithful and loving to his Livy, and incredibly brought his own writing powers back to another triumphant peak, and was even on the point of once again re-establishing some modicum of personal fulfillment and content when (this was almost an accursed house like that, later on, of Eugene O'Neill) the final blow fell — not yet visible to Sam Clemens, though already hinted at. Meanwhile at sixty, with Livy at fifty, the demonism also at the core of Mark Twain's spirit (not unlike the ragings of a Theodore Dreiser, later on, at a God of Justice and Mercy who yet allowed such senseless deeds of suffering and cruelty) was transfused into his art and his social vision. "I wish the Lord would disguise Himself in citizen's clothing & make a personal examination of the sufferings of the poor in London," Clemens jotted in his notebook, at this time. "He would be moved & would do something for them Himself."

This was the same London scene, of course, whose "lowest depths" Henry James found in the ignoble, mean-spirited middle classes of *The Wings of the Dove,* or even worse, the perfidious and unholy storybook "anarchists" of *The Princess Casamassima.* But Clemens was among the first of a whole series of more observant American writers who bore witness to the social misery in England.

Like all great writers he found his opiate and his salvation and his resurrection in the creative act itself. "I don't mean that I am miserable; no — worse than that — indifferent," he wrote to Howells. "Indifferent to nearly everything but work. I like that; I enjoy it, & stick to it. I do it without purpose & without ambition; merely for the love of it. Indeed, I am a mud-image; & it puzzles me to know what it is in me that writes & has comedy fancies & finds pleasure in phrasing them . . ." What it was in him, of course, was his genius — and not being able to sleep, he took pleasure in setting to work, sometimes, at four o'clock in the morning. It was during this period of darkness, too, that Clemens issued that celebrated statement to a newspaper reporter. (The press accounts of the time pictured him as abandoned by his family, deserted by all, drunk, sick, poor, and dying.) "Just say the report of my death has been grossly exaggerated." And when Livy kept on objecting to words like breech-clout, stench, offal, or to "a shady-principled cat" which had a family in every port, Clemens was mild. "You are steadily weakening the English tongue, Livy."

During this period, too, Clemens began developing his interest in dreams and in the dream life (or in illusion and reality) which almost every great writer has had, but which the Freudians find so portentously and ominously significant. Which was the dream, which was the reality, he asked himself, and sometimes he wondered if even his wife and family and his domestic life had been just a dream — a dreamlike fantasy which indeed he felt had now vanished. On the first anniversary of Susy's death, when the Clemenses were spending the summer in Switzerland, Livy took a small bag, went off for the day on a steamer to read over Susy's poetry, while Sam spent the day writing the beautiful ode "In Memoriam." The tension in the house was very great, Paine says. "A gloom settled on the household, a shadow of restraint" which was marked.

Clemens often worked in bed, and when a reporter came to see him, he refused to get up but made another concession to Livy's embarrassment. "Why, Livy, if you think so, we might have the other bed made up for him." And after all his debts had been paid off, his royalties were bringing in an income, and Rogers was investing his money for him, Clemens could hardly resist the old temptation of fascinating mechanical inventions which would yield him immense quick fortunes. He negotiated with the Austrian inventor Szezepanik for the rights to a carpet-pattern machine. He planned to obtain an option at five hundred thousand dollars and to organize a monopoly at a much larger amount to control the carpet-weaving of the world, if Rogers approved. Rogers did not approve; and Clemens did not always ask for Rogers' approval. He bought an interest, according to Paine, in a skimmed-milk invalid food called Plasmon, which would cure the human race of its ills; and meanwhile, in 1900, he published *The Man That Corrupted Hadleyburg and Other Stories and Essays.*

The volume as a whole included stories and articles, mainly in a popular vein and written for cash in the late nineties, but some as early as "The £1,000,000 Bank-Note" in 1893. Uneven in craft, rough in detail, "Hadleyburg" is a remarkable story, a fascinating sequel to *Pudd'nhead Wilson,* an important precursor to *The Mysterious Stranger* in the dark vein of Mark Twain's later fables. This western village was really a Hegelian reversal, or contradiction, of Hannibal, Missouri. Its fame was for its "commercial integrity," the moral virtue, the upright honesty and sobriety of its citizens. But who was the "mysterious stranger" himself who, having been wounded by the town, deliberately set out to corrupt it, to prove that all its pretenses of impeccable respectability were a fraud? This was again a dream-nightmare tale with a satanic figure as the mysterious activating presence; this was the dream turned inside out. Its satire followed that of the Virginia aristocrats in *Pudd'nhead,* those FFV's (First Families of Virginia) who were so honorable about everything except their subhuman slaves; and at base "Hadleyburg" was an eloquent example of the corruption of the old American republic by the great booming nineteenth century's notion of "progress."

The tone of the story was not realistic but symbolical, or closer, like *Pudd'nhead,* to a kind of native surrealism which Clemens invented for his own purposes. And "Hadleyburg" was also a brilliant study, psychological and social, of the influence of money upon the human spirit, or of the prevalence of greed in the human temperament when confronted by temptation. Clemens was projecting his own torment over a decade of financial ruin, surely, but he was projecting it into a specific historical context: the corruption of the town's earlier, more natural and less materialistic human types and social relationships. When the mysterious stranger leaves the sack of gold, poor Mrs. Richards immediately locks the house doors and bars the windows which had previously been open; her first thought is of thieves. The full, open, and easy quality of western frontier existence — the earlier democracy of small means and social equality in the older epochs of the national development — has been lost forever.

"It is dreadful to be poor," says Mr. Richards; but it is much more dreadful for them to be rich. His first thought was to destroy the stranger's written bequest and keep the sack of gold; the virtue of the frontier crumbled under the first temptation. Hadleyburg was indeed an "honest, narrow, self-righteous and stingy" town, as the village rebel, Barclay Goodson, had declared. In these symbolic or surrealist tales, Twain often used rather obvious names for his central figures.

And this is also a story of a terrible moral conformity, a fear of generous or bold human action, a show of public virtue as a mask for private gain, an overwhelming social hypocrisy which covers the contortions of small, if not evil souls.

The Richardses are really a terrible couple whom Clemens described with absolute accuracy; we flinch when we read about them because we understand them so well. The central logic, the developments in the early part of the story, the twists of human temperament and social circumstance alike, are invented by a diabolical intelligence. The greedy cunning of the Richardses is only equaled by their tormented anxiety — not an

anxiety about their scheming fancies but as to the possible appearance of their deeds. There is no question of morality in the
whole town of Hadleyburg; there is only a question of practical
consequences. "God forgive me — it's awful to think such
things," says Mary Richards, "but . . . Lord, how we are
made — how strangely we are made!" — and her guilt does
not prevent her from further manifestations of greed. During
the period of his own financial manipulations, Sam Clemens
had learned much about the desperate possibilities of the human temperament. "Hadleyburg" is a Balzacian tale of frontier
life.

But his financial experiences had added a depth and a bite
to Clemens' writing. The foolish artist, as the psychoanalytic
critics don't seem to understand, can enrich his art by his folly.
And one notices how often the central figures of these stories —
the "gambler," the "outcast," the "schemers," the respectable
hypocrites — are obvious projections of aspects of Twain's own
temperament, now used as his literary pawns.

Mary Richards again admits her guilt. "It is a mean town, a
hard, stingy town," and it is her belief that the town's honesty is
as rotten as hers is — and still she goes on scheming with her
anxiety-ridden husband to get the golden fortune. And the
"moral" struggles of the Richardses are repeated by the Coxes
and by "Pinkerton," the town banker. And Jack Halliday, who
is the loafing, good-natured, no-account, irreverent fisherman,
hunter, boys' friend, and bum of the town, Jack Halliday, or
Holiday, the pagan Huck Finn character of the story, becomes
a kind of a frontier Greek chorus which records the alternation
of joy (greed) and depression (fear of financial loss) in the
leading townspeople. It develops that the reward will go to
the person who knows what the social outcast Goodson told
the ruined gambler (the satanic stranger, or doubtless the
mask of Sam Clemens himself) which changed his whole life.

Everybody is trying to remember — or invent — that remark in order to get the money, in the malicious development of the story.

Each of the "Nineteen," the leading citizens of the town, gets a similar letter; each thinks he is the only recipient of the prize, each concludes he must have some special virtue to deserve this fortune — their only problem is *what* virtue? When Richards gets his clue to the fortune, his wife is ecstatic. "Oh, Edward, the money is ours, and I am so grateful, *oh,* so grateful — kiss me dear, it's forever since we kissed — and we needed it so — the money," she cries. Clemens is explicit about the repression of sexual pleasure in the face of financial anxiety.

For if Hadleyburg's had been a false virtue, untested by temptation, it is nevertheless true that the "deadly money" has now destroyed the town's whole social fabric and all its personal relations. Poor Richards — "Poor Richard," and one remembers the deadly animus of Twain's earliest attacks on Benjamin Franklin's hypocritical and pleasure-destroying materialism — poor Richards can't sleep for fear that he won't remember the good deed he has done to Goodson (he has done none) which has put him in such a favorable light with the mysterious stranger. "His imagination-mill was hard at work," Clemens remarks, and there is a brilliant section of the story on the endless processes of human rationalization. And then Richards suddenly realizes what the good deed was! Goodson had been engaged to a very sweet and pretty girl named Nancy Hewitt; the match had been broken off, and the girl had died:

Soon after the girl's death the village found out, or thought it had found out, that she carried a spoonful of negro blood in her veins. Richards worked at these details a good while . . .

[and] he seemed to dimly remember that it was *he* that found out about the negro blood; that it was he that told the village; that the village told Goodson where they got it; that he thus saved Goodson from marrying the tainted girl; that he had done him this great service without knowing that he *was* doing it; but that Goodson knew the value of it, and what a narrow escape he had had, and so went to his grave grateful to his benefactor and wishing he had a fortune to leave him.

What a remarkable "inversion" of truth has Mark Twain wrought here — or perhaps what a horrifying statement of truth as it appears to poor Richards. What a nice intuition it was to bring the race question into this parable of financial corruption in the new American Empire — as the small towns of the western frontier also fell under the spell of the great American fortunes in the vast sea change of the Old Republic toward the end of the nineteenth century.*

Just as the literary techniques of "Hadleyburg Corrupted" move from the psychological core of the story — the brilliant rationalizing of highly discreditable behavior — to a social scene of general corruption, so Clemens himself was now projecting the psychological tensions of his own financial crisis into the social and historical scene around him. So all art moves from the specific to the universal; and what is important to note, of course, is not only the foolish behavior of Clemens him-

* Yet it was this American artist, who, as we've seen, caught on to the evils and horror of world colonialism in *Following the Equator,* just as he had of racism and the Negro question in the United States, and of the whole political, financial, and moral corruption of his period in *The Gilded Age* — that the contemporary biographer, Justin Kaplan, could describe as turning away from the modern American scene after the *Connecticut Yankee,* and as actually becoming an "expatriate" after *Pudd'nhead Wilson.* Perhaps Mr. Kaplan doesn't appreciate the importance of Mark Twain's social criticism because he does not really understand it, or does not wish to. Perhaps it is Mr. Kaplan himself who is some kind of contemporary expatriate in a never-never land of psychic anxiety without any social context.

self during the whole period of his financial speculations, but the rich rewards which he reaped in his writing. His bankruptcy was not his undoing, as might have happened with a lesser talent, and as some Mark Twain critics have maintained about him — it was instead a kind of spiritual death and rebirth. What mattered in the end, as I say, was not so much his own suffering during this whole period as the new artistic purpose formed by his suffering; and he was to endure and, yes, *use,* in the highest artistic sense, even to the last ordeal of his domestic tragedy.

One notices also, in the central figures of "The Man That Corrupted Hadleyburg," not only the constant attempt to deceive others, but far worse, the continuous and unconscious process of *self-deception.* When Richards has finally reached the "solution" of the service he has done Goodson — the matter of the Negro blood in the "tainted girl" — his spirit is completely at peace. "It was all clear and simple now, and the more he went over it the more luminous and certain it grew; and at last, when he nestled to sleep satisfied and happy, he remembered the whole thing just as if it had been yesterday. In fact, he dimly remembered Goodson's *telling* him his gratitude once. Meantime Mary had spent six thousand dollars on a new house for herself and a pair of slippers for her pastor, and then had fallen peacefully to rest."

The whole community indulges in a spree of imaginary spending. The new architect in "this unpromising town" finds himself deluged by secret plans for palatial new houses. "The days drifted along, and the bill of future squanderings rose higher and higher, wilder and wilder, more and more foolish and reckless. It began to look as if every member of the 'Nineteen' would not only spend his whole forty thousand dollars before receiving-day, but be actually in debt by the time he got the money. In some cases lightheaded people did not stop with planning to spend, they really spent — on credit." And while Sam Clemens knew this from deep personal experience, he was also anticipating a whole new epoch of credit-financing and installment-buying on which a later American economy would come to rest — perhaps to thrive.

Hadleyburg was another early example of Thorstein Veblen's conspicuous consumption. What we see here is the disintegration of the whole town's structure, social and personal relationships alike, under the lure and pressure of an "imaginary fortune." While those great fortunes of Clemens' own period which were real did even more harm to the social patterns and moral values of the Old Republic than the symbolic one in Mark Twain's story. Clemens was also describing, in the chronicle of a disintegrating Hannibal — which became Hadleyburg, which became hell — the cultural impact of the titans and the trusts; of the new social-economic regime of monopoly capitalism in the United States. The rest of the mysterious message, which was *not* given to any of the aspiring "Nineteeners" in the town, read: "Go, and reform — or, mark my words — some day, for your sins, you will die and go to hell or Hadleyburg — *try and make it the former*."

Among the other stories and tales in the *Hadleyburg* volume, "The Esquimau Maiden's Romance," though poor fiction, is a parody of the impact of wealth upon a primitive society (a variation of the Hadleyburg Corrupted theme); just as we have already noticed how so many of Twain's stories, parables, fables of this period are almost obsessively concerned with the meaning of money as romance, fairy tale, delusion, disease, and nightmare. But listen to the Esquimau princess lamenting the moral decline of her father: "He has lowered the tone of all our tribe. Once they were a frank and manly race, now they are measly hypocrites and sodden with servility. In my heart of hearts I hate all the ways of millionaires. Our tribe was once plain, simple folk, contented with the bone fish-hooks of their fathers; now they are eaten up with avarice and would sacrifice every sentiment of honor and honesty to possess themselves of the debasing iron fish-hooks of the foreigner."

Even the Arctic Circle had its Hadleyburgs. During this period Clemens was writing sections of the *Autobiography* and revising certain parts of it for immediate publication, and "My First Lie and How I Got Out of It" may fall into this classification. He was now sixty-four, as he says, and his memory is not as good as it was. "If you had asked about my first truth it would have been easier for me and kinder of you, for I remember that fairly well; I remember it as if it were last week. The family think it was week before, but that is flattery and probably has a selfish project back of it." This is an entertaining familiar essay on the paucity of truth in the human spirit, with an unexpected conclusion. For Clemens' argument is, what does one individual liar amount to when compared to the gigantic conspiracy of lies upon which civilization rests?

The fact is, as Clemens stated, that "all lies are acts, and speech has no part in them" — a nice perception. And then "they" — by which he meant the students of lying in human development — "Then, if they examined a little further they recognized that all people are liars from the cradle onward, without exception, and that they begin to lie as soon as they wake in the morning, and keep it up, without rest or refreshment, until they go to sleep at night. If they arrived at that truth it probably grieved them — did, if they had been heedlessly and ignorantly educated by their books and teachers; for why should a person grieve over a thing which by the eternal law of his make he cannot help? He didn't invent the law; it is merely his business to obey it and keep still; join the universal conspiracy and keep so still that he shall deceive his fellow-conspirators into imagining that he doesn't know that the law exists."

History would absolve Sam Clemens of being cynical in these prophetic lines of prose; history would prove he was understating his case; but then, of course, he was working from history. "It is what we all do — we that know," he continued.

> I am speaking of the lie of silent assertion; we can tell it without saying a word, and we all do it — we that know. In the magnitude of its territorial spread it is one of the most majestic lies that the civilizations make it their sacred and anxious care to guard and watch and propagate.

The epoch of the Third Reich was in the distant future, the imperialistic horrors of the Belgian Congo, it may be, were resting in Clemens' prescient spirit, but meanwhile he gave a few other historical examples.

"For instance: It would not be possible for a humane and intelligent person to invent a rational excuse for slavery; yet you will remember that in the early days of the emancipation agitation in the North, the agitators got but small help or countenance from any one. Argue and plead and pray as they might, they could not break the universal stillness that reigned, from pulpit and press all the way down to the bottom of society — the clammy stillness created and maintained by the lie of silent assertion — the silent assertion that there wasn't anything going on in which humane and intelligent people were interested."

There would be those humane and intelligent German citizens who maintained the same silent assertion while the stench of the concentration camp filled their nostrils; those American citizens who maintained the same silent-assertion lie while Vietnamese villages and peasants were being bombed and massacred. But Asia and Africa were far away, and the Clemens who had written *Following the Equator* gave some closer examples. "From the beginning of the Dreyfus case to the end of it, all France, except a couple of dozen moral paladins, lay under the smother of the silent-assertion lie that no wrong was being done to a persecuted and unoffending man." During Mr. Chamberlain's South African war, Clemens continued, England lay under the like smother of silence, and "Now there we have instances of three prominent ostensible civilizations working the silent-assertion lie. Could one find other instances in the three countries? I think so. Not so very many, perhaps, but say a billion — just so as to keep within bounds." And this was polemical writing, of course, of high order. The familiar essay "On Lying" had turned into a brilliant social indictment.

"Are those countries working that kind of lie, day in and day out, in thousands and thousands of varieties, without ever resting? Yes, we know that to be true. The universal conspiracy of the silent-assertion lie is hard at work always and everywhere, and always in the interest of a stupidity or a sham, never in the interest of a thing fine or respectable."

This was a prose style of such distinction, a gravamen of such solidity and acuteness and consequence that one almost wants to quote every one of the sentences flowing so fully, so sweetly, from the brimming cup of Mark Twain's wrath. This universal conspiracy of silence upon which all civilization rested, was it the most timid and shabby of all lies? "It seems to have the look of it. For ages and ages it has mutely labored in the interest of the despotisms and aristocracies and chattel slaveries, and military slaveries, and religious slaveries, and has kept them alive; keeps them alive yet, here and there and yonder, all about the globe; and will go on keeping them alive until the silent-assertion lie retires from business — the silent assertion that nothing is going on which fair and intelligent men are aware of and are engaged by their duty to try to stop."

And then he reached his point, as though he had not made it yet. "What I am arriving at is this: When whole races and peoples conspire to propagate gigantic mute lies in the interest of tyrannies and shams, why should we care anything about the trifling lies told by individuals? Why should we try to make it appear that abstention from lying is a virtue? Why should we want to beguile ourselves in that way? Why should we without shame help the nation lie, and then be ashamed to do a little lying on our own account? Why shouldn't we be honest and honorable, and lie every time we get a chance?" Was there an echo of Huck Finn in this plaintive query? It was again a confrontation of primitive innocence and the ambiguities of civilization; but this was a sturdy, even impudent and ravishing innocence which did not flinch at whatever odd inversions of "reason" it reached. That is to say, Clemens concluded, "why shouldn't we be consistent, and either lie all the time or not at all? Why should we help the nation lie the whole day long and then object to telling one little individual private lie in our own interest, to go to bed on? Just for the refreshment of it, I mean, and to take the rancid taste out of our mouth." *

This was the high point, no doubt, of the other tales, sketches, and essays which were collected in the *Hadleyburg* volume, which constantly stressed, as Twain's treatise on lying did, the polar swing of the individual soul and the community. Among the other pieces, "The Belated Russian Passport" was an en-

* The "silent assertion" has just lately been paraphrased in the political rhetoric of the Nixon Administration as the "silent majority."

tertaining bit of popular fiction, as was the sketch about François Millet. "My Boyhood Dreams" was a takeoff on another
Victorian sanctity, and if Mark Twain had outraged the New
England sages at the notorious Whittier dinner, and had
sorely felt the subsequent disgrace and dishonor, now he could
spoof such illustrious figures of the period as Howells, John
Hay, Brander Matthews, Frank Stockton, Cable, and Aldrich
with equanimity. And he did. For all his heavy load of shame
or guilt or spiritual disgrace, the truth is that Sam Clemens was
incorrigible at heart, and kept on being himself.

Speaking about his own old age, he went Dada in a positively
proto-Lardnerian vein.

> From Cradle unto Grave I keep a House
> Of Entertainment where may drowse
>     Bacilli and kindred Germs — or feed — or breed
> Their festering Species in a deep Carouse.
>
> Think — in this battered Caravanserai,
> Whose Portals open stand all Night and Day,
> How Microbe after Microbe with his Pomp
> Arrives unasked and comes to stay.
>
> Our ivory Teeth, confessing to the Lust
> Of masticating, once, now own Disgust
>     Of Clay-plug'd Cavities — full soon our Snags
> Are emptied, and our Mouths are filled with Dust.*

But one must add that the rest of the stories and articles in
the *Hadleyburg* volume were an undistinguished lot, and the

---

* It is entertaining to compare Lardner's version of Cole Porter's "Night and
Day," including, "Night and day under the bark of me/ There's an Oh, such a
mob of microbes making a park of me."

But I do *not* think that Lardner was influenced by Mark Twain's verse; only
that in such instances Sam Clemens was peculiarly sophisticated for a nineteenth-century mind.

novelette *A Double-Barreled Detective Story,* in 1902, was a heavy-footed parody of the popular romance-detective story of the period.*

Perhaps this parody, which included a brief and calamitous appearance of Sherlock Holmes — only to be outwitted by a hero with a bloodhound's nose, because his mother had been attacked by dogs when she was pregnant — was intended as a kind of sequel to "The Stolen White Elephant," which the Russian critics enjoy so much as an attack on the "American police," which it was, though not a very good one. "A Dog's Tale," reprinted from *Harper's* magazine, Christmas Number, 1903, for the National Anti-Vivisection Society of London, is a rather horrifying little item contrasting animal virtue with scientific progress. And with *King Leopold's Soliloquy,* which created almost as much of a national sensation in 1905 as had *To the Person Sitting in Darkness* in 1901, we reach a new, bolder, even more outspoken period of Mark Twain's writings.

Perhaps the best account of Twain's radical social criticism is contained in Janet Smith's *Mark Twain on the Damned Human Race,* which opens with a quote by Clemens from John Macy's book about Twain:

> I am the only man living who understands human nature; God has put me in charge of this branch office; when I retire there will be no one to take my place. I shall keep on doing my duty, for when I get over on the other side, I shall use my influence to have the human race drowned again, and this time drowned good, no omissions, no Ark.

* Both this story and "My Debut as a Literary Person" (1903) are included in *The Man That Corrupted Hadleyburg and Other Stories* in the standard edition of Mark Twain's work. That is to say, in *my* standard edition of Mark Twain's work, Harper & Brothers, Authorized Edition, *The Complete Works of Mark Twain.* But there are several other editions of Twain's complete work, some more complete than others, and all having different groupings of his stories and essays.

To Mrs. Smith, *To the Person Sitting in Darkness* is Twain's masterpiece of this kind of polemics, and still the most timely of his short satires. (Though most modern critics disdain this whole vein of Clemens' writing as crude and vulgar "propaganda," or for a variety of personal and social reasons that I have suggested previously.) "When *To the Person Sitting in Darkness* appeared," she writes, "it produced a cyclone; the sections on the missionaries in China produced savage public warfare between Mark Twain and the American Board of Foreign Missions — a warfare which continued until the Board fell silent."

"The reparations extracted by the missionaries, which Mark Twain discusses, followed upon the victory of an international army, including two thousand Americans, which, in August, 1900, took the city of Peking from Chinese armies led by the Boxers . . . Supposedly, the international army was to punish antiforeign rioting by the Chinese, but, after China's defeat, the reparations extracted by the Great Powers, except the United States, were at least as rapacious as those extracted by the missionaries; the great difference was that they were not the work of professed men of God — and it was this work which Mark Twain ensured should live in infamy."

Meanwhile Clemens had prefaced his sermon to the Person in Darkness with a New Year's Greeting in the New York *Herald* of December 30, 1900.*

A GREETING FROM THE NINETEENTH TO THE
TWENTIETH CENTURY:

I bring you the stately nation named Christendom, returning bedraggled, besmirched, and dishonored from pirate raids in Kiao-Chou, Manchuria, South Africa and the Philippines, with her soul

---

* The present study of Mark Twain is also indebted to Philip S. Foner's pioneering book. *Mark Twain: Social Critic,* in 1958.

full of meanness, her pocket full of boodle, and her mouth full of hypocrisies. Give her soap and towel, but hide the looking glass.

And let us note incidentally that at the opening of the "American Century," the American press, despite the criticisms of Twain and Howells among others, still felt free enough to feature such indictments, and to accompany them with cartoons.

The pamphlet itself, *To the Person Sitting in Darkness,* reprinted from the *North American Review* by the Anti-Imperialist League in New York, was a loose documentary consisting of statements from newspapers, of quotations from members of the American Board of Foreign Missions, and Clemens' running commentary. Clemens opened with a smug and sanctimonious Christmas Eve editorial from the New York *Tribune* about a nation and a people "full of hope and aspiration and good cheer" who should ignore any carping grumblers. He continued with a vivid description of poverty and crime and corrupt politics in New York's lower East Side taken from the New York *Sun.* He quoted another news article from the same paper about the Reverend Mr. Ament's trip to collect indemnities for damages done by Boxers.

"Everywhere he went he compelled the Chinese to pay. He says that all his native Christians are now provided for. He had 700 of them under his charge, and 300 were killed. He has collected 300 taels for each of these murders and has compelled full payment for all the property belonging to Christians that was destroyed. He also assessed fines amounting to *thirteen times* the amount of the indemnity. *This money will be used for the propagation of the Gospel.* Mr. Ament declares that the compensation he has collected is *moderate* when compared with the amount secured by the Catholics, who demand, in addition to money, *head for head.* They collect 500 taels for each murder of a Catholic. In the Wenchu country 680 Catholics were killed, and for this the European Catholics here demand 750,000 strings of cash and 680 heads."

Mr. Ament denied that the missionaries were vindictive or that they generally looted or that they did anything after the siege that circumstances did not demand. "I criticize the Americans. *The soft hand of the Americans is not as good as the mailed fist of the Germans.* If you deal with the Chinese with a soft hand they will take advantage of it."

Now you can imagine what Sam Clemens did with such material as this; you should read his entire essay as a coruscation of polemical writing — since here I have only room for a little summary. The Reverend Ament, said Clemens, was surely the right man in the right place. "What we want of our missionaries out there is not that they shall merely represent in their acts and persons the grace and gentleness and charity and loving-kindness of our religion, but that they shall also represent the American spirit. The oldest Americans are the Pawnees." And he went on to describe examples of Pawnee Indian "justice" which were equivalent to that of the white American missionaries. He went on to console the Reverend Mr. Ament for the larger profits the Catholic missionaries had made from these murders; he proposed a monument for Mr. Ament composed of the indemnity payments and skulls of murdered Chinese peasants. "Mr. Ament's financial feat of squeezing a thirteenfold indemnity out of the pauper peasants to square other people's offenses, thus condemning them and their women and innocent little children to inevitable starvation and lingering death, in order that the blood money so acquired might be *'used for the propagation of the Gospel,'* does not flutter my serenity; although the act and the words, taken together, concrete a blasphemy so hideous and so colossal that, without doubt, its mate is not findable in the history of this, or of any other age.* Yet, if a layman had done that thing and justified it with those words, I should have shuddered, I know. Or, if I had done the thing and said the words myself — however, the thought is unthinkable, irreverent as some imperfectly informed people think me. Sometimes an ordained minister sets out to be blasphemous. When this happens, the layman is out of the running; he stands no chance."

So much for the Reverend Mr. Ament. Clemens went on to quote "barbaric" Japanese opinion to the effect that the missionary organizations constituted a constant menace to peaceful international relations, and then posed the crucial question.

*Shall we?* That is, shall we go on conferring our civilization upon the peoples that sit in darkness, or shall we give those poor things a rest? Shall we bang right ahead in our old-time, loud, pious way, and commit the new century to the game; or shall we sober up and sit down and think it over first? Would it not be prudent to get our civilizational tools together, and see how much stock is left on hand in the way of glass beads and theology, and maxim guns and hymn books, and trade gin and torches of progress and enlightenment (patent adjustable ones, good to fire villages with, upon occasion), and balance the books, and arrive at the profit and loss, so that we may intelligently decide whether to continue the business or sell out the property and start a new civilizational scheme on the proceeds?

* Clemens' descriptions of American missionary behavior in China during the Boxer crisis are confirmed and indeed surpassed by similar accounts, which are more detailed, intimate, and illuminating, contained in the first three volumes of Han Suyin's memoirs. These books. *The Crippled Tree, A Mortal Flower,* and *Birdless Summer,* though little recognized in the United States, have already proved to be one of the few literary epics of the contemporary period in the English language; and they come as a revelation to even "informed" western opinion.

And indeed, if only the avaricious colonial powers of the early 1900s had listened to the advice of this "idealistic" and moral literary genius of the time, the new century might have been spared fifty years — and surely another fifty more to come — of what was essentially race war under the guise of such ambiguous and shifting concepts as socialism, communism, nationalism, capitalism, and imperialism. Nor would the profits of individuals, corporations, and nations, however large, however tempting and momentarily rewarding, ever compensate for the national losses, the sufferings of the entire human community, the universal sacrifice and destruction which were already implicit to Mark Twain in the colonizing process. Much more likely, the twentieth century's wars of liberation, in Asia, Africa, and South America — in the United States itself, divided and torn as it was by racial warfare and ghetto insurrections — would threaten the whole base and future of western European democratic institutions.

And furthermore, in *To the Person Sitting in Darkness* (who became the twentieth century's person striving to discover life and light), Clemens went on to prophesy exactly that.

"Extending the blessings of civilization to our brother who sits in darkness has been a good trade and has paid well, on the whole; and there is money in it yet, if carefully worked — but not enough, in my judgment, to make any considerable risk advisable. The people that sit in darkness are getting to be too scarce — too scarce and too shy. And such darkness as is now left is really of but an indifferent quality, and not dark enough for the game. The most of those people that sit in darkness have been furnished with more light than was good for them or profitable for us. We have been injudicious."

"The blessings-of-civilization trust, wisely and cautiously administered, is a daisy," Clemens continued. "There is more money in it, more territory, more sovereignty, and other kinds of emolument than there is in any other game that is played. But Christendom has been playing it badly of late years, and must certainly suffer by it, in my opinion. She has been so eager to get every stake that appeared on the green cloth, that the people who sit in darkness have noticed it — they have noticed it, and have begun to show alarm. They have become suspicious of the blessings of civilization. More — they have begun to examine them. This is not well. The blessings of civilization are all right, and a good commercial property; there could not be a better, in a dim light. In the right kind of light, and at a proper distance, with the goods a little out of focus, they furnish this desirable exhibit to the gentlemen who sit in darkness."

He listed such virtues of civilization as Love, Justice, Gentleness, Temperance, Liberty, Equality, Mercy, and so on. But, he said, this was merely an outside cover, gay and pretty and attractive, while *inside* the bale "is the actual thing that the customer sitting in darkness buys with his blood and tears and land and liberty." And the civilization-export business was being ruined.

*To the Person Sitting in Darkness* went on to describe some of the more obvious examples of imperialism's careless mistakes. It explained the manufacture of the Boer War by the English Colonial Secretary Chamberlain in order to acquire the vast wealth of the diamond mines and black slave labor. It related the history of the German Kaiser as an energetic new partner in dividing up the spoils of China. "He lost a couple of missionaries in a riot in Shantung, and in his account he made an overcharge for them. China had to pay a hundred thousand dollars apiece for them in money; twelve miles of territory containing several millions of inhabitants and worth twenty million dollars; and to build a monument, and also a

Christian church; whereas the people of China could have been depended on to remember the missionaries without the help of these expensive memorials." * The person in outer darkness knew this was an overcharge, and Clemens went on to evaluate the cash value of a missionary with that of an intelligent country editor. "It is no proper figure for an editor or a missionary; one can get shopworn kings for less . . . It got this property, true; but it *produced the Chinese revolt,* the indignant uprising of China's traduced patriots, the Boxers. The results have been expensive to Germany, and to the other disseminators of progress and the blessings of civilization."

Clemens believed that the Chinese were not unreflective. They would muse upon the event, and be likely to say: "Civilization is gracious and beautiful, for such is its reputation; but can we afford it? There are rich Chinamen, perhaps they can afford it; but this tax is not laid upon them, it is laid upon the peasants of Shantung; it is they who must pay this mighty sum, and their wages are but four cents a day. Is this a better civilization than ours, and holier, and higher and nobler? Is not this rapacity? Is not this extortion?" He asked if Germany would have treated America in the same way if the missionaries had been slaughtered in the United States. "And later would Germany say to her soldiers: 'March through America and slay, *giving no quarter;* make the German face there, as has been our Hun-face here, a terror for a thousand years; march through the great republic and slay, slay, slay, carving a road for our offended religion through its heart and bowels'? Would Germany do this to America, to England, to France, to Russia? Or only to China, the helpless . . ."

---

* Incredible to read today, unbelievable and impossible? Much worse follows in Twain's account, all confirmed and elaborated in detail in the Han Suyin memoirs.

He reported the final reflection of the Chinese person. "Can we afford civilization?" These were eloquent passages of immense prophetic weight in *To the Person Sitting in Darkness,* which twentieth-century history would vindicate in full, even while the western mind would be terrified by the "obscure" Chinese revolution.

And next Russia was playing the imperialist game by robbing Japan of its hard-earned spoil: Port Arthur "all swimming in Chinese blood." With the person in darkness again observing and noting, Russia then

> seizes Manchuria, raids its villages, and chokes its great river with the swollen corpses of countless massacred peasants — that astonished person still observing and noting. And perhaps he is saying to himself: "It is yet *another* civilized power, with its banner of the Prince of Peace in one hand and its loot basket and its butcher knife in the other. Is there no salvation for us but to adopt civilization and lift ourselves down to its level?"

And then it was America itself which began playing the imperialist game.

Clemens still felt the American purpose in Cuba, in the Spanish-American War, had been honest and in the tradition of the Old Republic. (During the course of the article, nevertheless, he began to have his doubts about this, too.) But the conquest of the Philippines was horrifying to him, and he said so in some detail.

In particular Clemens was enraged by the treacherous cunning through which the American army had destroyed the small, ill-armed native Filipino army under the guise of assisting its struggle against the Spanish oppressor. This campaign to secure the Philippines for the United States, rather than to allow them the freedom they had fought for, was particularly brutal, like all colonial wars against the colored peoples. And finally the American government announced that it was adopting General Kitchener's methods against the Boers: massacre, extermination, and denudation of the land. Clemens also described the relative casualty rates of Filipino and American soldiers:

> We must stand ready to grab the person sitting in darkness, for he will swoon away at this confession saying "Good God! those 'niggers' spare their wounded, and the Americans massacre theirs!"*

What Kitchener's and General MacArthur's methods meant in detail was illustrated by the words of an American soldier in the Philippines. "We never left one alive. If one was wounded, we would run our bayonets through him." And now, said Clemens, having laid all the historical facts before the person in outer darkness, we should bring him to again, and explain them to him. We should say to him:

"They look doubtful, but in reality they are not. There have been lies; yes, but they were told in a good cause. We have been treacherous; but that was only in order that real good might come out of apparent evil. True, we have crushed a deceived and confiding people; we have turned against the weak and friendless who trusted us; we have stamped out a just and intelligent and well-ordered republic; we have stabbed an ally in the back and slapped the face of a guest; we have bought a shadow from an enemy that hadn't it to sell; we have robbed a trusting friend of his land and his liberty; we have invited

---

* By now Clemens was using quotes around the word "nigger," when he used it ironically, or as part of folk speech, or on the tongue of those people who despised the colored races whom Clemens himself admired and defended. Surely those contemporary critics, like Fiedler and Leavis, who espouse the word "nigger" with such delight, and seemingly with Mark Twain's precedent and authority, can be said to be wholly unaware of this writer's craft.

our clean young men to shoulder a discredited musket and do bandits' work under a flag which bandits have been accustomed to fear, not to follow; we have debauched America's honor and blackened her face before the world; but each detail was for the best. We know this. The head of every state and sovereignty in Christendom and 90 per cent of every legislative body in Christendom, including our Congress and our fifty [sic] state legislatures, are members not only of the church but also of the blessings-of-civilization trust. This world-girdling accumulation of trained morals, high principles, and justice cannot do an unright thing, an unfair thing, an ungenerous thing, an unclean thing. It knows what it is about. Give yourself no uneasiness; it is all right."

And he went on to propose a new American flag with the white stripes painted black and the stars replaced by the skull and crossbones — and to suggest that the U.S. could slip out of its congressional contract with Cuba and give her something better in place of it. "It is a rich country, and many of us are already beginning to see that the contract was a sentimental mistake."

Great history, great writing, and great art, yes, in the polemical tradition of art! Perhaps in this sense *To the Person Sitting in Darkness* is the classic work of all the social tracts written in the fury of Mark Twain's outraged sensibilities during the opening years of the new century. Some of these essays, like "Corn-Pone Opinions," "As Regards Patriotism," "Bible Teaching and Religious Practice," "The War Prayer," we shall discuss later on.* But meanwhile we have noted that this hatred of colonialism, of racism, of slavery in any guise, of cruelty,

* All collected recently, with other articles in the same vein, in Janet Smith's book, but some of them published previously in a volume of Twain's posthumous essays edited by Paine, *Europe and Elsewhere,* in 1923; and in Paine's — but not Charles Neider's — edition of *Mark Twain's Autobiography.*

exploitation, suffering, and misery, was not of course a "new vein" in Clemens' work, nor was it the sick product of his financial ruin and domestic tragedy. What marks all these essays of social protest and personal outrage, instead, is the vein of hilarious humor which Clemens invoked in the midst of his brilliant irony and scathing moral indignation. As early as 1873, writing in the New York *Tribune* about the proposed annexation of the Hawaiian Islands, Clemens had invoked almost the same themes and tone.

We *must* annex those people. We can afflict them with our wise and beneficent government. We can introduce the novelty of thieves, all the way up from streetcar pick-pockets to municipal robbers and Government defaulters and show them how amusing it is to arrest them and try them and turn them loose — some for cash, and some for "political influence." We can make them ashamed of their simple and primitive justice . . . We can give them juries composed of the most simple and charming leather-heads. We can give them railway corporations who will buy their Legislatures like old clothes, and run over their best citizens. We can furnish them some Jay Goulds who will do away their old-time notions that stealing is not respectable . . . We can give them lecturers! I will go myself.

We can make that bunch of sleepy islands the hottest corner on earth, and array it in the moral splendor of our high and holy civilization. Annexation is what the poor islanders need. "Shall we to men benighted the lamp of life deny?"

The difference was not so much in Mark Twain, indeed, as in his subject matter. As we said, his world had changed more swiftly and brutally and savagely than Sam Clemens had. His series of personal tragedies may have sorrowed and embittered him — but they had not defiled and debauched him, nor made him brutal, savage, ruthless, and avaricious. What we are witnessing in these eloquent, bold, and radical social satires of Twain is not at all the rantings of an embittered old man — how could any serious Mark Twain scholar ever think so? — but the eventful and fateful meeting of the man and the time which creates art. Or of a unique personality, hardened and deepened, as it may be, by life, and of a historical period gone bad, vicious, grasping, and barbaric.

We may only be grateful that the proper chronicler was there, the recording angel indeed of art, civilization, and life.

There are other essays which Clemens wrote at this time about a changing America — moving from the moral simplicity and grandeur of the Old Republic at its best to the imperial dynasty of an industrial-military complex which was to cast its shadow over the land masses of Europe, Asia, and Africa. "A Defence of General Funston," in 1902, was a kind of appendix to *The Person Sitting in Darkness*. This was the specific account of the capture of the Filipino General Emilio Aguinaldo as accomplished by General Funston, and widely acclaimed as a heroic exploit of American military prowess. Mark Twain did not agree. Funston had also characterized all Americans who opposed the conquest of the Philippines as "traitors," a term that would be used recurrently thereafter in American politics — and which Clemens made a point of accepting with pleasure, when compared, say, with the official American "patriots" of the period. Writing his essay on Washington's Birthday, Clemens made a comparison of the two military figures; and he was fearful that General Funston, with all his duplicity, cruelty, and sadism, would become the model of the new American military hero. Describing how the helpless and starving Funston, disguised as a Filipino guerrilla fighter, and accompanied by the treacherous Macabebe tribe of natives, was rescued and refreshed by the Filipino President

Aguinaldo — only to shoot down Aguinaldo's guard and then to wantonly sport with the remnants of Aguinaldo's military staff through shootings and beatings, Clemens commented: "It was left to a Brigadier General of Volunteers in the American army to put shame upon a custom which even the degraded Spanish friars had respected. *We promoted him for it.*"

But just here Clemens reverted to his notorious notion of a kind of dark determinism in human life,\* and using it for passages of savage irony, Clemens confessed that he could not really condemn Funston for his savage behavior but only Funston's *It*.

"These being the facts, we come now to the question: Is Funston to blame? I think not. And for that reason I think too much is being made of this matter. He did not make his own disposition, It was born with him. It chose his ideals for him, he did not choose them. It chose the kind of society It liked, the kind of comrades It preferred . . . It, and It only, was to blame, not Funston . . . It had a native predilection for unsavory conduct, but it would be in the last degree unfair to hold Funston to blame for the outcome of his infirmity; as clearly

---

\* We shall discuss this later on; but meanwhile what is curious to note in our literary history of the 1950s is the degree of distaste, or even anger, with which the leading critics of the Cold War epoch attacked the concept of "determinism" in a whole line of American writers from Mark Twain to Theodore Dreiser. During this epoch there was apparently presumed to be some underground and devious link between philosophic determinism and radical social criticism, or even Marxism and Communism . . . It is worth remembering that almost every great writer has adhered to some form or another of a deterministic philosophy which has held his own talent as "accidental" and of lesser consequence than the environmental aspects which happened to cause the flowering of the talent — just as Dreiser held a Clyde Griffiths to be the victim of a corrupted American society, and as Mark Twain here views, though ironically, General Funston.

*But this is the disclaimer of genius.* It is only the small souls of the world who flaunt their own "individualism," or "will power," or "spiritual strength" as superior to the conditioning forces of society, culture, and history. Or even of events, or chance, or accident!

unfair as it would be to blame him because his conscience leaked out through one of his pores when he was little — a thing which he could not have helped, and he couldn't have raised it anyway; It was able to say to an enemy, 'Have pity on me, I am starving; I am too weak to move, give me food; I am your friend, I am your fellow patriot, your fellow Filipino, and am fighting for our dear country's liberties, like you — have pity, give me food, save my life, there is no other help!' and It was able to refresh and restore Its marionette with the food, and then shoot down the giver of it while his hand was stretched out in welcome . . . It has the noble gift of humor, and can make a banquet almost die with laughter when It has a funny incident to tell about; this one will bear reading again — and over and over again, in fact." And Clemens repeated the sadistic episode of the slaughter of Aguinaldo's bodyguard and military staff with which Funston had entertained his American audiences as an example of American military cunning and power.

They had fished the wounded Filipino officer Villia out of the river and kicked him up the bank with coarse jokes. This was a wounded man, said Clemens. "But it is only It that is speaking, not Funston. With youthful glee It can see sink down in death the simple creatures who had answered Its fainting prayer for food, and without remorse It can note the reproachful look in their dimming eyes, but in fairness we must remember that this is only It, not Funston . . . And It — not Funston — comes home now to teach us children what patriotism is! Surely It ought to know."

Burning words, etched by the acid of Clemens' contempt at such military behavior in the Philippines, where his America, too, had joined in the racist conquest and social degradation which he had already witnessed on the part of the "corrupted"

Old World's imperialism in Asia and Africa. The essay called "Comments on the Killing of 600 Moros," in 1906, was in effect a sequel to Mark Twain's "Defence of General Funston" — a "defence" which only Satan could have devised to cope with human nature.*

A tribe of these "dark-skinned savages," as Clemens called them, had entrenched themselves in the bowl of an extinct crater near Jolo. Since they were "hostiles, and bitter at us because we have been trying for eight years to take their liberties away from them, their presence in that position was a menace." The American commander, General Leonard Wood, discovered that the Moros numbered six hundred including women and children; and that their crater bowl was on a mountain peak 2200 feet above sea level, "and very difficult of access for Christian troops and artillery." There were finally the six hundred savages in the mountain bowl, and about the same number of American troops and allies on the mountain summit overlooking the bowl, with artillery, when General Wood issued his order to attack.

The depth of the crater bowl was about fifty feet, as Mark Twain noted. "The battle began — it is officially called by that name — our forces firing down into the crater with their artillery and their deadly small arms of precision; the savages furiously returning the fire, probably with brickbats — though this is merely a surmise of mine. Heretofore the Moros have used knives and clubs mainly; also ineffectual trade-muskets when they had any. The official report stated that the battle was fought with prodigious energy on both sides during a day and a half, and that it ended with a complete victory for the

---

* The Moro essay was written as part of Mark Twain's *Autobiography*, and first published in 1924, in Albert Bigelow Paine's edition of this book. It is omitted from Charles Neider's "new" version of the *Autobiography*, in 1959, for reasons of "personal taste" and "esthetic values" which the present writer finds both mysterious and meretricious.

American arms. The completeness of the victory is established by this fact: that of the six hundred Moros not one was left alive. The brilliancy of the victory is established by this other fact, to wit: that of our six hundred heroes only fifteen lost their lives.

"General Wood was present and looking on. His order had been, 'Kill *or* capture those savages.' Apparently our little army considered that the "or" left them authorized to kill *or* capture according to taste, and that their taste had remained what it has been for eight years, in our army out there — the taste of Christian butchers."

Clemens pointed out that, then as now, the American newspaper dispatches on the battle extolled and magnified the "heroism" and "gallantry" of the American troops, lamented the loss of a few white men, elaborated the wounds of a few others — and ignored the six hundred dead Moros. He mentioned the casualty rates on both sides in the Civil War, at Waterloo, and in the "pathetic comedy" called the Cuban War. "Contrast these things with the great statistics which have arrived from that Moro crater! There, with six hundred engaged on each side, we lost fifteen men killed outright, and we had thirty-two wounded . . . The enemy numbered six hundred — including women and children — and we abolished them utterly, leaving not even a baby alive to cry for its dead mother. *This is incomparably the greatest victory that was ever achieved by the Christian soldiers of the United States.*"

Then, as public revulsion mounted in the United States when the true nature of the bloody massacre began to emerge, and as General Wood's tone changed from enthusiastic admiration for the American military "triumph" to an uneasy rationalization of the slaughter, Clemens added his final comments to the "Killing of 600 Moros": "Doctor Wood will find that explaining things is not in his line. He will find that where a man has a proper spirit in him and the proper force at his command, it is easier to massacre nine hundred [as it turned out to be] unarmed animals than it is to explain why he made it so remorselessly complete . . . The inference seems plain. We cleaned up our four days' work and made it complete by butchering these helpless people."

But among the polemical writings of this period we can hardly omit what was in its time the most popular pamphlet of all, *King Leopold's Soliloquy*. We have already noticed how the Belgian reign in the Congo can be interpreted historically as the dark rehearsal for the Nazi Terror in Europe. (And to some degree, though in a quite different historical context, the Stalin purges in Russia.) Once this could happen in "savage" Africa, it was made possible in "civilized" Europe; and once mass extermination had been practiced for profit on the black races, it could be used in the name of the highest of patriotic reasons upon the "inferior" white races. No end to this game once started; and whatever the validity of this comparison, it is certain that there were ten million murders in the Belgian Congo between 1885 and 1905; no mean comparison in an earlier age, without the "scientific" and prefabricated death factories that the Nazis developed.

In Jacob Blanck's *Biography of American Literature,* one notes also that *King Leopold's Soliloquy,* described as another "Defence" of the Congo rule, had four reprintings of the first edition in 1905, and a second edition in the next year (Twain refused any royalties for this pamphlet written for the Congo Reform Association) and still two more American editions before the London-Unwin edition in 1907.* The essay itself, as with all Mark Twain's polemical writings, was "crude" and rough in

* In Janet Smith's background material for this essay she quotes another voice from an older world, Vachel Lindsay's *The Congo*: "Listen to the yell of Leopold's ghost/ Burning in Hell for his hand-mained host./ Hear how the demons chuckle and yell,/ Cutting his hands off, down in Hell."

form, even apparently formless to those esthetic and conformist critics who, particularly in the 1950s, used such criteria to rule out this whole phase of Mark Twain's work. The point is, of course, that Clemens had devised his own native form for this whole genre of writing which, rough and careless and "mixed," or even mixed-up, as it appeared to be, was still an extraordinary eloquent, forceful, and historically valuable kind of writing.

In *King Leopold,* as in the previous essays we have discussed, he threw together newspaper headlines, firsthand journalistic accounts of the Congo, photographs of mutilated savages taken by the invaluable new witness of the period, the Kodak, missionary reports, official documents of Congolese administrators, plus his own imaginative reconstructions, and passages of raging moral anger and satire. Clemens has Leopold speaking in person, surrounded by the documents and records of his infamous doings, swearing violently, kissing his crucifix, apologizing, admitting certain errors, rationalizing, defending himself full force without a trace of guilt or conscience for the immeasurable evil he had perpetrated upon an innocent and helpless people. "I have spent millions to keep the press of the two hemispheres quiet . . . I have spent other millions on religion and art, and what do I get?" Leopold asks. "In print I get nothing but slanders — and slanders again . . . Miscreants — they are telling *everything!*" And Clemens then told the story of how Leopold obtained the territory of the Congo from the Great Powers, including America, in order to root out slavery and stop the slave raids, "and to lift up those twenty-five millions of gentle and harmless blacks out of darkness into light, the light of our blessed Redeemer." But the documents surrounding Leopold, which have at last brought *him* to light, record that for twenty years he had ruled the Congo State as the absolute sovereign of a fruitful domain four times as large as the German Empire, claiming millions of inhabitants as his private property, his serfs, his slaves. "Yes, they go on telling everything, these chatterers! They tell how I levy incredibly burdensome taxes upon the natives — taxes which are a pure theft; taxes which they must satisfy by gathering rubber under hard and constantly harder conditions, and by raising and furnishing food supplies gratis — and it all comes out that, when they fall short of their task through hunger, sickness, despair, and ceaseless and exhausting labor without rest, and forsake their homes and flee to the woods to escape punishment, my black soldiers, drawn from unfriendly tribes, and instigated and directed by my Belgians" — those "unspeakable Belgians" as Clemens declared — "hunt them 'down and butcher them and burn their villages — reserving some of the girls."

Leopold then begins to rage at the diary of a Belgian official in the Congo which was published by the British consul. "Here he leaves it to be recognized that a thousand killings and mutilations a month is a large output for so small a region as the Mambogo River concession, silently indicating the dimensions of it by accompanying his report with a map of the prodigious Congo State in which there is not room for so small an object as that river" . . . And Leopold reads:

Two hundred and forty persons, *men, women and children,* compelled to supply government with *one ton* of carefully prepared foodstuffs *per week,* receiving in remuneration, all told the princely sum of 15s. 10d!

"Very well, it was liberal! It was not much short of a penny a week for each nigger.* It suits this consul to belittle it, yet he knows very well that I could have had both the food and the

---

* See previous footnotes on the use of this word by Mark Twain. By now, indeed, it is clear that he placed this word only on the lips of white men whom he utterly despised; which could have been a long list, however.

labor for nothing. I can prove it by a thousand instances . . . Mm — here is some more of the consul's delicacy! He reports a conversation he had with some natives." And Clemens put down some further direct testimony of Belgian barbarism in dealing with the Congo blacks. He quoted the testimony of the Reverend W. H. Sheppard, talking with a black raider of Leopold's who collected all the chiefs, subchiefs, men and women of one of these native tribes within a compound, demanded slaves and other gifts from them, and massacred the whole lot remorselessly when his demands were refused. Some of the eighty or ninety corpses were still lying in the fields with the flesh carved away from the skeletons.

"*Another* detail, as we see! — cannibalism. The report cites it with a most offensive frequency," cries Leopold in despair. "My traducers do not forget to remark that inasmuch as I am absolute and with a word can prevent in the Congo anything I choose to prevent, then whatsoever is done there . . . is my act, my *personal* act . . . that the hand of my agent is as truly *my* hand as if it were attached to my own arm; and so they picture me in my robes of state, with my crown on my head, munching human flesh, saying grace, mumbling thanks to Him from whom all good things come . . . They speak out profanely and reproach Heaven for allowing such a fiend to live. Meaning me. They think it irregular. They go shuddering around, brooding over the reduction of that Congo population from 25,000,000 to 15,000,000 in the twenty years of my administration; then they burst out and call me 'the King with Ten Million Murders on his Soul." They call me a record."

What is remarkable, of course, is the mixture of complacency, rationalizing, indignation, and high moral dudgeon on the part of Mark Twain's King Leopold. And the usual self-deception or hypocrisy about black lives.

Clemens compared Leopold's work with the Great Famine in

India, and with such previous tyrants as Attila, Torquemada, Genghis Khan, Ivan the Terrible, and concluded that the only match in history for Leopold was the Flood. He went on to report that "another madman" wanted to construct a memorial for the perpetuation of Leopold's name out of the fifteen million skulls and skeletons killed by Leopold's order. He, Clemens, got carried away by this idea and went into elaborate detail for such an elegant memorial which would serve as a permanent museum to convey the enormity of human destruction in the Congo. (The world does not care for such museums, and they are poorly attended in general, like those of the Nazi holocaust.)

Leopold reads more of the missionary and journalistic reports of the day detailing the individual horrors which occurred daily under a regime designed to make a norm out of human atrocities. Leopold becomes specially irritated at noting that a widow had been forced to sell her little girl. And he is profoundly disturbed by the crucifixion of sixty women. This is profanation of the sacred emblem of Christianity, he cries, and the wrong way to do it. He studies some photographs of mutilated Negroes (which were printed in the pamphlet editions of *King Leopold*) and declaims against the "incorruptible Kodak," when for years the pulpit and press had denied all such rumors. He reads a final journalist summary (written presumably by Clemens):

> But enough of trying to tally off his crimes! His list is interminable, we should never get to the end of it. His awful shadow lies across his Congo Free State . . . It is a land of graves; it is *The* Land of Graves; it is the Congo Free Graveyard. It is a majestic thought: that is, this ghastliest episode in all human history is the work of *one man alone;* one solitary man; just a single individual — Leopold, King of the Belgians . . . Lust of conquest is royal; kings have always exercised that stately vice; but lust of money

— lust of shillings — lust of nickels — lust of dirty coin, not for the nation's enrichment but for *the king's alone* — this is new . . . we shrink from hearing the particulars of how it happened. *We shudder and turn away* when we come up to them in print.

And that, says Mark Twain's Leopold, concluding his reverie, "Why, certainly — *that* is my protection. And you will continue to do it. I know the human race."

And surely his prediction of the weakness of the human race in not wishing to acknowledge deeds of cruelty and suffering — of turning its head away, of pretending to be unaware of what lies in front of its eyes; and then of a swift "forgetting," a repression of all unpleasant memories or associations: surely this prediction is justified by history. But perhaps without this trait of callous indifference, of suppression and evasion, humanity itself, facing such recurrent crises of human evil and suffering, could hardly continue its struggle.

"The Czar's Soliloquy", in 1905, was in a sense a sequel to *King Leopold*; it was not so well understood or so popular, but in literary terms it was more compact, direct, and impressive writing. Clemens was one of the few Americans who did not regard Theodore Roosevelt's mediation of the Russo-Japanese war with approval. The Portsmouth, New Hampshire, peace treaty won the Nobel Prize for "the windy and flamboyant President," as Clemens wrote in his *Autobiography,* but it destroyed all of Mark Twain's hopes that a defeated Russia might find a revolutionary release from "an insane and intolerable slavery." "I was hoping that there would be no peace until Russian liberty was safe," he said to the Associated Press at the time. "I think there can be no doubt that that mission is now defeated and Russia's chains riveted; this time to stay. I think the Czar will now withdraw the small humanities that have been forced from him, and resume his medieval barbarisms with a relieved spirit and an immeasurable joy . . . I think nothing has been gained by the peace that is remotely comparable to what has been sacrificed by it."

"The Czar's Soliloquy" was, among other things, a plea for immediate and bloody action, as Janet Smith says: "But what Mark Twain had in mind was not revolution, but a program of assassination. This program various Russian groups — mainly Anarchists and Nihilists, and mainly young people — had been enthusiastically pursuing since before 1881, when they assassinated Alexander II, one of the most liberal of the Russian Czars. But Alexander III, who succeeded his father, was of the same stripe as Nicholas II, who came to the throne in 1894" — and was the Czar Clemens described. As early as 1890, too, he had stated his views about Russia in an unmailed letter to the editor of the American magazine *Free Russia*. "Of course I know that the properest way to demolish the Russian throne would be by revolution. But it is not possible to get up a revolution there; so the only thing left to do, apparently, is to keep the throne vacant by dynamite until a day when candidates shall decline with thanks . . ." In the same letter he made it clear that his vision of history was hardly pacifist. "My privilege to write these sanguinary sentences in soft security was bought for me by rivers of blood poured upon many fields, in many lands, but I possess not one single little paltry right or privilege that came to me as a result of petition, persuasion, agitation for reform, or any kindred method of procedure. When we consider that not even the most responsible English monarch ever yielded back a stolen public right until it was wrenched from him by bloody violence, is it rational to suppose that gentler methods can win privileges in Russia?" *

For these reasons, and others to come, it is easy to see why

---

* Compare the writings of the contemporary theoretician of the Third World, and of the Revolution there, Frantz Fanon, who in far different context repeats Mark Twain's prophetic words.

Mark Twain is regarded with such reverence by modern Russian scholars; why they are so well informed about his work — and why they objected when this whole area of Twain's writing was omitted by American scholars, during the epoch of the fifties on such grounds (as we know) as that it was "too controversial," "too roughly written," "too violent," or "in bad taste." Charles Neider's "reply" to the Russian critics — who pointed out that his version of the *Autobiography* omitted all the episodes of radical social criticism which Clemens had particularly delighted in writing for it — was a particularly blatant example of such Cold War "scholarship," as is Justin Kaplan's *Mr. Clemens and Mark Twain*. The Russians were right, in this case, and the Americans were wrong. As any reader of the polemical essays can testify, this whole area of Mark Twain's social criticism is one of the adornments of his art, as it should be of his country's culture.

In the *Soliloquy* itself, Clemens seized upon a London newspaper item which declared that the Russian Czar, after his morning bath, meditated an hour before getting dressed. Clemens expatiated upon Carlyle's thesis of "clothes" marking human rank and power, and then, "A curious invention, an unaccountable invention — the human race!" continues this blood brother of King Leopold. "The swarming Russian millions have for centuries meekly allowed our family to rob them, insult them, trample them under foot, while they lived and suffered and died with no purpose and no function but to make that family comfortable! These people are horses — just that — horses with clothes and a religion. A horse with the strength of a hundred men will let one man beat him, starve him, drive him; the Russian millions allow a mere handful of soldiers to hold them in slavery — and these very soldiers are their own sons and brothers!"

There was another strange thing, continued Mark Twain's

Russian Czar, "to wit, the world applies to Czar and system the same moral axioms that have vogue and acceptance in civilized countries! Because, in civilized countries, it is wrong to remove oppressors otherwise than by process of law, it is held that the same rule applies in Russia, where there is no such thing as law — except for our family. Laws are merely restraints — they have no other function. In civilized countries they restrain all persons and restrain them all alike, which is fair and righteous, but in Russia such laws as exist make an exception — our family. We do as we please; we have done as we pleased for centuries. Our common trade has been crime, our common pastime murder, our common beverage blood — the blood of the nation. Upon our heads lie millions of murders. Yet the pious moralist says it is a crime to assassinate us. We and our uncles are a family of cobras set over a hundred and forty million rabbits, whom we torture and murder and feed upon all our days; yet the moralist urges that to kill us is a crime, not a duty."

Inspired writing, again, from an outraged soul! The central debate in the radical sector of American thinking in the mid-1960s was that between the advocates of passive resistance and of revolutionary violence in both the civil-rights movement and the shameful war in Vietnam. How was it that Mark Twain had reached such conclusions of revolutionary violence as the essential lever in history, so easily, so naturally, so forcefully — while a half century later it was officially declared, also, that such revolutionary violence was repugnant to the American notion of justice and progress, of evolutionary history and the democratic process itself? Well, that is to say, violence was condemned *within* the United States; while outside its borders, in every portion of the still under-developed world, the American military felt free to obliterate a whole countryside, a whole nation's population if necessary, all the cities, towns, villages, fields, crops of any small country, in a policy of instant armed resistance to social upheavals it did not approve of. Which had changed most, the American nation or its artistic consciousness as exemplified in Sam Clemens?

And which was the obvious historical truth in this argument, and which the transparent historical fabrication for the plain purpose of imperial power, control, exploitation, and plunder in the name of a senseless (but cunningly contrived) "national security"? What a shameful, wicked, devastating kind of lie was perpetrated in the national consciousness during the Cold War epoch; and what can one say of the nation's intellectuals who either accepted this lie, or went along with it because of cowardly or selfish reasons? (I am not speaking here of the truly revolutionary pacifist movements.) And meanwhile Sam Clemens was continuing, with his ruthless and lacerating logic, to expose the pious fraud that the Russian monarchy — like the slave-holding Southern plantation owners of the Civil War period — would willingly abdicate all its power and profits peacefully, under the duress of civilized or religious morality.

"It is not for me to say it aloud," continued Mark Twain's ruminating Czar to himself, unaware that he was giving out his secrets to the whole world of the mid-1900s, unaware that the diabolical Sam Clemens had caught him without his clothes on, and that the Emperor was indeed naked in the full sight of this "childlike" and incorruptible artist: "But to one on the inside — like me — this is naively funny; on its face illogical. Our family is above all law, there is no law that can reach us, restrain us, protect the people from us. Therefore, we are outlaws. Outlaws are a proper mark for anyone's bullet. Ah! what could our family do without the moralist? He has been our stay, our support, our friend; today, he is our only friend. Whenever there has been dark talk of assassination, he has come forward and saved us with his impressive maxim, 'Forbear: nothing politically valuable was ever yet achieved by violence.' He probably believes it. It is because he has by him no child's book of world history to teach him that his maxim lacks the backing of statistics. All thrones have been established by violence; no regal tyranny has ever been overthrown except by violence; by violence my fathers set up our throne; by murder, treachery, perjury, torture, banishment, and the prison they have held it for four centuries, and by these same arts I hold it today. There is no Romanoff of learning and experience but would reverse the maxim and say: 'Nothing politically valuable was ever yet achieved *except* by violence.' "

Thus Mark Twain combined his early rejection of conventional religion and morality, his scornful attacks on the missionaries under the subterfuge and cover of Christianity, with the true workings of history. Here he saw clearly that conventional morality and conventional Christianity were being used as the main prop and "moral support" of the implacable tyranny perpetuated by the Russian emperors. In "The Czar's Soliloquy", he continued with a recital of the Czar's most recent crimes, after the conclusion of the Russo-Japanese War and of the Russian nation's stirrings of revolt. The Czar reads two parallel newspaper clippings: one of the Cossacks' brutalities against the Polish people; the other of the religious awe and servile adulation with which the Russian masses still regarded the presence and "the hallowed features of *the Lord's Anointed*." The Czar is moved: "And it was I that got that grovelling and awe-smitten worship! I — this thing in the mirror — this carrot! With one hand I flogged unoffending women to death and tortured prisoners to unconsciousness; and with the other I held up the fetish toward my fellow deity in heaven and called down His blessing upon my adoring animals whom and whose forebears, with His holy approval, I and mine have been instructing in the pains of hell for four lagging centuries. It is a picture! To think that this thing in the mirror — this vegetable — is an accepted deity to a mighty nation, an innumerable host, and nobody laughs; and at the same time is a diligent and practical professional devil, and nobody marvels, nobody murmurs about incongruities and inconsistencies! Is the human race a joke? Was it devised and patched together in a dull time when there was nothing important to do? Has it no respect for itself?"

Let us remember these words in relation to Twain's celebrated and ambiguous novelette, *The Mysterious Stranger*. And surely Sam Clemens' respect for the human race was drooping, sinking, as he concluded the Czar's Soliloquy — though his writing was strangely exalted. This essay too has been subjected by leading critics to the usual objections I have listed — yes, this "rude and vulgar" and tasteless, formless Mark Twain, who precisely for this sector of his writing even above the rest is reverenced in Russia, Asia, Africa, and South America as America's great literary genius! In this case, to paraphrase Robert Burns, if only *indeed* we could see ourselves as others see us! It should be clear now there is no true note of purely personal frustration in these essays; they are the sentiments of a master artist who was enraged by blatant and callous social injustice — that is to say, human injustice on a mass scale. They are Twain's testimony to his time; and the time's testimony to Mark Twain.

In "The United States of Lyncherdom" (1901), moreover, Twain took a look at his own country in this period of raw colonialism, savage imperialism, and racial genocide. This was indeed such an indignant and heartbroken article that Clemens put it away, and decided not to publish it; while even Paine, using it some twenty years later in the collection of posthumous essays, *Europe and Elsewhere,* was still concerned about its effect.*

"And so Missouri has fallen, that great state!" so Clemens opened his piece. "Certain of her children have joined the lynchers, and the smirch is upon the rest of us. That handful of her children have given us a character and labeled us with a name, and to the dwellers in the four quarters of the earth we are 'lynchers,' now and ever shall be." The world would not stop and think, said Clemens with a familiar irony, that the bulk of Missourians building an honorable name for themselves did not endorse the action; that the hundred Missourians who were lynchers were in fact renegades. "No, that truth will not enter its mind; it will generalize from the one or two misleading samples and say, 'The Missourians are lynchers.' It has no reflection, no logic, no sense of proportion. With it figures go for nothing; to it, figures reveal nothing, it cannot reason upon them rationally . . . It would say, 'There are a hundred lynchers there, therefore the Missourians are lynchers'; the considerable fact that there are two and a half million Missourians who are *not* lynchers would not affect their verdict . . . Oh, Missouri!"

A young white woman had been found murdered, and perhaps raped — the "usual crime" of that period, or the common pretext for lynching Negroes. "Although it was a region of churches and schools," Clemens continued, "the people rose, lynched three Negroes — two of them very aged ones — burned out five Negro households, and drove thirty Negro families into

---

* In a letter to Clemens quoted by Kaplan, Bernard Shaw remarked that he believed Mark Twain was one of the greatest masters of the English language — as indeed almost all of the leading English writers did, with the notable exception of the uncomprehending Matthew Arnold — and that "I am persuaded that the future historian of America will find your works as indispensable to him as a French historian finds the political tracts of Voltaire."

the woods." Churches indeed; one could ask, as Clemens did, what kind of Christianity was practiced in the southern Churches, and what part the ministry played in opposing such mobs. (The ministers looked the other way; or not approving the lynching of Negroes for "rape," deplored the "necessity" for it.) Clemens, moreover, went on to point out that every time a Negro was lynched on the supposition of rape, it encouraged more Negroes to consider the possibility of raping, and more white men to perform the act of lynching. In 1900 there had been eight more cases of lynching than in 1899, and in 1901 he thought there would be more cases than in 1900, mainly in the four southern states of Alabama, Georgia, Louisiana, and Mississippi. The other reason Clemens attributed to the rising rate of lynching during these terrible years in the south was simply the moral cowardice of man:

> It has been supposed — and said — that the people at a lynching enjoy the spectacle and are glad of a chance to see it. It cannot be true; all experience is against it. The people in the South are made like the people in the North — the vast majority of whom are right-hearted and compassionate, and would be cruelly pained by such a spectacle — and *would attend it,* and let on to be pleased with it, if the public approval seemed to require it. We are made like that and we cannot help it. The other animals are not so, but we cannot help that, either. They lack the moral sense; we have no way of trading ours off, for a nickel or some other thing above its value. The moral sense teaches us what is right, and how to avoid it — when unpopular.

Thus Mark Twain on the "moral sense" in man, a favorite source of ironical commentary in his later period of work. Now against the mass drive and mob instinct of man, he asked, why were there not a few bolder spirits to oppose this, like those sheriffs of the period who did hold back the lynchers, or the perhaps more courageous outlaws who could terrorize such mobs? But no, he concluded, his scheme would not work. "There are not enough morally brave men in stock. We are out of moral-courage material; we are in a condition of profound poverty." In the meantime, there was another plan. "Let us import American missionaries from China, and send them into the lynching field. With 1,511 of them out there converting two Chinamen apiece per annum against an uphill birth rate of 33,000 pagans per day, it will take upward of a million years to make the conversions balance the output and bring the Christianizing of the country in sight to the naked eye; therefore, if we can offer our missionaries as rich a field at home, at lighter expense and quite satisfactory in the matter of danger, why shouldn't they find it fair and right to come back and give us a trial?"

The Chinese were universally conceded to be excellent people, honorable, industrious, trustworthy, and all that, Clemens continued. "Leave them alone, they are plenty good enough just as they are; and besides, almost every convert runs a risk of catching our civilization. We ought to be careful. We ought to think twice before we encourage a risk like that; for, *once civilized, China can never be uncivilized again.* We have not been thinking about that. Very well, we ought to think of it now. Our missionaries will find that we have a field for them — and not only for the 1,511 but for 15,011 . . . We must implore them to come back and help us in our need," added Clemens after citing a particularly nasty account of the white man's cruelty in these lynchings. "Patriotism imposes this duty on them. Our country is worse off than China; they are our countrymen, their motherland supplicates their aid in this, her hour of deep distress. They are competent; our people are not. They are used to scoffs, sneers, revilings, danger; our people are not. They have the martyr spirit; nothing but the martyr spirit can brave a lynching mob, and cow it and scatter it. They can save the country, we beseech them to come home and do it."

He referred again to the description of the lynching of one Negro which he multiplied by 115 (the estimated figure for lynchings in 1900), and added 88 (the figures already recorded for lynchings in 1901), and said: "Place the 203 in a row, allowing 600 feet of space for each human torch, so that there may be viewing room around it for 5,000 Christian American men, women, and children, youths and maidens; make it night for grim effect, have the show in a gradually rising plain, and let the course of the stakes be uphill; the eye can then take in the whole line of twenty-four miles of blood-and-flesh bonfires unbroken, whereas if it occupied ground level the ends of the line would bend down and be hidden from view by the curvature of the earth. All being ready, now, and the darkness opaque, the stillness impressive — for there should be no sound but the soft moaning of the night wind and the muffled sobbing of the sacrifices — let all the far stretch of kerosened pyres be touched off simultaneously and the glare and the shrieks and the agonies burst heavenward to the Throne . . . There are more than a million persons present; the light from the fires flushes into vague outline against the night the spires of five thousand churches. O kind missionary, O compassionate missionary, leave China! Come home and convert these Christians!"

Thus the flaming conclusion of "The United States of Lyncherdom" which was indeed "dramatic" and "visual" and "scenic" and "rendered" enough to satisfy all the deepest yearnings of a Henry James. Although this celebrated American expatriate, James I mean, in his own book called *The American Scene*, written during the same years, and in his wanderings southward, would expatiate only on the rude, barbaric, lazy

African tribal types he found there, and on the terrible eco-
nomic and domestic exigencies forced upon the former southern
aristocrats whose cause and whose sentiments James found himself comprehending more and more clearly and intimately, as it
were.*

And so, as Mark Twain recalled to their mother country
those American missionaries whom he had ridiculed and attacked in the first of the later polemical essays mentioned here
— *To the Person Sitting in Darkness* — he had come full
circle from what he had first felt to be the Old World's evil imperialism, and then discovered right at hand, before his nose,
in the New World's own burgeoning colonialism and racism.
The cycle was complete.

But that is not to say that he had by any means finished writing in this altogether imperial and majestic vein of radical
social criticism which the Mark Twain scholarship of the Cold
War period would find so regrettable, offensive, and unbecom-
ing. No, Sam Clemens himself knew that he had discovered an
altogether new mood of inspiration in his later and last periods of
writing; a rich and golden realm in these areas of colonialism,
imperialism, and racism as the salient features of his society.

* In what should be a classic literary history of this period but is instead a misleading document, Edmund Wilson's *Patriotic Gore,* this leading American
critic is completely taken in by James' romantic (and at base pathological)
rhetoric about both the Civil War and the post-Civil War scene, in both the
grotesque travelogue, *The American Scene,* and in the baroque *Memoirs.* Somewhat like his alma mater, Princeton, Wilson can now be described as the
northernmost-situated of all the southern critics. Similarly, he has little use
for (or apparent knowledge of) Twain's brilliant social criticism of the scene
of James' snobbish romance, and Wilson himself seems infatuated by Twain's
wealth, social position, and acquaintanceship with the financial tycoons . . .
Wilson's work has been described earlier as that of a genius without any
"center"; in his late period it is obvious that his brilliant esthetic superstructure
lacks any solid social ground. And Irving Howe's "Introduction" to the most
recent edition of *The American Scene* reads as though it were composed some
fifteen years ago. Perhaps the Jamesian cultists cannot *afford* to keep up with
the times.

Returning to such themes would renew his failing fancy and restore his faltering pen, and carry it to new and higher flights of brilliant, ironical, comic, and often quite marvelous passages of polemical prose, both of its time and timeless. With a sounder sense of art and life than his future critics, those who were becoming ever more intimidated by the increasingly repressive nature of their own culture, he would return to this aspect of his art until the end of his life, taking a diabolical pleasure in it, purging his turbulent spirit, refreshing his genius.

# SIX

# DEATH OF AN EPIC POET

By August of 1908 Samuel Clemens had made his final and astounding comeback to an atmosphere of comfort, pleasure, luxury, of world fame and, odd as it may have seemed, to domestic happiness.* Howells' son John, an architect, had designed the Italian-looking mansion. How many gorgeous mansions had the poor western boy, Sam Clemens, dwelt in with glory and munificence; how many had he exited from in bankruptcy and disgrace; and still he came back to another one (in Redding, Connecticut), called Stormfield from Twain's ironical vision of heaven.

There he surrounded himself with his familiar pleasures once more and abandoned himself to the small happinesses of his declining years. The girls were away; even when Jean, apparently restored and buoyant in health, became her father's secretary she appeared only at meals, and the aging Clemens depended more and more on the never-failing amanuensis, diarist, and chronicler, Paine. In this final relationship of the declining master and the worshipful, obsequious apprentice, the syco-

---

*After a prolonged illness, Olivia Clemens had died in Florence in June, 1904, never having recovered from the death of their daughter Susy. "At a quarter past 9 this evening she that was the life of my life passed to the relief & the peace of death after 22 months of unjust and unearned suffering," Clemens wrote. He was heart-broken and distraught and these years were filled with his tributes to Livy as the "Eve" of his earthly paradise; and yet from this blow too his resilient spirit finally rebounded.

phantic note of Paine's *Mark Twain: A Biography* intrudes itself to a small (Jamesian) degree. Indeed, "I have dismissed my secretary," Clemens wrote to the Howellses, "and have entered upon a holiday whose other end is the grave."

He had already piled up, during a period of two and a half years, about half a million words for the *Autobiography*. At Stormfield he spent the morning in bed reading and answering letters; in the afternoons there were two regular games for himself and guests: cards and billiards, still his great domestic pastime. In the evening, as Paine tells us, there was the music, the stately measures of the orchestrelle which he had brought along from his 21 Fifth Avenue house.

Even then, without experience of fascism, Clemens believed the American republic was already doomed to become a monarchy, because in the nature of man there was a deep desire to reverence a king, and because, secondly, while little republics have lasted long, protected by their poverty and insignificance, great ones have not. "And the condition is, vast power and wealth, which breed commercial and political corruptions, and incite public favorites to dangerous ambitions."

It was clear to Clemens, and should be pointed out to our own sactimonious business community, that it was *commercial* corruption which led to (and actually controlled) political corruption; just as the Christian plans and schemes for "universal peace" during these years were a hypocritical mask for armed imperialism, and for the First World War. "The gospel of peace is always making a deal of noise, always rejoicing in its progress but always neglecting to furnish statistics. There are no peaceful nations now. All Christendom is a soldier-camp. The poor have been taxed in some nations to the starvation point to support the giant armaments which Christian governments have built up, each to protect itself from the rest of the Christian brotherhood, and incidentally to snatch any scrap of real estate left exposed by a weaker owner." Clemens went on to recap the history of King Leopold II of Belgium — "the most intensely Christian monarch since Alexander VI, that has escaped hell thus far, has stolen an entire kingdom in Africa, and in fourteen years of Christian endeavor there has reduced the population from thirty millions to fifteen." And then:

> Within the last generation each Christian power has turned the bulk of its attention to finding out newer and still newer and more and more effective ways of killing Christians, and, incidentally, a pagan now and then; and the surest way to get rich quickly in Christ's earthly kingdom is to invent a gun that can kill more Christians at one shot than any other existing kind. All the Christian nations are at it. The more advanced they are, the bigger and more destructive engines of war they create.

Prophetic words again in which Clemens saw not only the First World War already on his horizon, but perhaps even the Second, and the whole nature of "modern civilization." During the same period he had, rather oddly, and to a certain degree reminiscent of Lewis Carroll's intense interest in young girls (not to mention many other writers of great stature such as Theodore Dreiser, who had the same uneasy yearnings), formed an association of little "Angel-Fish" admirers and companions at home and in Bermuda. In the Mark Twain who is not primarily to be viewed in orthodox psychoanalytic terms at all, there was still a curious strain — or a complex — about youthful innocence and "virginity" (as in his deplorable version of Joan of Arc) which commonly shows up in the later years of intensely sensual artists.

"My child," Clemens wrote to one of his young and adoring companions, "it's as tranquil & contenting as Bermuda. You will be very welcome here, dear"; and there are other curious intimations and associations with Dreiser's erotic baby-talk in *The "Genius"* and *An American Tragedy,* and elsewhere.

At Stormfield he debated the existence of Jesus Christ with Paine, and reading two books on the Baconian viewpoint of Shakespeare, one of which he used and literally, as was his wont, and embellished with his own asides and conclusions, he began to write *Is Shakespeare Dead?* Started as a hobby, it became in familiar fashion almost one of his obsessions, though with less disastrous consequences than most, and with much more comedy attached to it. Harpers' demurring, Clemens had the volume printed on his own, another example, as we've seen, of Mark Twain's publishing "cowardice."

Clara had recovered from her troubles, Jean was still improving in health as her father's secretary. He had a home once more with his children around him; he who had already survived so many tragic epochs and domestic disasters, until one admires Sam Clemens' enduring personal fortitude, in these last years, as well as his still effervescent literary talent. But now too, at this brief moment of personal fulfillment and happiness in Samuel Clemens' long and full life, he was on the edge of a new series of disasters. In May, 1909, he made a final trip to consult Henry Rogers on business only to learn that the valued friend who had rescued him from bankruptcy and ruin had died the night before. Clemens felt that he had been cast adrift, his old friends dissolving all around him. Nevertheless he worked hard and long, with his political friend Champ Clark, for the establishment of a new copyright bill for which he had been working since 1906. He was attacked for plagiarizing George Greenwood's book, *The Shakespeare Problem Restated*, which of course he had, in his own inimitable way. And he suffered the first pains of the heart disease which would kill him.

As usual, he went on with his reading, just now Suetonius and — "When I take up one of Jane Austen's books, such as *Pride and Prejudice,* I feel like a barkeeper entering the king-

dom of heaven. I know what his sensations would be and his
private comments." But he liked the early verse of Willa Cather;
a curious little encounter in our letters. As his heart attacks increased during this year, he began to make preparations, both
private and public, for his own departure:

> I came in with Halley's comet in 1835 [he said to Paine]. It is
> coming again next year, and I expect to go out with it. It will be
> the greatest disappointment of my life if I don't go out with
> Halley's comet. The Almighty has said, no doubt: "Now here are
> these two unaccountable freaks; they came in together, they must
> go out together.

In these final notes and jottings of Mark Twain, according to
Paine's *Autobiography,* he still remained a natural (and unconscious) Marxist in part of his thinking: "Morals are not the
important thing — nor enlightenment — nor civilization," he
noted. "A man can do absolutely well without them, but he
can't do without *something to eat.* The supremest thing is the
*needs of the body,* not of the mind & spirit." He still remained
pagan. "I am old now and once was a sinner. I often think of it
with a kind of soft regret. I trust my days are numbered. I
would not have that detail overlooked." And he was still enchanted by Livy. "She was always a girl, she was always young
because her heart was young; & I was young because she lived
in my heart & preserved its youth from decay."

There was even one more peak of happiness and joy. There
was a concert for the Redding library, planned by Clemens
around the musical careers of the talented pianist Ossip Gabrilowitsch, and Clara Clemens whom he was courting. The library
concert was an immense success; the subsequent marriage of
Clara and Ossip brought felicitations from Mark Twain's friends
and admirers the world over. Ossip was handsome, gay, and al-

ready famous; Clara was stately, rather heavy-bodied and of a brooding disposition, even at the moment of their wedding.*

When the aging Mark Twain was asked whether he was pleased with the marriage, his answer reflected his life's anguish. He was pleased, he said, as fully as any marriage could please him. "There are two or three solemn things in life, and a happy marriage is one of them, for the terrors of life are to come. I am glad of this marriage, and Mrs. Clemens would be glad, for she always had a warm affection for Gabrilowitsch."

His health was running down seriously during this time, and he should perhaps have been happier than he was at Clara's marriage; and, as usual, he would not follow his doctor's orders about smoking and exercise. To Miss Wallace, part of the Bermuda "Angel-fish" group of Mark Twain's little girls, he wrote: "I can't walk. I can't drive. I'm not down-stairs much, and I don't see company, but I drink barrels of water to keep the pain quiet; I read, and read, and read, and smoke and smoke all the time (as formerly) and it's a contented and comfortable life." (It even appears that the medical advice incited Sam Clemens to smoking.) He revised his will.† And he began writing another

---

* She had had an uneasy childhood and adolescence, both physically and psychologically. Perhaps her early life was burdened by the extravagant affection which the Clemenses had extended to her sister Susy, and the extended and exorbitant period of mourning over Susy's death. At any rate Clara's daughter, and Ossip's, was institutionalized and died at an early age, and there are no living descendants of Mark Twain. There was indeed a certain curse which afflicted all of the Clemens children — the baby son who died early, the three daughters who led such inbred, domestic and tragic lives. Some biographers attribute their fates to Clemens' own devoted but jealous and overbearing fatherly arrogance; but we should not forget Livy's delicate health and temperament which had also presided over the domestic menage. The combination of events which doomed the Clemens daughters was physical as well as psychological; in the blood stream as well as in the mind. But then too, how obviously and how extravagantly these parents, Sam and Livy, loved each other to the very end; and perhaps all unconsciously the children were paying for *that*.

† According to Paine (whose *Mark Twain, a Biography* I am following in this account), Twain's estate was valued at over $600,000, which was not a bad recovery for an artist bankrupt in his prime of life.

book, *Letters from the Earth,* which Clemens said would never be published, but which was published, as he must have known it would be.

*Letters from the Earth* was in fact to contain some of Mark Twain's best writing, polemical and otherwise, just as into all these late books "never intended for publication" and written, as he said, purely for his own pleasure (but what major artist does not write for posterity?), he poured forth all the hidden depths of his nature and all its prophetic peaks in that "last style" which was infinitely his best style. A style which he had taken a lifetime to fashion in all its deceptive simplicity and brilliant lucidity.

Clemens was considering the idea of the new American empire following the way of Rome. Reading always, he was attracted to memoirs and history: Saint-Simon, Casanova, Pepys, Carlyle's *French Revolution* still at hand, Francis Parkman — and Clemens could hardly refrain from remarking about *The Jesuits in North America*:

> That men would be willing to leave their happy homes and endure what the missionaries endured in order to teach these Indians the road to hell would be rational, understandable, but why they should want to teach them a way to heaven is a thing which the mind somehow cannot grasp.

After Parkman, there was Greville's *Memoirs,* Plutarch, P. T. Barnum, the *Letters of Madame De Sévigné,* Dana's *Two Years Before the Mast,* and the great Darwin's *Descent of Man.* And Clemens still kept his admiration for Kipling's poems, even while his own thinking had advanced far ahead of the illustrious bard of imperialism and the white man's burden, which meant, in effect, the black man's destruction.

In mid-November, 1909, Clemens and Paine went together for another vacation in Bermuda, the blessed isles; on Clemens' seventy-fourth birthday he appeared to Paine as looking "wonderfully well." Upon their return to Stormfield for the Christmas holidays, Jean was busy with her holiday preparations on December 23, and on that night she was struck by an epileptic fit (or heart failure) and died in the bathtub. It was the "final disaster," as Clemens said. It marked the failure of his last attempt at rebuilding his domestic life; it marked the end of his writing (as it was the final section of the *Autobiography*) and it hastened his impending death. Although Paine believes that Clemens was hardened and inured to the deaths of his friends and his family, anybody who reads the last section of the *Autobiography* may feel differently. Despite all of Clemens' irony and factualism as to death being the only true gift of life, his description of Jean's death is one of his most touching, affectionate, lyrical, bitter-sweet paeans to life, his daughter's life, and, ever again, her mother's life. Here again, as often with Mark Twain, this great comedian brings tears to our eyes.

He spent the next two days after Jean's death writing the full account of it. "I am setting it down — everything. It is a relief for me to write it. It furnishes me an excuse for thinking." On Christmas Day, 1909, he watched Jean's baby nurse, Katie Leary, accompany Jean's body as it set out on its last pilgrimage to the Elmira cemetery.

> From my windows I saw the hearse and the carriages wind along the road and gradually grow vague and spectral in the falling snow, and presently disappear. Jean was gone out of my life, and would not come back any more. Jervis, the cousin she had played with when they were babies together — he and her beloved old Katie — were conducting her to her distant childhood home, where she will lie by her mother's side once more, in the company of Susy and Langdon.

He was too weary and too disheartened to make the journey, but later that day, according to Paine's account, he felt a cold current of air around him in the bathroom which he associated with Jean's burial.

Reading the many letters of condolence, to the ones which offered the orthodox Christian view that God does not willingly punish us, Mark Twain replied: "Well, why does he do it then? We don't invite. Why does He give Himself the trouble?" And to Mrs. Gabrilowitsch, he poured out his anguished heart. "You can't imagine what a darling she was that last two or three days; & how *fine,* & good, & sweet, & noble — & *joyful,* thank Heaven! — & how intellectually brilliant. I had never been acquainted with Jean before. I recognized that . . . But I mustn't try to write about her — I *can't.* I have already poured my heart out with the pen, recording that last day or two. I will send you that — & you must let no one but Ossip read it. Good-by. I love you so! And Ossip." *

According to Paine, also, Clemens really attempted no further writing after Jean's death; it was the last disaster of his life, and the rest was a brief epilogue. There was another "gorgeous letter" from Howells on an essay which Twain published in *Harper's Bazar*; there was a final meeting with this old friend and literary adviser. Clemens went back to Bermuda briefly, but in April, 1910, he was suffering severe pains around his heart and was living on hypodermic injections and opiates. Paine went to Bermuda to fetch him back home; as we know, Sam Clemens did not want either to die in a foreign place or to return as a corpse. It was a question for a while whether he could make the trip back; he recovered enough to

* Clemens, like most geniuses, was undoubtedly a difficult father. The Clemens children, as we've noted, had a strong vein, hereditary or environmental, of neurosis and physical illness; in the later years we've seen how the household was darkened by financial worries, grief, and sickness. But letters such as this from Clemens to Clara, do much to recall the essential harmony, grace, and sweetness of their domestic life at its best, and to refute studies (Freudian for the most part, but including to a degree Edith Colgate Salsbury's *Susy and Mark Twain*) of Twain's oppressive effect upon his daughters, and their covert hostility or enmity.

reach his home, dying, in a horrible trip. "I am sorry for you, Paine," he is reported as saying, "but I can't help it — I can't hurry this dying business. Can't you give me enough of the hypnotic injunction [as he called the needle] to put an end to me?" And then: "After forty years of public effort I have become just a target for medicines." And, only half awake, or half alive: "Isn't there something I can resign and be out of all this . . . I am like a bird in a cage: always expecting to get out, and always beaten back by the wires . . . Oh, it is such a mystery, and it takes so long."

Great men, it is said, die great deaths, and the last days of Samuel Clemens have this mark upon them. At the end of the first day he asked Paine how many days and nights were left for his trip home: "We'll never make it. It's an eternity . . . It's a losing race; no ship can outsail death" — but nevertheless he arrived in New York, and was driven back to Stormfield.

"There was never anybody like him; there never will be," William Dean Howells said after their final meeting in New York, and after a loving relationship of over forty years between two men so strangely assorted, and despite such differences of opinion as theirs on the Haymarket Riots, when Howells spoke out publicly in favor of the "anarchist criminals" falsely condemned for the crime, and Mark Twain did not. Howells suffered from public persecution and literary boycott for his great act of moral courage. Twain, for whatever reasons, made no public statement. Yet there is no discussion of this matter in their public papers so far available; and their deep friendship apparently remained undisturbed.

On a still, sweet April night, Thursday the fourteenth, 1910, according to Paine, Clemens returned home to Stormfield, and by Sunday, when Clara arrived, he was still articulate. "This is a peculiar kind of disease," he said. "It does not invite you to read; it does not invite you to be read to; it does not invite you to talk, nor to enjoy any of the usual sick-room methods of treatment. What kind of a disease is *that?*" On Tuesday the nineteenth, he asked Clara to sing for him some of the Scotch songs he loved; when she left, he said goodbye, he might never see her again. On April 20, Halley's Comet, which had accompanied his birth, appeared in the heavens again, as Clemens had predicted; and on Thursday, the twenty-first, in the peaceful spring evening, he died in his seventy-fifth year.

# SEVEN

# SATAN AS PRANKSTER

THE MYSTERIOUS STRANGER had a somewhat mysterious history. Was it never published during Clemens' lifetime because, as he believed, he never could find "the right end" for it? That was usually the trouble with his stories, as we know. Or because he was afraid in truth of this dark fable which was the highest and best climax of this vein in his work, from *The Tragedy of Pudd'nhead Wilson* in 1894 to *The Man That Corrupted Hadleyburg* in 1900 and *The $30,000 Bequest* in 1906. At the base of *The Mysterious Stranger* was the nihilistic philosophy of *What Is Man?* too, only here that pounding and persistent pessimism of Clemens' lowest period was transmuted into highly complex, ambiguous art. In its tone *The Mysterious Stranger* is light, satirical, even gay just when its message is most horrid. Talk about Melville! Talk about the *Piazza Tales* such as "Bartleby the Scrivener," "The Encantadas," and perhaps the greatest of them, "Benito Cereno." Mark Twain's vision of life in *The Mysterious Stranger* was just as demonic, nihilistic, and enigmatic.

This is one of the major short stories of evil and emptiness at the core of life; and both Melville and Twain eclipsed in their depth and range of vision the short stories of Ernest Hemingway on the same theme. But just as Melville was to live on and write, in his last fable of *Billy Budd,* of a more mixed universe of both good and evil, or perhaps beyond good and evil, so Twain's somber view of man's life in *The Mysterious Stranger* was curiously balanced by a sense of light and joy, mysterious to behold, in the story itself. The background history of the story still remains obscure. (*I am not here concerned with the academic controversy over the various editions of this book.*\*) One might speculate it was started in the lowest depths of Clemens' life, the period of Livy's last illness and the family's collapse, and then refined and refined, subtly altered, in his last years. For the story's opening is full of paradoxes, enigma upon enigma, which bewilder and dazzle us — which are resolved slowly in the story's development . . . if they are resolved.

The scene was Austria in 1590. The town was called Eseldorf (or "Jackassville"), as the successor to Hannibal, Hadleyburg, and Dawson's Landing. This little transposed frontier settlement was still "a paradise for us boys," but this time a paradise ringed round with more ominous taboos and evil omens. Of the village's two priests, Father Adolf was held in more respect because "he had absolutely no fear of the Devil." He mocked at him in fact, and had actually met Satan face to face and defied him. "This was known to be so. Father Adolf said it himself." The other priest, Father Peter, believed that God was all goodness and would find a way to save his poor human children; the villagers loved but were sorry for him. The village Astrologer was the third member of this peculiar trinity, the possessor of occult wisdom and ancient magic, pre-religious

---

\*Despite the academic controversy about "the Mysterious Stranger manuscripts," and the alleged three versions of the story extant, there is only one version that makes sense, the final version that Twain wrote, and to which A. B. Paine added an ending from one of the previous two scripts. But the main thrust of the story has nothing to do with the ending, and Twain's endings were almost always poor.

in essence, whom the good Father Peter denounced but Father Adolf and the Bishop respected.

As the story opens, Father Peter is already on the road to ruin, along with his niece Marget. The village money-lender, Solomon Isaacs, is about to foreclose the mortgage on their house. Against the prevailing trinity of religious and superstitious authority Clemens set up a kind of pagan trinity of three boys who were always together and had been so from the cradle. Theodor Fischer, son of the church organist, is the story's narrator; his friends are Nikolaus Bauman and Seppi Wohlmeyer. As in *Huck Finn* these three are natural boys. "We knew the hills and the woods as well as the birds knew them; for we were always roaming them when we had leisure — at least, when we were not swimming or boating or fishing, or playing on the ice or sliding down hill." But here the castle park is a feudal scene and the castle servingman, Felix Brandt, provides the aura of primitive mysticism — of ghosts, witches, enchanters, bats, and incubae — formerly supplied by the Negro slaves . . . Yet the Mysterious Stranger seems far away from all this.

He is a handsome and well-turned-out young man with a winning face and a pleasant voice, "and was easy and graceful and unembarrassed, not slouchy and awkward and diffident like other boys." He wins over the three youths by his charm and beguilements, while he makes fire out of air and ice out of water and fills their pockets with goodies. He makes living animals out of clay after he has told them he is an angel, and proceeds to make a toy castle filled with five hundred active little people as a replica of medieval life. He outfits a cavalry division and lets the boys make the horses and cannon. It is then he tells them his name is Satan, named after his uncle who was blameless before the Fall, and this fills the boys with divine wonder. "I should not be able to make any one understand how exciting it all was. You know that kind of quiver that trembles around through you when you are seeing something so strange and enchanting and wonderful that it is just a fearful joy to be alive and look at it — "

> and you know how you gaze, and your lips turn dry and your breath comes short, but you wouldn't be anywhere but there, not for the world.

And this theme of satanic enchantment — of a revelatory excitement that thrills the mind and the senses alike — is a persistent one throughout *The Mysterious Stranger* and we must ask ourselves what its true meaning is, both to Samuel Clemens and in the larger realm of psychological feeling.

Satan also answers the unasked questions of the boys. "Have I seen him? Millions of times. From the time that I was a little child a thousand years old I was his second favorite among the nursery angels of our blood and lineage — to use a human phrase — yes, from that time until the Fall, eight thousand years, measured as you count time." But which "Him" is Clemens referring to, even while he is careful not to use the customary capitalization — God or the Devil? In point of fact they are equated in the story; it is actually the Devil — or to minimize man's nature and destiny even more — it is the Devil's nephew who is the Acting God, to all purposes the real God, of the chronicle.

There is another favorite notion of the later Mark Twain, the notion of time being imaginary and man-made, and hence important only to man in his delusionary universe. The youthful Satan is sixteen thousand years old, by human count, and as he says, without sin. "No, the Fall did not affect me nor the rest of the relationship. It was only he that I was named for who ate of the fruit of the tree and then beguiled the man and the woman with it. We others are still ignorant of sin; we are not able to commit it; we are without blemish, and shall abide in that estate always. We — " And then he squeezes the life blood out of two of the toy workmen he has created, wipes off the stain of blood with his handkerchief, and continues. "We cannot do wrong; neither have we any disposition to do it, for we do not know what it is."

The boys are horrified by this act of wanton bloodshed on the part of their dazzling young friend while he is uttering the strange speech about being without sin. Then, in the toy kingdom, the wives of the dead men start to lament, a priest arrives, masses of people assemble to grieve and weep — and Satan, annoyed by the tiny tumult, wipes out the whole assemblage. "It made us sick to see that awful deed," says Clemens' young narrator, and these people had not been prepared by the Church for death, and the boys feel it their duty to bring their supernatural acquaintance to worldly justice. And yet —

He went on talking right along, and worked his enchantments upon us again with that fatal music of his voice. He made us forget everything; we could only listen to him and love him, and be his slaves, to do with us as he would. He made us drunk with the joy of being with him, and of looking into the heaven of his eyes, and of feeling the ecstasy that thrilled along our veins from the touch of his hand.

Accents of enchantment and love indeed, of a fatal charm, a divine and diabolical and utterly thrilling bondage! Was Clemens' symbolical man-child thus profoundly linked to a cruel and hostile force, to a personage of super-evil? The Stranger, moreover, "had seen everything, he had been everywhere, he knew everything, and he forgot nothing," and he made, for his enthralled trio of boys, the entire history of creation come alive to their eyes. "He told of the daily life in heaven; he had seen the damned writhing in the red waves of hell; and he made us see all those things, and it was as if we were on the spot and looking at them with our own eyes. And we felt them, too but there was no sign that they were anything to him beyond mere entertainments. Those visions of hell, those poor babes and women and girls and lads and men shrieking and supplicating in anguish — why, we could hardly bear it, but he was as bland about it as if it had been so many imitation rats in artificial fire."

With these lines Clemens was of course achieving a double purpose. He was presenting his familiar parody of religious superstition; and at the same time he is pointing out how man's notion of religion — for which so much has been endured, suffered, and sacrificed during the long course of history — is irrelevant to any cosmic Being, or in any cosmic sense. When Satan describes men and women, here on earth, even in their most sublime moments, the boys are ashamed, "for his manner showed that to him they and their doings were of paltry poor consequence," and Satan's (Clemens'?) comparison of mankind was with flies. What strikes Theodor Fischer in the story is that Satan is not even angry; his tone is matter-of-fact. The truth of this kind of revelation to the eager young eyes of childhood is so clear as not to be questioned. Meanwhile, when the boys have finished every detail of the medieval clay castle, complete with halberdiers and cavalry, the Stranger invokes storm, earthquake, fire in order for them to witness the sudden and complete destruction of all their work. "Our hearts were broken; we could not keep from crying. 'Don't cry,' Satan said, 'they were of no value.' 'But they are gone to hell!' 'Oh, it is no matter; we can make plenty more.'" The castle and people have disappeared into a common grave.

Satan's consistent answer, in fact, to the boys' horrified plea that he is destroying human lives is that he can make more of them. "It was no use to try to move him; evidently he was wholly without feeling, and could not understand. He was full of bubbling spirits, and as gay as if this were a wedding instead of a fiendish massacre. And he was bent on making us feel as he did, and of course his magic accomplished his desire. It was no trouble to him; he did whatever he pleased with us."

In a little while we were dancing on that grave, and he was playing to us on a strange, sweet instrument which he took out of his pocket; and the music — but there is no music like that, unless perhaps in heaven, and that was where he brought it from, he said. It made one mad, for pleasure; and we could not take our eyes from him, and the looks that went out of our eyes came from our hearts, and their dumb speech was worship. He brought the dance from heaven, too, and the bliss of paradise was in it.

This is the conclusion of the prelude, introduction, or invocation, to *The Mysterious Stranger*. The Devil leaves the boys on an errand, though they beg and beseech him not to. He announces that while to them he is Satan, he is taking the worldly name of Traum, or "Dream." But what a mysterious, complex, beguiling introduction this is; which is almost a short story in itself. What is the meaning of this divine and diabolical music that Satan brings from "heaven," while the boys rejoice in his presence, bow down to his power, his charm, and dance on the grave of the feudal castle and its inhabitants, so casually created, so casually obliterated. On the premise that more can be made, they are of no consequence. Many of Mark Twain's critics have stressed the utter dark despair and cynicism of this story, which is yet, however, cast in these accents of joy and gaiety, of comedy and boundless pleasure. From where did Mark Twain himself evoke the note of delicious pleasure, of almost uncontrollable and orgiastic delight, of a complete sensuous pleasure on the boys' part even while they are witness to these scenes of crime and evil in terms of the little clay figures of human life? What is the strange and haunting esthetic medium and message of *The Mysterious Stranger*?

We should notice Clemens' own pleasure and identification with his Satan, the master magician whose creation and destruction of human life is so casual, sadistic, good-humored, and ironical. If indeed this strange story was written during Sam Clemens' own period of deepest human suffering, there are elements again of a creative projection and catharsis. The artist was in a sense taking his revenge on those forces of life and death which had so deeply tormented him. If you can't beat them, join them.

There are other notes here of a return to a religious kind of debate about life and death on the part of a writer who so very early had decided to cast aside all religious superstitions and formalities. And to those critics who have stressed Sam's guilt at having deprived Livy of her own religious solace in the later years of sorrow and need, it can be pointed out that Mark Twain's Satan is a patent justification of Twain's own convictions . . . But on a deeper and wider level of historical or metaphysical content, we notice that the Clemens who, in his *Carnival of Crime,* had rejected social conventions to embark on a life of pagan "crime" and pleasure, now was deriving a mysterious sense of joy and exaltation from the spectacle of social crime itself, and human suffering. And here he was closer to the speculations of Wilhelm Reich, along with Rank, that the social repression of our primary nature can lead only to the corrupted sexuality and social blood baths of Hitler's Germany, or Fascism's true appeal. Was it not strange that he was describing the "Satanic enchantment" of the sexually

innocent and pagan boys in almost purely sexual terms? In
the almost classic terms of black magic, the witchcraft cult, the
underground worship of Priapus-Satan from the oldest of ancient days?

In the story itself, meanwhile, Father Peter is helped by Satan,
at the boys' urging, and in Satan's most satanic manner, by
discovering eleven hundred ducats which will rescue him from
his worldly troubles — and lead to his further persecution.
Gold and money, as a symbol of human disaster to Clemens,
are viewed here just as in *The Man That Corrupted Hadleyburg, The $30,000 Bequest,* and *Pudd'nhead Wilson*; just as
it had been at the core of Clemens' own tragedy and the whole
American social tragedy of his period.

With Father Peter's mysterious "redemption" comes the fact
that the whole village is gossiping about the mysterious money;
and the Astrologer emerges in the story as Father Peter's per-
secutor by declaring the money was stolen from him. Father
Peter is put in jail pending the outcome of his trial, while the
boys and their "protector," Satan, now devote their efforts to
saving Father Peter's niece Marget. Her serving maid, the poverty-stricken old peasant, Ursula, "discovers" a mysterious
kitten who produces four silver groschen (and much, much
more) every day. And Clemens described this peasant spirit
as the human matrix. "In her heart she probably believed it
was a witch-cat and an agent of the Devil; but no matter, it was
all the more certain to be able to keep its contract and furnish a
daily good living for the family, for in matters of finance even
the piousest of our peasants would have more confidence in an
arrangement with the Devil than with an archangel."

Satan appears himself at Marget's house, in the person of
Philip Traum, and is so beautiful that Marget can hardly keep
her eyes off him. "That gratified me, and made me proud. I

hoped he would show off some, but he didn't. He seemed only interested in being friendly and telling lies. He said he was an orphan." In fact Satan declares he hardly knows his own parents. "But he had an uncle in business down in the tropics, and he was very well off and had a monopoly, and it was from this uncle that he drew his support."

The Huck Finn "tone" appears steadily in this last tale of enchanted and illusioned (and yes, comic) youth which was set against such a gloomy background. Philip Traum even declares he was studying for the ministry, while a mysterious and abundant meal is produced for all of them, and poor Ursula, corrupted by Satan's compliments, begins on the course of her own downfall. And Marget's also; but the boys still do not understand that anything is preferable, in one sense, to Satan's — or God's? — "sympathy." And meanwhile, on another level of the story's plot, Satan conducts the boys to a medieval torture chamber where a heretic is being "questioned," and to a French village where the peasant-workers are condemned to lives of utmost poverty, shame, and horror. "Have they committed a crime, these mangy things?" Satan asks. "No. What have they done, that they are punished so? Nothing at all, except getting themselves born into your foolish race." It is the "Moral Sense," cries Satan-Twain again, which sets off man from the innocent beasts, and enables him to perform, with clear conscience, all the atrocious acts that no animal would think of.

The story shifts back to the present, and to Seppi Wohlmeyer, who is also intoxicated by Satan's presence.

He had felt his blood leap and his spirits rise in a way that could mean only one thing, and he knew Satan was near, although it was too dark to see him. He came to us, and we walked along

together, and Seppi poured out his gladness like water. It was as
if he were a lover and had found his sweetheart who had been lost.

A lost lover, a lost sweetheart indeed. Some lover, some sweetheart! while Seppi proceeds to say that the village loafer, Hans
Oppert, has disappeared after clubbing his dog and knocking
out one of its eyes. Seppi calls Hans a "heartless brute," and
Satan becomes severe. "There is that misused word again —
that shabby slander. Brutes do not act like that, but only
men." Well, says Seppi, it was inhuman. "No, it wasn't, Seppi;
it was human, quite distinctly human. It is not pleasant to hear
you libel the higher animals by attributing to them dispositions
which they are free from, and which are found nowhere but
in the human heart. None of the higher animals is tainted with
the disease called the Moral Sense. Purify your language,
Seppi; drop those lying phrases out of it."

In these pages perhaps Clemens stressed his old enemy,
man's "moral sense," too heavily; there are passages which
are as if taken directly from the moralistic sermons of *What Is
Man?* — but on the whole *The Mysterious Stranger* is the creative *product,* and filled with creative fancy, of that simplistic
and tedious volume of philosophy. In art, to stress and repeat
an essential concept, one must never take an artist's ideology
literally. It is what develops *artistically* from the artist's "philosophy" which really counts; as for example again, in the difference between Theodore Dreiser's philosophical "determinism"
(or mechanism), so heavily stressed by Dreiser's recent biographers and critics, and Dreiser's truly remarkable creativity,
which seems to be ignored.

Even when Clemens was being most blunt and bitter about
man's destiny — as *The Mysterious Stranger* itself, so entertaining and humorous in its opening texture, begins to assume

a darker and more deadly hue — there are passages of devastating, bitter eloquence. Man is made of dirt, Satan says when the boys question him about mortal and immortal beings: "I saw him made . . . Man is a museum of diseases, a home of impurities; he comes today and is gone to-morrow; he begins as dirt and departs as stench." And the difference between man and the angels is again that man has the Moral Sense which offends everything Satan believes in. There is a dull week or so in the story's action when Satan is absent, while Marget and Ursula are prospering mightily through their wishing-kitten, and have hired Gottfried Narr as an errand boy. A mistake, the boys know, since Gottfried, while personally a dull, good creature, is under a cloud. "And properly so, for it had not been six months since a social blight had mildewed the family — his grandmother had been burned as a witch. When that kind of malady is in the blood it does not always come out with just one burning."

There follows the remarkable section on witches in *The Mysterious Stranger* which Clemens adduced to illustrate still another phase of man's temperament — or was there a still more sinister import to these pages? The witch terror had risen higher than ever before in Eseldorf, befuddling everybody's wits, and yet "This was natural enough because of late years there were more kinds of witches than there used to be."

In old times it had been only old women, but of late years they were all ages — even children of eight and nine; it was getting so that anybody might turn out to be a familiar of the Devil — age and sex hadn't anything to do with it. In our little region we had tried to extirpate the witches, but the more of them we burned the more of the breed rose up in their places.

This was a variation on a familiar thesis of Mark Twain's about lynchings among other things; and as Twain's Satan might have added: It proved once more the development and "progress" of human society. Just recently there had been a mass burning of little-girl witches, Clemens added in a passage that might remind one of Salem, Massachusetts; and the story moved into the subplot, or parallel plot, of Marget and Ursula's doom as incurred by Satan's kindness. Father Adolf suspects Marget's abundant household of witchcraft and orders the villagers to gather together there and discover the truth. "The bars were down, and we could all go there now, and we did — our parents and all — day after day." The cat began to strain herself, adds Theodor Fischer. The meals and parties became more and more opulent.

The sorry history of Marget's "good fortune" is replete with ambiguous irony: a combination of satanic "kindness" and human frailty . . . and mob hysteria. For Marget, being human, is delighted with her opulence and popularity in the village society; she tries to surpass herself in providing foods and wines for her neighbors, out of her kindness and her vanity. Her "innocence" is terrible to behold; Clemens seems to be saying that the victim deserves his punishment.

One party is so celebrated that even Satan arrives, along with the Astrologer and Father Adolf, and there is much village gossip about the charming stranger. Satan "defends" Marget — temporarily, for his own purposes, and for a worse fate. Theodor (the last or lost Huck) even has the idea of "reforming" his charming and beloved friend:

We talked together, and I had the idea of trying to reform Satan and persuade him to lead a better life. I told him about all these things he had been doing, and begged him to be more considerate and stop making people unhappy. I said I knew he did not mean any harm, but that he ought to stop and consider the possible consequences of a thing before launching it in that impulsive and random way of his; then he would not make so much trouble.

Alas, for our youthful illusions. In passages such as these Clemens conveyed all the delightful and nostalgic and sweet-sounding and sweet-feeling "innocence" of childhood quite as accurately as he had in *Huck Finn,* though with far deeper and deadlier undertones. A remarkable achievement for such an aging and tragic and weary writer who yet retained the inviolate pagan core of his earliest being. Maybe it is just this series, or sequence, or delicate fusion of such different and almost incompatible emotions which makes *The Mysterious Stranger* so interesting and puzzling to read.

And Satan is indeed a much blacker version of Huck's wisest teacher, "Nigger Jim." He only looks amused at Theodor's statement and declares that none of his acts are random. "I know what the consequences are going to be — always." And he adds: "I have wrought well for the villagers, though it does not look like it on the surface. Your race never knows good fortune from ill. You are always mistaking the one for the other. It is because they cannot see into the future." (A happy thought indeed.) Satan then expands on Twain's earlier theme of determinism in human life — but says that he can change this if they want him to. Then comes the harrowing episode of Lisa and Nikolaus in *The Mysterious Stranger,* when Satan arranges for their early and immediate death — one of Clemens' own boons of life — rather than a prolonged existence of illness and misery and pain. At this time Satan also assures the boys that Father Peter's name will be cleared in the court trial about his magic fortune, and he too will be "happy" — an ominous word in the satanic lexicon.

Theodor is allowed to tell Seppi about Nick's impending death; but in this subplot Clemens invoked too much of the romance-melodrama — the sentiment he was wont to fall back upon when inspiration failed. The action is contrived, but the

theme that Mark Twain stressed was not: in childhood, man
— this vile and lowly being — in childhood even man is good,
and closer to the animal levels of life which Twain also equated
with the angelic. The boy is closer to pure feeling than the
analytic "reasoning powers" bent on manipulation and power,
and using the "moral sense" as the cover for all sorts of hypocrisy. Here Theo learns, both from Satan and from Mark Twain,
not only that death is life's single blessing, but perhaps an early
death is best of all. "Many a time since I have heard people
pray to God to spare the life of sick persons, but I have never
done it." (Twain himself said this elsewhere.)

In despair over her daughter's death, Lisa's mother has sworn
that she will never pray to God again; and the weaver Fischer
has betrayed her to the church authorities to have her burned
at the stake; but Satan reassures the boys that she is going to
heaven and escaping twenty-nine years of misery on earth.
On the other hand Fischer, the informer, will have a long life
full of joy — and go to hell. Satan even disperses the lynch
mob which follows Frau Brandt to the stake, but the boys
have learned their lesson:

> We did not ask if he had brought poor Fischer's luck to any of
> them. We did not wish to know. We fully believed in Satan's
> desire to do us kindnesses, but we were losing confidence in his
> judgment. It was at this time that our growing anxiety to have
> him look over our life-charts and suggest improvements began to
> fade out and give place to other interests.

In this statement, couched in Twain's deadpan irony, Theodor
has learned one of life's great lessons.

Frau Brandt also echoes the pagan-infancy-edenic theme
at the base of *The Mysterious Stranger*. She is tired of village
society, of life itself, and goes willingly to the stake; yet her final

words are "We played together once, in long-gone days when we were innocent little creatures. For the sake of that, I forgive you." Satan then provides the boys with a kaleidoscopic view of the race's development from the Garden of Eden to Cain and Abel and a long series of crimes, murders, and massacres. Next the Flood and the Ark, and Satan declares, "The progress of your race was not satisfactory. It is to have another chance now." And the boys see Noah overcome with wine, Sodom and Gomorrah, Lot and his daughters, the Hebraic wars, the Egyptian wars, the Greek wars, the Roman wars, and the birth of Christianity. "Then those ages of Europe passed in review before us, and we saw Christianity and Civilization march hand in hand through those ages, leaving famine and death and desolation in their wake, and other signs of the progress of the human race." And always there were wars, as Satan added, and more wars, "but never a war started by an aggressor for any clean purpose — there is no such war in the history of the race." While the future contained only "slaughters more terrible in their destruction of life, more devastating in their engines of war, than any we had seen."

There is another statement by Theodor in *The Mysterious Stranger*. "Then he began to laugh in the most unfeeling way, and make fun of the human race, although he knew what he had been saying shamed us and wounded us. No one but an angel could have acted so; but suffering is nothing to them; they do not know what it is, except by hearsay." For these children still have the capacity for shame, in a true sense, which most adults have long repressed except in a vanity, ego and face-saving sense. And is mental or psychological suffering denied to the angels because human suffering, to the later Twain, no longer had any meaning? But Christianity, Satan concluded, had done the most of all for human progress; and here, in those swift interchanges of both feeling and intellect which mark *The Mysterious Stranger,* Clemens moved imperceptibly from "human" or biopsychic evil and sin to social-historical evil. The ironical and devastating theologian of man's heart was simultaneously the radical social critic. "It is a remarkable progress. In five or six thousand years five or six high civilizations have risen, flourished, commanded the wonder of the world, then faded out and disappeared; and not one of them except the latest ever invented any sweeping and adequate way to kill people. They all did their best — to kill being the chief ambition of the human race and the earliest incident in its history — but only the Christian civilization has scored a triumph to be proud of. Two or three centuries from now it will be recognized that all the competent killers are Christians; then the pagan world will go to school to the Christian — not to acquire his religion but his guns."

And Clemens was not too far off in *this* prophecy. In a later age much different from the still-placid, peaceful, and "established" society at the turn of the century, Asiatic China, minus the missionaries, was busily developing its own atomic weaponry, after the Christian world of Western European society had produced Hitler and the Bomb as its civilizational end products. There is another witch-hunt and stone-throwing in these pages, a denunciation of those human spirits who don't join the celebration, and then again Twain's account of the martial (and the mob) spirit operating on the modern civilizational matrix. There has never been a just war, Satan repeats, never an honorable one on the part of the instigator, but "the loud little handful — as usual — will shout for the war. The pulpit will — warily and cautiously — object — at first; the great, big, dull bulk of the nation will rub its sleepy eyes and try to make out why there should be a war, and will say, earnestly and indignantly, 'It is unjust and dishonorable, and there is no necessity for it.' Then the handful will shout louder. A few fair men on the other side will argue and reason against the war with speech and pen, and at first will have a hearing and be applauded; but it will not last long; those others will out-shout them, and presently the anti-war audiences will thin out and lose popularity. Before long you will see this curious thing: the speakers stoned from the platform, and free speech stran-gled by hordes of furious men who in their secret hearts are still at one with those stoned speakers — as earlier — but do not dare to say so. And now the whole nation — pulpit and all — will take up the war-cry, and shout itself hoarse, and mob any honest man who ventures to open his mouth, and presently such mouths will cease to open. Next the statesmen will invent cheap lies, putting the blame upon the nation that is attacked, and every man will be glad of those conscience-soothing falsities, and will diligently study them, and refuse to examine any refutations of them; and thus he will by and by convince himself that the war is just, and will thank God for the better sleep he enjoys after this process of grotesque self-deception."

In such passages as these in *The Mysterious Stranger,* the logic flows almost imperceptibly from the individual to his social order and back again to the individual, so that the re-sult is a complex interwoven net of human-social deception, which is perhaps the most accurate description of what actu-ally happens. Even though Sam Clemens had seen only "minor" wars, and the simpler imperialistic campaigns of his period, it was just as though he stood at the outbreak of World War I, World War II, of the wars in Korea and Vietnam, and the pos-sible inception of World War III. That is the way it happened. In the narrative, the trial of Father Peter (and by implication

of his unfortunate niece Marget) proceeds apace, while the
boys worry about Satan's absence. "If Satan would only
come! That was my constant thought," says Theodor Fischer.
And Satan does come, and in the person of Wilhelm Meidling,
Marget's suitor, wins the case for Father Peter handily. (Meidling, alas, soon loses "that luminous look in his eyes" that he
had when Satan was in him.) They bring the good news to
Father Peter in jail only to discover he has lost his san-
ity. When the boys rebuke Satan for accomplishing this deed,
he reminds them of his promise to restore Father Peter's good
name — and to make him happy for the rest of his life.

"There it was, you see," says Theodor. "He didn't seem to
know any way to do a person a favor except by killing him or
making a lunatic out of him. I apologized, as well as I could;
but privately I did not think much of his processes — at that
time." In the course of this macabre tale we come to realize
that Theodor is indeed learning much for his age; is beginning
to understand the satanic logic of life. He is becoming, as it
were, the Devil's disciple. Satan pursues the argument with his
familiar contention "that our race lived a life of continuous and
uninterrupted self-deception. It duped itself from cradle to
grave with shams and delusions which it mistook for realities,
and this made its entire life a sham." The one great weapon it
possessed, added Satan-Twain, was humor, the assault of
laughter against which no sham, hypocrisy, or evil could really
stand; and this kind of humor, too, the human race hardly
ever understood.

There follows the final, complex, and elusive chapter of *The
Mysterious Stranger*: the disappearance of Satan.

"For as much as a year Satan continued these visits, but at
last he did not come at all. This always made me feel lonely
and melancholy. I felt he was losing interest in our tiny world

and might at any time abandon his visits entirely." Thus the boys' deepest thrill at the satanic presence is compounded by their sense of loss in his departure. "When one day he finally came to me," says Theodor, "I was overjoyed, but only for a little while. He had come to say good-by, he told me, and for the last time. He had investigations and undertakings in other corners of the universe, he said, that would keep him busy for a longer period than I could wait for his return."

Beneath the surface irony of this statement, that the human race was no longer worthy of Satan's interest, there was a deeper chord, perhaps not entirely known but surely felt by Sam Clemens. If the world was to lose all its satanic thrills of pleasure and excitement, then the pagan yearnings of which Clemens himself was such a deep and devout exponent, were yielding, in the Freudian-Rankian thesis, to all the discontents and repressions of civilization. And a "civilizing" process had indeed happened in the American scene of Mark Twain's own life. Primitive, wild Nature was being devoured and conquered by the scientific-industrial and urban complex. The rebellious Satan would surely lose interest in such a dehumanized area which finally denied him and his works. Such a world would be without interest to Sam Clemens too, since it was simultaneously narrowing and suppressing that area of personal rebellion, human dissent, and social questioning which he, above all, had always typified. This was indeed the United States at the turn of the century, at its "watershed," or that deep, impassable canyon-gulf between the Old Republic and the conquering Empire.

Older human evils disappearing, new and much worse, abstract and dehumanized (industrialized, mass-produced) evils would follow. Vainly Theodor pleads with Satan, who admits it has been a pleasant and comradely experience. "But I must go now, and we shall not see each other any more." "In this life, Satan, but in another? We shall meet in another, surely?" pleads Theodor in a variation of Sam Clemens' contention he would always rather go to hell than to any human heaven. Then, all tranquilly and soberly, Satan made his strange answer. *"There is no other."* And thus Mark Twain's final parable demolished his own lifelong artistic mythology of heaven and hell — and accomplished even more in Theodor's response to this assertion. "A subtle influence blew upon my spirit from his, bringing with it a vague, dim, but blessed and hopeful feeling that the incredible words might be true — even *must* be true." A blessed and hopeful feeling indeed reflecting the maturer Clemens' deepest intuition that one taste of life was sufficient for any human being. When Theodor asks again if this could be true, outstripping all his own religious beliefs and superstitions in the story, and Satan reaffirms it is true, and that all visions of future life are merely visions without real existence, Theodor can hardly breathe "for the great hope that was struggling in me." *"Life itself is only a vision, a dream,"* Satan repeats, and Clemens, like Shakespeare in *The Tempest,* steps out of his own fiction. "It was electrical. By God! I had had that very thought a thousand times in my musings!" — *"Nothing* exists," Satan adds. "All is a dream. God — man — the world — the sun, the moon, the wilderness of stars — a dream, all a dream; they have no existence. *Nothing exists save empty space — and you!"*

And this "you" was not Theodor but only the *thought* of Theodor, so Twain ended this mysterious story with a thought "alone in shoreless space, to wander its limitless solitudes without friend or comrade forever." And there followed one of the most curious and imperfect ending-passages of *The Mysterious Stranger,* in which Clemens vented all his rage and bit-

terness at the cruel and savage universe of nature upon the
religious God that he and Satan alike had already dismissed as
a fiction. (Some of these ending passages were in fact too close
to the grim sermonizing of *What Is Man?*, and perhaps that is
why Clemens was not satisfied with the story's end and refused
to print it in his own lifetime.) Not to mention that they appear
to contradict themselves in part; for Clemens seems to be saying there is and is not a God, or a meaning to life. "You perceive *now,* that these things are all impossible except in a
dream," Satan concludes. "You perceive that they are pure
and puerile insanities, the silly creations of an imagination that
is not conscious of its freaks — in a word, that they are a
dream, and you the maker of it. The dream-marks are all
present; you should have recognized them earlier."

Once more Satan repeats a passage that was compulsive in
this late artist despite his own sense of art. "It is true, that which
I have revealed to you; there is no God, no universe, no human
race, no earthly life, no heaven, no hell. It is all a dream — a
grotesque and foolish dream . . ." "He vanished, and left me
appalled; for I knew, and realized, that all he had said was
true." Thus the famous ending line of *The Mysterious Stranger,*
and despite the repetitions and confusions of the story's ending which never satisfied Mark Twain himself, it is still an effective if a perplexing conclusion.* There has been much discussion of this conclusion among the Mark Twain critics, too,
but what has not been stressed in this case is the psychological
rather than the philosophical impact. The philosophic vision
here is as simplistic as in *What Is Man?*; and the psycho-
esthetic meaning is very interesting. There is no doubt that
Clemens himself, along with Satan, is bidding farewell to human life, is indeed denigrating human beings to the point of
not being worthy of Satan's or God's interest — of indeed having really created a monstrous God, an amiable but disinter-

*See footnote on page 206 on this ending.

ested and sadistic Satan. And quite like the Shakespeare of
*The Tempest* (of which there are other echoes here), Clemens was dismissing not only life itself but the life of his own
artistic kingdom! Even while he and Shakespeare and Satan
still stood apart from their work as the Master Magicians
who created and could just as easily obliterate it.

There was certainly also a form of spiritual confessional as
well as esthetic release in this dark ending to an otherwise
ironical, entertaining, and even gay fiction.

During his later period Clemens, as we know, was constantly
playing on the theme of dream and reality, both in published
and unpublished material. It is a theme that every great writer
has dealt with, like that of innocence and evil. It is such an
integral factor in art that with some writers it becomes almost
a *technique.* Any mature artist, any mature person, looking
back upon his own life experience from the peak, or the mo-
tionless plateau, of his career — in that period when we know
that "we are all defeated," as Willa Cather said, enemies and
friends, successes or failures, healthy and sick, rich and poor —
must wonder at a certain dreamlike texture that the past begins to assume; must wonder if life is life and death is death;
and which is dream, and which reality? And what does it
matter, all the things we fought so hard for, all the victories
which were gained at such cost, all the failures we mourned so
bitterly? Who comes out ahead — except the complacent, the
unseeing, the totally self-immersed, who do not understand the
blind and chance meaning of human life? This is in the complex texture of *The Mysterious Stranger,* as well as in the sermonizing end; this is a central element which makes the story
great and which did not need the explicit statement that Clemens concluded with. (And how many forms of human euphoria
are invoked to conceal and becloud the true moral of life.)

In those dark years of his mature life, Clemens, moreover,

might well have thought the glorious triumphs of his youth were but a dream, illusionary victories, compared with the black nightmare of "reality." In his blackest periods, he must, like Melville, have questioned all the false semblances of success, wealth, love, and happiness which he had previously reveled in so innocently. In terms of personal guilt too, his own tender and smarting conscience, how much more comforting, if also equally illusionary, to see the whole processes of being and existence as a passing dream, and man himself as irrelevant and inconsequential even in the midst of his cruelty, stupidity, and hypocrisy.

Thus if *The Mysterious Stranger* shares, in a curious way, some of the enigmatic obscurity, the ironical twists and turns of plot, of a typical Henry James novella, say, it has at base a much more profound vision — since James, to the very end, was obsessed by all those special privileges and worldly honors, all those "goodies" of life, which Mark Twain had enjoyed so abundantly, and had discarded as so meaningless and empty. And whereas Melville, at the peak of his own literary achievement in *Moby Dick,* and in the chasm of worldly disgrace which attended upon his epic, had seen life, as in the *Piazza Tales,* purely in terms of horrors and evils and crimes, Sam Clemens, much closer to a Theodore Dreiser, saw it as a matter of cosmic indifference, or as the *plaything* of vast cosmic forces who indifferently created and destroyed our world as of no consequence, and indeed of a questionable reality.

In this sense human life, and nature as the creating force of life are not evil, as so many lesser writers and other injured souls have proclaimed, but a matter of cosmic indifference, which is beyond such anthropomorphic terms as good and evil. More profound, this is also a less paranoid view of existence in which man is the puppet (free will or not) of natural forces that can create him, advance him, or maim him and destroy him with Mark Twain's satanic indifference. This was the true end, the esthetic projection and climax of Sam Clemens' own happiness and sorrow: this dream and nightmare of life as felt by an especially gay, pagan, and pleasure-loving spirit.

But despite the black ending of this fable (and Twain's familiar penchant for lurid melodrama in such cases) what is the quality which really sets off *The Mysterious Stranger* from all other stories on the same theme both in American and world literature? Which makes it so priceless and unique? We have noticed its enchantment with crime and evil, couched not merely in sexual but almost orgiastic emotional terms. Was there a difference here between Satan's joy and gaiety even at his worst, and the dull inhumanity of man? If life was evil on all levels, perhaps it was preferable to join with the Evil Life Spirit itself, as only Mark Twain could portray it, in all its delight and charm? Now this is close to the story's underlying, never stated theme. This desperate nihilism turns out to be very entertaining. This black despair is undergoing the purgation of humor — that humor which, as Twain himself declared, was the only possible defense against man's poor little existence on earth. Evil is not quite evil when it becomes a parody, a comedy of evil. (Yes, this does lead back to the plenary-pagan childhood world of comic make-believe in *Tom Sawyer* and *Huckleberry Finn*. Exactly.) And when evil itself can become as charming and beguiling as Satan was at Marget's party! What an extraordinary view this was of Satan himself, this charming young "pretender" spreading his "favors" — his fatal gifts — with such an insouciant style. The beautiful and devastating irony of *The Mysterious Stranger* is touched by Twain's irrepressible comedy; the Twainian man has been down into the black pit of mortal disaster, and has emerged laughing.

Though it is important to stress that Mark Twain, like all

great writers, never attempted to deny the basic tragedy of life. He was only discounting its long history of sordid evil. In this sense, just as Nigger Jim had been Huck's first great counselor in this life, so Mark Twain's Satan was Theodor Fischer's far more sophisticated counselor in the matter of death. And that is to say, paralleling the form of *Life on the Mississippi,* the mature and elderly Twain is now looking back on the more youthful Twain of life and letters. (This double vision is of course an intuitive part of the double soul.) And here Mark Twain was repeating that laughter belongs to man as well as the Gods, in perhaps the only area of existence where man achieves equality with the careless and indifferent, rather than evil or malevolent, life forces. If Satan disposed those ironic "favors" with such equanimity, man could still receive them with equal and knowing composure. Talk about the "frustrated and bitter and old" Mark Twain! *The Mysterious Stranger* is the purest bit of divine sunlight to illuminate all the long, dark, endless abyss of human history. Satan as the Great Prankster, yes; and laughter as the only salvation for the whole muddy mess of man's life — this was Mark Twain's final (or nearly final) verdict. And that is why *The Mysterious Stranger* is so very special among the great stories of the world which deal with the problem of human existence.

# EIGHT

# THE STORY OF A LIFE

Most of Mark Twain's work is autobiographical in essence from *Roughing It* and *Life on the Mississippi* to his *Autobiography* in 1924; and the final (semifinal) period of his work was even more directly filled with the personal utterances which are almost always his best statements. Twain was not essentially a novelist or fiction writer; that is why all the criticism concerned with his "formlessness," lack of structure, uneven texture, has little relevance to his work. It takes a bard, a large and various talent, to talk always about himself without tedium, since he is in fact talking about the world with which he is inextricably and pantheistically joined at the very moment he is so separate and original as an individual voice. Clemens had started jotting down notes for the *Autobiography* as early as 1870. In Vienna in the late nineties, solvent again and recognized for the world figure he was, he began jotting down notes of his youth in Missouri: those curious frontier river towns whose color shifts so suddenly from white to black, from innocence to guilt, from Eden to the

Fall, from happy childhood to the unpleasant maturity of both an individual and a nation.

Some years later in Florence, where Livy had gone in a last effort to regain her health, Clemens returned to the *Autobiography,* and again in 1906, linking himself with his amanuensis and future biographer and editor, Albert Bigelow Paine, he set to work in earnest dictating his last work. Paine brought along a secretary, and Clemens talked to a select audience of two, often from his bed. "It was his custom to stay in bed until noon, and he remained there during most of the earlier dictations, clad in a handsome dressing-gown, propped against great snowy pillows . . ." Snowy white pillows, and Mark Twain's famous white suits: symbol of that lost innocence which Clemens still wanted to preserve symbolically; and that "whiteness" which Melville, even more desperate and outraged at the world, inveighed against as the very color of evil, parading as innocence. (Twain, knowing this also, preferred to keep the illusion, which he had also lost.) "He loved this loose luxury and ease," Paine tells us, "and found it conducive to thought," while it was also Clemens' way of avoiding as long as he could the societal straightjacket. It was Bill Nye, Clemens' friend and early associate on the lecture platform, who said he always slept as much as he could, and only regretted he could not carry his bed around with him.

It was in these circumstances that Twain evolved the "formless form" of the *Autobiography,* as an extension of the form he had to a large degree used in all his writing; an early mode of the "stream of consciousness" which became fashionable in the epoch of James Joyce. "Often he did not know until the moment of beginning what was to be his subject for the day," Paine tells us. "Then he was likely to go drifting among his memories in a quite irresponsible fashion, the fashion of table conversation, as he said, the methodless method of the human mind. 'Start at no particular time of your life; wander at your free will all over your life; talk only about the things which interest you for the moment; drop it the moment its interest threatens to pale, and turn your talk upon the new and more interesting thing that has intruded itself into your mind and meantime.' "

But in a certain sense Clemens was conning his confidante Paine in dramatizing this form of the *Autobiography*; in another sense he conned himself into allowing himself too much freedom in using this system of natural thought association. This may be the way that thinking does think itself; this is the source and inspiration of art perhaps, but art is the end product of this source and inspiration when it is formed and disciplined to its own shape, as it is in the best of Mark Twain, too. Clemens was also aware of some of the flaws of pure dictation and free association. "When I was younger I could remember anything, whether it happened or not; but I am getting old and soon I shall remember only the latter."

Paraphrasing Josh Billings, another of the gifted frontier humorists from whom Sam Clemens descended, he added: "It isn't so astonishing the things that I can remember, as the number of things I can remember that aren't so." But he was on safer ground and more profound in the Preface to his final book. "In this Autobiography I shall keep in mind the fact that I am speaking from the grave. I am literally speaking from the grave, because I shall be dead when the book issues from the press . . . I speak from the grave rather than with my living tongue, for a good reason: I can speak thence freely." He declared that all men shrink from expressing their private lives in public, and he argued that "the frankest and freest and privatest product of the human mind and heart is a love letter; the writer gets his limitless freedom of statement and expression from his sense that no stranger is going to see what he is writing. Everybody would hesitate to write such letters if they faced the possibility of publication, Twain added, and such letters indeed were embarrassing when they were published. But yet, "It has seemed to me that I could be as frank and free and unembarrassed as a love letter if I knew that what I was writing would be exposed to no eye until I was dead, and unaware, and indifferent."

These words are as though carved in stone, and it is interesting that Mark Twain concurred with Freud, if unconsciously, when he equated the love letter with death (Eros and "Death Wish") in such a balancing of the life forces.

The earlier sections of the *Autobiography*, titled "Early Fragments, 1870-77," are just that. As in the case of Mark Twain's *Christian Science*, he played and toyed with his subject for around a decade before he got seriously interested and produced, mainly in the second volume of the book, a solid narrative. "What a wee little part of a person's life are his acts and his words!" so Clemens declared in his opening "text" or little sermon. "His real life is led in his head and is known to none but himself. All day long, and every day, the mill of his brain is grinding, and his *thoughts*, not those other things, are his history . . ." He said this to prove that the mass of any man is hidden, that biographies are but the clothing of the true man whose biography cannot be written. But it suggests also that the *work* — the literary production of a writer — rather than his life and actions, is the writer's true biography, his thoughts preserved in his art.

The volume opens with his reflections on "The Tennessee Land," which his father had purchased to make his family wealthy, and which, as the illusion of great sudden, miraculous wealth, pursued Samuel Clemens' life in other guises as well. Written around the later seventies also, the section on Clemens' early life in Florida and Hannibal, Missouri, is beautiful, crisp, nostalgic writing about frontier life in the 1830s. Yet this is broken off shortly by the account of Twain's friendship with General Grant, the days of Grant's power and poverty, the writing of the famous *Memoirs* while the epical hero of the Old Republic was in his terminal illness. This also marked the beginning of Mark Twain's publishing house, the Charles Webster Company whose failure contributed to Twain's bankruptcy in the nineties. Elsewhere Clemens remarked it would have been better if he had been struck dead the moment he decided to publish the *Memoirs*. But the account of Grant himself is touching, warm, affectionate, illuminating, one of the best original sources about this historical figure. The Freudian concept of Grant as a "surrogate father" of Clemens is again nonsensical, since it precludes the notion of mutual friendship between two such different geniuses of the American past. Or even more accurately, Freudism misses the sense of awe, and respect and worship at the base of Clemens' pantheistic temperament; those noble emotions which alone make life worth living, which are also at the core of art; and are viewed always as ignoble "sublimations" to the Freudian orthodoxy — thus making of art and life alike a kind of mean and narrow subterfuge. It is true that Grant was the symbol of that military science which Clemens always derided, ridiculed, and attacked; there was perhaps a touch of vanity and self-justification in the fact that *he,* Mark Twain, was the General's friend and benefactor. But Grant admired *him.*

The memoir of Grant, fascinating as it is, was too close to Clemens' heart in those days, and it takes up too much space in the wrong part of the *Autobiography*. Although, as by some unknown sense of esthetic balance, Clemens followed the long, glowing account of the heroic general by a short biting sketch of the inventor James W. Paige whose typesetting machine cost him a total of $150,000, as Clemens asserted at the time of his writing, and $190,000 in the end, as Paine asserts. This marked the beginning, along with the publishing house, of the financial crisis which was such a critical point in Twain's later life and art. Yet Clemens' account of Paige is still marked by the kind of genial tolerance (amid much malevolent wit) he always accorded to the great frauds and scoundrels of the world with whom he had his secret affinity. Shades of Mary Baker Eddy whom Clemens remorsely pursued with such a love-hate: he still shook his head in puzzled awe over Paige's business behavior. "Paige and I always meet on effusively affectionate terms, and yet he knows perfectly well that if I had him in a steel trap I would shut out all human succor and watch that trap till he died."

The reverse was really true; Paige had Clemens in a trap of steel until the artist, not the inventor, almost died. But here Clemens went back to his childhood once more and to another "false claimant" or "false claim" which had bewitched his family. This was the story of the Clemenses' connection with the American-born English earldom of Fairfax which also figures in Mark Twain's work — and which, along with the Tennessee Land, gave the Clemens family such a false sense of great wealth and hereditary aristocracy. As for Sam, he went back to Noah, so he said, or better yet, to Adam and to Satan. There is an account of Twain's mother's ancestry, including the James Lampton who was the prototype of Colonel Mulberry (or Beriah) Sellers in *The Gilded Age* and elsewhere, and another close relative of Sam Clemens in person and in spirit. There is a glowing account of Uncle John Quarles' farm in Missouri which, whether in fact or in fancy or both, was in effect the true Edenlike home of Clemens' boyhood. A series of American writers, from Edith Wharton to H. L. Mencken and Sinclair Lewis, have condemned and ridiculed the American west; another group including Theodore Dreiser and Sherwood Anderson have looked back upon it with affection and nostalgic sadness. But Mark Twain's description of Missouri life in the *Autobiography* is just about the best thing we have on this scene, western and southwestern, in the national letters. What forces changed his later view of his origins into a blackened and debased literary scene we have already noticed; but here again, toward the close of his life, it shines forth in all its pristine pleasure, joy, and beauty.

Including the Negroes, whom Mark Twain described here with his customary affection and insight. Among the boys, black and white, they were friends and comrades and yet not quite. "Color and condition interposed a subtle line which both parties were conscious of and which rendered complete fusion impossible."

Among the slaves there was the famous "Uncle Dan'l," who was used in several books under his own name and under the better-known name of Jim in *Huck Finn*. And Clemens added frankly: "In my schoolboy days I had no aversion to slavery. I was not aware that there was anything wrong about it. No one arraigned it in my hearing; the local papers said nothing against it; the local pulpit taught us that God approved it, that it was a holy thing, and that the doubter need only look in the Bible if he wished to settle his mind — and then the texts were read aloud to us to make the matter sure; if the slaves themselves had an aversion to slavery, they were wise and said nothing."

Maybe it was in the course of his self-education about slavery that Sam Clemens saw the true nature of the forces of social conformity: the press, the pulpit, the false use of the Bible and Christianity itself. Certainly it was a long way from the slaveowner to the anti-imperialist radical critic of American society; while the issue of human property, of slavery and the darker races, was crucial in the spiritual development of Mark Twain.

And Clemens went on to describe some other details in the texture of frontier life on his uncle's farm, including the caves and
the half-breed "Injun Joe" of *Tom Sawyer*; the snakes, the countryside, the games and sports and accidents of childhood existence there; the practice of medicine and of dentistry in those
days.

In the most nostalgic and pleasing pages of the *Autobiography*, Clemens described "education" in the river towns,
childhood loves (though still either puritanically or curiously
without sexual overtones), and the ritual of childhood smoking.
"As I have said, I spent some part of every year at the farm until
I was twelve or thirteen years old. The life which I led there
with my cousins was full of charm, and so is the memory of it
yet. I can call back the solemn twilight and mystery of the deep
woods, the earthy smells, the faint odors of the wild flowers, the
sheen of rain-washed foliage, the rattling clatter of drops when
the wind shook the trees, the far-off hammering of woodpeckers
and the muffled drumming of wood pheasants in the remoteness
of the forest, the snapshot glimpses of disturbed wild creatures
scurrying through the grass — I can call it all back and make it
as real as it ever was, and as blessed. I can call back the prairie,
and its loneliness and peace, and a vast hawk hanging motion-
less in the sky, with his wings spread wide, and the blue of the
vault showing through the fringe of their end feathers. I can see
the woods in their autumn dress, the oaks purple, the hickories
washed with gold, the maples and the sumachs luminous with
crimson fires, and I can hear the rustle made by the fallen leaves
as we plowed through them. I can see the blue clusters of wild
grapes hanging among the foliage of the saplings, and I remember the taste of them and the smell. I know how the wild blackberries looked, and how they tasted, and the same with the
pawpaws, the hazelnuts, and the persimmons; and I can feel the

thumping rain, upon my head, of hickory nuts and walnuts when we were out in the frosty dawn to scramble for them with the pigs and the gusts of wind loosed them and sent them down. I know the stain of blackberries, and how pretty it is, and I know the stain of walnut hulls, and how little it minds soap and water, also what grudged experience it had of either of them. I know the taste of maple sap, and when to gather it, and how to arrange the troughs and the delivery tubes, and how to boil down the juice, and how to hook the sugar after it is made, also how much better hooked sugar tastes than any that is honestly come by, let bigots say what they will."

These sections of the *Autobiography* are simply lovely to read or to listen to, as the lyrical side of Mark Twain's genius which is often overlooked — and there are many more of them. This essential worship and awe before the beauty of natural life lie back of his great satire, humor, and parody; and are fused with them to establish his unique tone: tender, haunting, touching, affectionate as well as angry, aroused, irascible, ironical, and comic. In a tradition of nature worship which is peculiarly American from Thoreau and Emerson to Whitman, Mark Twain, as I say, is joined with but surpasses the frontier reminiscences of Dreiser and Sherwood Anderson and Willa Cather among the last of our "nature writers" — before a modern generation of urban, even industrial, and now computerized, novelists took over the literary scene.

Probably this was also a key distinction between the writers of the Old Republic — our "older world" — and the generations of American writers who grew up in the modern U.S.A. In the *Autobiography,* meanwhile, Clemens went on to eulogize watermelons and their eating. "I know how a boy looks behind a yard-long slice of that melon, and I know how he feels; for I have been there. I know the taste of the watermelon

which has been honestly come by, and I know the taste of the
watermelon which has been acquired by art. Both taste good,
but the experienced know which tastes best. I know the look of
green apples and peaches and pears on the trees, and I know
how entertaining they are when they are inside of a person." He
went on, in this haunting ode to the western frontier life of his
childhood, to discuss frozen apples in barrels, and apples that
are roasting on a hearth in wintertime, and hot apples along
with sugar and a drench of cream.

He described Uncle Dan'l's kitchen with the white and black
children grouped on the hearth, and Uncle Dan'l's tales of black
folklore. He remembered the howling of the wind and the
quaking of the house on stormy nights, and the dismal hoo-
hooing of the owl, and the wailing of a wolf sent mourning
by on the night wind. "I remember the raging of the rain on
that roof, summer nights, and how pleasant it was to lie and
listen to it, and enjoy the white splendor of the lightning and the
majestic booming and crashing of the thunder." There was a
lightning rod atop his room on that farm, "an adorable and
skittish thing to climb up and down, summer nights, when there
were duties on hand of a sort to make privacy desirable . . .
I remember the 'coon and 'possum hunts, nights, with the
negroes, and the long marches through the black gloom of the
woods . . . I remember the pigeon seasons, when the birds
would come in millions and cover the trees and by their weight
break down the branches . . . I remember the squirrel hunts,
and prairie-chicken hunts, and wild-turkey hunts, and all that;
and how we turned out, mornings, while it was still dark, to go
on these expeditions, and how chilly and dismal it was, and
how often I regretted that I was well enough to go . . . But
presently the gray dawn stole over the world, the birds piped up,
then the sun rose and poured light and comfort all around,

everything was fresh and dewy and fragrant, and life was a boon again. After three hours of tramping we arrived back wholesomely tired, overladen with game, very hungry, and just in time for breakfast."

Shades of those later American writers, uneasy provincials moving to the eastern culture centers, who decried their western childhood and background as sterile, oppressive, bleak, and colorless. For the older generations, if not for figures like Sinclair Lewis, these western origins gave them a sense of life, of nature — that young dawn when everything was indeed "fresh and dewy and fragrant." There followed in the *Autobiography* the great tribute of Sam Clemens to his mother Jane Lampton Clemens — a field day for psychoanalysts, if you like, but which ended up, as Mark Twain himself did, by being super- or post-Freudian, or by simply going beyond and surpassing the narrow Freudian strictures. Clemens made no secret of his admiration for and adoration of "this first and closest friend" of his whole life. "She had a slender, small body, but a large heart — a heart so large that everybody's grief and everybody's joys found welcome in it, and hospitable accommodation." Like her famous son — and all innocently and happily Clemens described in her many of his own traits of temperament and character — Jane Clemens had a continuous curiosity about the world around her. In all her life, "she never knew such a thing as a half-hearted interest in affairs and people, or an interest which drew a line and left out certain affairs and was indifferent to certain people. The invalid who takes a strenuous and indestructible interest in everything and everybody but himself, and to whom a dull moment is an unknown thing and an impossibility, is a formidable adversary for disease and a hard invalid to vanquish. I am certain that it was this feature of my mother's makeup that carried her so far toward ninety."

And thus we learn of a certain relationship between Sam Clemens' invalid mother and his invalid wife. But what invalids! And it is possible that the deepest emotional rhythms of this remarkable human being were contained in this sequence between his "first and closest friend," Jane Lampton Clemens, and his first, last, and deepest love, Olivia Langdon Clemens. There is a curious phonetic connection between the two names, of course, but rather than expressing any traits of the embedded infantile or autistic personality, such as Henry James par excellence, Mark Twain was describing through his mother, perhaps by inference his wife, all the symptoms of the outgoing and life-embracing soul. His mother's interest "in people and other animals" was warm, personal, friendly. She always found something to excuse and to love in the toughest of characters, said Clemens, "even if she had to put it there herself. She was the natural ally and friend of the friendless." And it comes as no surprise in this maternal profile that "she could be beguiled into saying a soft word for the devil himself." Whether it was Clemens' own arguments in defense of Satan that he put into his mother's words is not important. "Who prays for Satan," asked these two spirits as one. "Who, in eighteen centuries, has had the common humanity to pray for the one sinner that needed it most, our one fellow and brother who most needed a friend yet had not a single one, the one sinner among us all who had the highest and clearest *right* to every Christian's daily and nightly prayers, for the plain and unassailable reason that his was the first and greatest need, he being among sinners the supremest?"

But the tone of these arguments was in fact that of the mother —this "friend of Satan" who was a most gentle spirit and yet was the most eloquent person that Clemens had heard when defending weakness against force or cruelty, or hurt or shame.

Here too was one obvious source of Clemens' identification with that animal race which was in so many ways superior to the reasoning animal called man. "All the race of dumb animals had a friend in her." This profile of Jane Clemens had more detail as it merged, in the *Autobiography,* with another description of the environment, the habits and manners, the social structure of those bygone western towns in which Sam Clemens had lived so fully and so happily. There was the detailed description of the "Boys' Town" in Hannibal in 1849, when Clemens was fourteen years old, which formed the background of *Tom Sawyer* and *Huck Finn.* Howells had also written on the same subject; but his memoirs lacked the spice of Clemens' account, and then the *Autobiography* ventured almost into the forbidden area of childhood sexuality.

But a boy's life is not all comedy; much of the tragic enters into it; and Clemens went into those areas of his youth which were dominated by anxiety, fears, and torments; the whole "underside" of life and art alike, which so often appears to be the only side. He went into the enforced Presbyterian morality of his youth which later on he defied, and was tormented by — and still defied. "But no matter, mine was a trained Presbyterian conscience and knew but the one duty — to hunt and harry its slave upon all pretexts and on all occasions, particularly when there was no sense nor reason in it." There are the familiar episodes of Clemens' early life which became such integral parts of his writing, described here with great precision as examples of the somber side of "innocent" provincial life. And then Clemens proceeded to "analyze" a little further that whole tortured, neurotic, superstitious, moral-religious strain of his temperament which his modern critics have seized upon.

The cases of raw frontier violence and sudden death obsessed the young Clemens, it is true, and furnished many of his night-

mares. "I went home to dream, and was not disappointed."
But he had his own view of them even at an early age. "My
teaching and training enabled me to see deeper into these tragedies than an ignorant person could have done. I knew what
they were for. I tried to disguise it from myself, but down in
the secret depths of my troubled heart I knew — and I *knew*
I knew. They were inventions of Providence to beguile me to a
better life. It sounds curiously innocent and conceited, now,
but to me there was nothing strange about it; it was quite in accordance with the thoughtful and judicious ways of Providence
as I understood them. It would not have surprised me, nor even
overflattered me, if Providence had killed off that whole community in trying to save an asset like me. Educated as I had
been, it would have seemed just the thing and well worth the expense. *Why* Providence should take such an anxious interest
in such a property, that idea never entered my head, and there
was no one in that simple hamlet who would have dreamed of
putting it there. For one thing no one was equipped with it."

Thus Clemens' "explanation" of the singular conscience
which indeed informed his life and work, the early sense of life's
torment and horror which accompanied the very early sense of
his own singular destiny. What is remarkable is that while, in
the *Autobiography,* he was in the throes of these compulsions,
he could examine them so objectively, so eloquently, and with
such a comic sense. Perhaps he was here, at least, as he claimed
for the whole book, speaking from the grave, from beyond the
limited horizons of life. And thus he himself described that
"morbidity" or "blackness" or "pessimism" or "cynicism," or
that "rigid, mechanical determinism" which his critics have
speculated about so much. "It is quite true, I took all the tragedies to myself, and tallied them off in turn as they happened,
saying to myself in each case with a sigh, 'Another one gone —

and on my account; this ought to bring me to repentance; the patience of God will not always endure.' And yet privately I believed it would."

There follows Twain's description of his own daylight and nighttime existence — the polarized daylight and night-dark aspects of his temperament and work — which, despite all the later critical discussion of this theme, still remains as the definitive statement. And why not? Sam Clemens knew himself better than anybody else would ever know him. He remains in literary history as a prime example of the outgoing and life-gathering spirit combined with the most acute sense of self-knowledge and self-vision. That is, he added, he believed in the endurance of God's patience with him in the daytime, but not at night. "With the going down of the sun my faith failed and the clammy fears gathered about my heart. It was then that I repented. Those were awful nights, nights of despair, nights charged with the bitterness of death. After each tragedy I recognized the warning and repented; repented and begged; begged like a coward, begged like a dog; and not in the interest of those poor people who had been extinguished for my sake, but only in my *own* interest. It seems selfish, when I look back on it now."

Selfish indeed! What a description of the human soul: of sin, guilt, atonement — and sin. Of bravado and fear. Of the utterly self-centered sources of religious or superstitious worship. And Clemens went on to describe the meaning of these nights of fear and guilt, despair and death. "My repentances were very real, very earnest; and after each tragedy they happened every night for a long time. But as a rule they could not stand the daylight. They faded out and shredded away and disappeared in the glad splendor of the sun. They were the creatures of fear and darkness, and they could not live out of their own place. The day gave me cheer and peace, and at night I repented again. In all my boyhood life I am not sure that I ever tried to lead a better life in the daytime — or wanted to. In my age I should never think of wishing to do such a thing. But in my age, as in my youth, night brings me many a deep remorse. I realize that from the cradle up I have been like the rest of the race — never quite sane in the night. When 'Injun Joe' died . . . But never mind. Somewhere I have already described what a raging hell of repentance I passed through then. I believe that for months I was as pure as the driven snow. After dark."

It is interesting to note, at the climax of his self-analysis, that Mark Twain described himself in the classical terms, not so much of Freudian individualism, as of the racial consciousness of Jung. And so, despite the experiences of failure, pain, despair, and death, the guilt of the bankruptcy, the series of domestic tragedies; even so, with all these visions of suffering described in the *Autobiography,* and still more to come as in all human experience, so that life without its elements of death is hardly to be called life — even so, Mark Twain's biggest and best and last book emerges as a "daylight book," full of life, love, and laughter. Revealing all his nighttime fears only to smile at them, Mark Twain himself emerges, not as a split, divided, tormented figure. But rather, if he still acknowledged and bowed down to all this in a yet rebellious mood of comedy, as a daylight writer of the highest sort who gives us, so many years later, a chronicle full of sweetness, affection, tenderness, and humor *about* the tragic experience of life.*

* Bernard DeVoto, discussing without much humor some of Twain's excoriating anger in the *Autobiography,* concluded it was a black book written in the framework of Twain's financial troubles and family difficulties. But this is to miss the real point of the *Autobiography* completely — as a book which allows its author to indulge in personal wrath, envy, parody, and satire fully, and yet is itself beyond anger and hatred and fear in its main stress, almost achieving an angelic peace and tenderness in its comic vision of human motives.

The *Autobiography* is in fact the last great spiritual legacy of the Old Republic to the modern American Empire, more truly living out its destiny in a mood of nightmarish fear and darkness. Despite all the critics and editors who had their own reasons for disparaging the original edition of this work (Kaplan describes it as "magnificent talk" — taken from De-Voto's "table talk," which DeVoto took from Twain's own words), it is a gem of a book — even though we have barely begun to discuss it here, and must try to limit the scope of its treatment. In the series of keys it provides for the real meaning of Mark Twain's work, it is the comic rebellion of a Tom Sawyer, and the edenic flight of a Huck Finn which still remains at the center of Mark Twain's earthly vision — but again we must stress that while this writer was centered in childhood, as many critics have observed, he was hardly limited to it. It is a fatal mistake to assume this about Mark Twain, since *all* great artists remain "childlike" in their vision of social and civilizational repressions, and Twain was only the most obviously and brilliantly so. His last great work, the *Autobiography* itself, was a work of the highest and most sophisticated maturity.

It was a maturity which had learned, despite all the risks and gambles and losses and disasters and farces of experience, that the main purpose of life-in-death is to enjoy itself, and to play, and take what soft pleasures it can in its tiny and dubious span of existence. What else do we live for? Then Clemens moved on to the story of "Jim Wolfe and the Cats," which became another bit of legendary comic folklore in the later sixties, at the start of his writing career. He moved from here to reminiscences of his lecturing period, including such figures as George Dolby, the famous theatrical agent of the time, Petroleum Vesuvius Nasby, Josh Billings, and the other frontier humorists who were collected, together with such eastern celebrities as Henry Ward

Beecher, Horace Greeley, and Wendell Phillips, under the auspices of the Redpath lecture bureau. There were famous women on the lecture platform in those days, too; and Clemens described certain "house-emptiers" like Olive Logan and Kate Field. Lecturing was a craft of its own, and some of its tricks are described here by probably the most famous lecturer of all time. There was another example of "The Beauties of the German Language," and Clemens went on to describe Viennese life in the late nineties, including a great parade that he loved, the best parade he had ever seen — while adding: "At the end of this year I shall be sixty-three — if alive — and about the same if dead."

In discussing the background of *Innocents Abroad,* Clemens was, after all this time in the first volume of the *Autobiography,* describing the origins of his first book, the true start of his literary career; no wonder he dwelt upon it with such a multitude of facts, and probably too fully. He went on to some of his earliest literary friends and acquaintances: Robert Louis Stevenson, Thomas Bailey Aldrich, and the unspeakable Bret Harte upon whose memory Clemens summoned all his powers of abuse and invective.

But more on this later on. There was an interesting and touching account of Twain's friendship with Henry Huttleston Rogers: that ruthless, cunning, arrogant, and heartless Standard Oil mogul, who was also a most charming and cultivated personality, and who did indeed befriend Sam Clemens in his hour of need, and in effect made him a new fortune, and presented him, like a Machiavellian patron perhaps, or a Medici, to the whole circle of powerful American financiers. The barons and titans and tycoons almost considered Mark Twain their court jester, the more fools they not to realize what was really happening — as Twain's later portraits of them would show. This was

invaluable experience for a great American writer in the heyday
of finance industrialism, to be close to the very center of the
structure, and, so to speak, the favorite guest in Capitalism's
house.

Mark Twain never missed a chance like this, which we've
already seen, which we are seeing right here, and which we
shall see in the future pages of this book. If I seem to bear down
on this a little heavily, it is because Biographer Kaplan has
stated that the price of Rogers' friendship and aid was that Mark
Twain was henceforth gagged and mute in regard to any free
opinions about his society, or capitalism or the Standard Oil trust
in particular. Well, we already know that just the opposite is
true; it was *after* Twain's bankruptcy that both his fiction and
his social criticism took on all its bite and brilliance; not to mention the allusions he made to the Rockefellers and Standard Oil
particularly. In fact Mark Twain's *personal* ties, with a few
intimate exceptions, never, in the end, prevented him from
speaking as he pleased. The reverse was more likely with this
perverse and satanic spirit, as almost anybody should know.

Perhaps it was Mr. Kaplan, rather than Sam Clemens, who
was incapable of social criticism, as I've said, and was unable
to recognize it when it rose into flaming print right before his
eyes. Meanwhile, dictating the *Autobiography* (and telling
Paine to fashion the final book out of all this raw material), Clemens reminisced about another millionaire friend of
his, John Mackay, from the early days of the great Bonanza in
Nevada in 1871. This was another fine section of history and
reporting about the silver-mine epoch in the west. Men who
were penniless prospectors, living by dint of the worst physical
labor, became fantastically wealthy overnight. The Bonanza
rose in value from $26,000 to $16,000,000 in six years. These
new millionaires became multimillionaires after that, and then,
naturally, United States Senators.

If Sam Clemens did not already have the gambling fever in his bloodstream, he would have been sure to acquire it in his years of apprenticeship. Together the two were too much for him, and the end — for him, though not for some others — could have been foreseen. As a result of the Bonanza strike, all the mines in that area, so he recorded here ironically, rose to a value of $400,000,000 in the stock market — "And six months after that, that value had been reduced by three-quarters; and by 1880, five years later, the stock of the Consolidated Virginia was under $2 a share, and the stock in the California was only $1.75" — for the Bonanza was now exhausted. (This was background material for the epical *Roughing It* of 1872.)

A period of fairy-tale success and of sudden disaster which almost prophesied, and to a certain extent helped to shape, Sam Clemens' future career. From the silver mines his narrative moved to the notorious Morris incident of the period. A respectable matron, trying to see President Roosevelt, was dragged away screaming by the White House police, maltreated physically, and then, overcome by the shock of her experience, languished in bed while the nation was horrified. While noting the affair was hardly of great historical importance, Clemens was possessed by this episode which added fuel to his dislike of the heroic Teddy, whose Cuban military campaign, as Clemens said elsewhere, compared well with Waterloo.

But the Morris case led him into other comments about the state of the nation. "I wonder what the Morris incident will look like in history fifty years from now. Consider these circumstances: that here at our own doors the mighty insurance upheaval has not settled down to a level yet. Even yesterday, and day before, the discredited millionaire insurance magnates had not all been flung out and buried from sight under the maledictions of the nation, but some of the McCurdies, McCalls, Hydes, and Alexanders were still lingering in positions of trust, such as directorships in banks. Also we have to-day the whole nation's attention centered upon the Standard Oil corporation, the most prodigious commercial force existing upon the planet . . . Also we have Congress threatening to overhaul the Panama Canal Commission to see what it has done with the fifty-nine millions, and to find out what it prosposes to do with the recently added eleven millions. Also there are three or four other matters of colossal public interest on the board to-day. And on the other side of the ocean we have Church and State separated in France; we have a threat of war between France and Germany upon the Morocco question; we have a crushed revolution in Russia, with the Czar and his family of thieves — the grand dukes — recovering from their long fright and beginning to butcher the remnants of the revolutionaries in the old confident way that was the Russian way in former days for three centuries; we have China furnishing a solemn and awful mystery. Nobody knows what it is, but we are sending three regiments in a hurry from the Philippines to China, under the generalship of Funston, the man who captured Aguinaldo by methods which would disgrace the lowest blatherskite that is doing time in any penitentiary."

After this, Clemens still pursued the Morris case, not of course for its own sake, as he realized, but for the light it threw upon President Roosevelt. "Roosevelt's biographer will light up the President's career step by step, mile after mile, through his life's course with illuminating episodes and incidents. He should set one of the lamps by the Morris incident, for it indicates character. It is a thing which probably could not have happened in the White House under any other President who has ever occupied those premises. Washington wouldn't call the police and throw a lady out over the fence!" And there followed an acerbic attack upon the blustering, warmongering, and imperialistic President whom Mark Twain hated both on principle and in person. Well, he conceded that he enjoyed Roosevelt's qualities when he was acting in the capacity of a private citizen. "But when he is acting under their impulse as President, they make of him a sufficiently queer President. He flies from one thing to another with incredible dispatch — throws a somersault and is straightway back again where he was last week. He will then throw some more somersaults and nobody can foretell where he is finally going to land after the series. Each act of his, and each opinion expressed, is likely to abolish or controvert some previous act or expressed opinion. This is what is happening to him all the time as President. But every opinion that he expresses is certainly his sincere opinion at that moment, and it is as certainly not the opinion which he was carrying around in his system three or four weeks earlier, and which was just as sincere and honest as the latest one. No, he can't be accused of insincerity — that is not the trouble. His trouble is that his newest interest is the one that absorbs him; absorbs the whole of him from his head to his feet, and for the time being it annihilates all previous opinions and feelings and convictions. He is the most popular human being that has ever existed in the United States, and that popularity springs from just these enthusiasms of his — these joyous ebullitions of excited sincerity. It makes him so much like the rest of the people. They see themselves reflected in him. They also see that his impulses are not often mean. They are almost always large, fine, generous. He can't stick to one of them long enough to find out what kind of a chick it would hatch if it had a chance, but everybody recognizes the generosity of the intention and admires it and loves him for it." *

* This brilliant profile of Theodore Roosevelt — along with the Morris case and Twain's caustic summary of the world around him — was omitted in Charles Neider's later version of the *Autobiography* on grounds of "taste" or "esthetics," as Neider claimed, but really because of the prevailing Cold War theology in the American fifties whose narrow values many critics accepted so blandly, so smugly, so piously. And still do.

Mark Twain was seventy when he wrote this, but how interested he was both in his own country and the world around him when compared with some of his later critics who viewed the same material with such artistic disdain; and how this outside world, in turn, enriched and revitalized the aging artist and his work. What good prose this was, in short, which has been claimed not to be "art," and how Clemens pursued Teddy Roosevelt with the familiar satirical animosity he had shown toward some previous objects of his wrath. It was good for him, he knew, and good for his writing; and this was only a part of some further reflections on Thanksgiving, the Congo, and other world events.*

Thanksgiving Day, said Clemens, had originated in New England when the Puritans realized they had succeeded in exterminating their neighbors, the Indians, instead of getting exterminated by their neighbors, the Indians.

> Thanksgiving Day became a habit, for the reason that in the course of time, as the years drifted on, it was perceived that the exterminating had ceased to be mutual and was all on the white man's side, consequently on the Lord's side; hence it was proper to thank the Lord for it and extend the usual annual compliments.

The original reason for Thanksgiving Day had long since ceased to exist, he added, since "the Indians have long ago been comprehensively and satisfactorily exterminated and the account closed with the Lord, with the thanks due." But still the habit persisted as a national holiday, and every year the American presidents and state governors set themselves the task "to hunt up something to be thankful for, and then they put these thanks into a few crisp and reverent phrases, in the form of a procla-

* Also omitted by Neider, and by the rest of his generation of "silent" American scholars.

mation, and this is read from all the pulpits in the land, the national conscience is wiped clean with one swipe, and sin is resumed at the old stand."

The year 1906, when Mark Twain's birthday fell on Thanksgiving, was particularly noted for having very little to be thankful for. Clemens wanted to put off the whole holiday on the ground that nothing had happened during the previous twelvemonth except several vicious and inexcusable wars, and King Leopold of Belgium's usual annual slaughters and robberies in the Congo State, together with the insurance revelations in New York.

He reminisced about the Clemenses' best and oldest friend, the Reverend Joseph Twichell, and Twichell's Civil War experience under General Sickles — whose monotonous conversation reminded Clemens of Bill Nye's remark about Wagner's music. "I have been told that Wagner's music is better than it sounds." The Civil War led Twain back to his own lack of martial valor, his dislike (for such a revolutionary thinker) of any force or violence in his own life, his brilliant and comic evasions of danger, his open admission of his own cowardice. If Clemens was at all guilty about his military failure, and if this entered into his worship of General Grant (as Freudians suggest), let us remember, more importantly, that this "guilt" produced some of the greatest antiwar writing in our literature. In January of 1906 Clemens began dictating the second volume of the *Autobiography* with some discussions of Booker T. Washington's Tuskegee Institute, which he supported, and of that fashionable New York society which, lionizing Twain himself, included such figures as Joseph H. Choate, Chauncey Depew, and Colonel (George) Harvey. That February was the thirty-sixth anniversary of the Clemenses' marriage, and Livy had been dead for one year and eight months, and there followed another of those lyrical and touching passages about her. She was always cheerful, said Clemens, even in the worst of times. "During the nine years that we spent in poverty and debt she was always able to reason me out of my despairs and find a bright side to the clouds and make me see it. In all that time I never knew her to utter a word of regret concerning our altered circumstances, nor did I ever know her children to do the like."

> For she had taught them, and they drew their fortitude from her. The love which she bestowed upon those whom she loved took the form of worship, and in that form it was returned — returned by relatives, friends, and the servants of her household. It was a strange combination which wrought into one individual, so to speak, by marriage — her disposition and character and mine. She poured out her prodigal affection in kisses and caresses, and in a vocabulary of endearments whose profusion was always an astonishment to me. I was born *reserved* as to endearments of speech, and caresses, and hers broke upon me as the summer waves break upon Gibraltar.

Samuel Clemens went on to describe their early home life together, Sam and Livy and the children, and the Hartford mansion and their cherished servants — the whole domestic scene of their younger years — in one of the most tender and poignant sections of the *Autobiography*. The artist's recall is complete, the tone is touching and affectionate and entertaining; these pages of Twain's memoirs couldn't be better. It *is* a fairy tale that Mark Twain creates again of their youthful peak of fame, success, happiness, and grand living: the house that Livy's father "surprised" them with in Buffalo, the newspaper which was given to Mark Twain in part ownership, the servants including the young Irish coachman, Patrick McAleer, the housekeeper Katie Leary, the cook Ellen, and later on the other Hartford domestics who always remained part of the Clemens family. What is fascinating again is the childlike joy of the young Clemens' acceptance of all these material splendors with no qualms of conscience and no concern about his own ability to live up to this totally new (kingly) role in life. Prince and Pauper he was indeed, in about equal fashion, in another of those ingenious dualisms of his temperament.

There is in particular a loving tribute by Twain to Patrick McAleer, who had just died, and whose funeral he attended. There is the death of their first son, Langdon, for which Clemens always held himself guilty (wrongly, it would appear today), and had never spoken about until the *Autobiography*. There is Susy's death again, which now Mark Twain almost regarded as a kind of sacrificial atonement for the success of his world-wide lecture tour. The details of her meningitis attack and suffering are so blunt here as to be harrowing, and Clemens went on to talk about her childhood and her character — "she that had been our wonder and our worship." As a little child she was already oppressed and perplexed, said Clemens,

by the maddening repetition of the stock incidents of our race's fleeting sojourn here, just as the same thing has oppressed and perplexed maturer minds from the beginning of time. A myriad of men are born; they labor and sweat and struggle for bread; they squabble and scold and fight; they scramble for little mean advantages over each other. Age creeps upon them; infirmities follow; shames and humiliations bring down their prides and vanities. Those they love are taken from them, and the joy of life is turned to aching grief. The burden of pain, care, misery, grows heavier year by year. At length ambition is dead; pride is dead; vanity is dead; longing for release is in their place. It comes at last — the only unpoisoned gift earth ever had for them — and they vanish from a world where they were of no consequence; where they achieved nothing; where they were a mistake and a failure and a foolishness; where they have left no sign that they have existed — a world which will lament them a day and forget them forever. Then another myriad takes their place, and copies all they did, and goes along the same profitless road, and vanishes as they vanished — to make room for another and another and a million other myriads to follow the same arid path through the same desert and accomplish what the first myriad, and all the other myriads that came after it, accomplished — nothing!

And here indeed was the classical statement, in almost the same words as the later novelist Theodore Dreiser was to say it in, of the tragic view of life for modern man. A tragic view, let us note, which lay at the base of all Mark Twain's humor and gave it that remarkable and complex tone and shading; a tragic view of man's destiny which joined inexorably the high individuality of Mark Twain's genius (as it did Dreiser's) with the struggling, suffering obscure hordes of mankind. And a view of life which, moreover, for just this reason — this loss of mutual affinity, this lack of bond and union between the individual and the community — is almost completely lacking in contemporary American literature.

For this view of Sam Clemens', and this bond of the great and the little, the exalted and the lowly, the special and the general, is at the base of all great art. When the artist is too removed, or society too oppressive, no great art is possible — as we can see from all the high renascences of art; and from all the bleak and sterile periods like our own, when literary fads and fashions are mistaken for literary achievement; when both artists and critics alike are ignorant of their true literary heritage in the United States, and the real horizons and boundaries of literature itself.

In a sense Susy now dominated the second volume of the *Autobiography,* and in one of those remarkable intuitions of Mark Twain, it is she who gives shape to the remaining events of his own life, and to the soft and loving memories of life in Hartford. He proceeded by using extracts of Susy's "Biography" of her father written when he was in his fiftieth year and she in her fourteenth. "We are a very happy family. We consist of Papa, Mamma, Jean, Clara and me. It is Papa I am writing about, and I shall have no trouble in not knowing what to say about him, as he is a *very* striking character." And then Clemens went off into a scathing denunciation of the herdlike tendencies of the literary critics of his own time, and a shameless explanation of how he had always let Howells set the tone of the reviews of his new books.

He pointed out that his critics had gone so far in describing his personal appearance as to create the impression that he was distinctly and distressingly unhandsome. "That description floated around the country in the papers, and was in constant use and wear for a quarter of a century. It seems strange to me that apparently no critic in the country could be found who could look at me and have the courage to take up his pen and destroy that lie. That lie began its course on the Pacific coast, in 1864, and it likened me in personal appearance to Petroleum V. Nasby, who had been out there lecturing. For twenty-five years afterward, no critic could furnish a description of me without fetching in Nasby to help out my portrait. I knew Nasby well, and he was a good fellow, but in my life I have not felt malignantly enough about any more than three persons to charge those persons with resembling Nasby."

It is Mark Twain presenting Susy's biography of Mark Twain which incites Mark Twain to further memories. (This reflection of a reflection which Clemens apparently just stumbled on, was to become a familiar technique in a later and more sophisticated age of writers such as Virginia Woolf and Gide.) "That burglar alarm which Susy mentions," said Clemens, "led a gay and careless life, and had no principles." And there follows an episode of Livy, Sam, the burglars, and the burglar alarm in the Hartford house that I can only touch on. As the burglar advanced from one floor to another in the house, Clemens kept turning off the alarm for that floor and "explaining" to Livy just what the burglars were doing and how he (Sam) could be of no help to them. "Suppose he comes up here!" Livy exclaims at last. "I said: 'It is all right. He will give us notice.' She said: 'What shall we do then?' I said, 'Climb out of the window.' She said: 'Well, what is the use of a burglar alarm for us?' I said: 'You have seen that it has been useful up to the present moment, and I have explained to you how it will be continuously useful after he gets up here.'"

There is the episode in the Clemenses' early life when Sam, who had prided himself on keeping the secret of his obscene language and spirited profanity away from the rest of his family, made the mistake of indulging in it while the bathroom door was open. A hushed silence fell upon the house and when he returned to his bedroom, unable to meet Livy's eye, she repeated his terrible vocabulary in her cultivated voice, and they broke up in laughter together. Echoes of Tom Sawyer and Huck Finn were in this marriage too, and Clemens' memory of that exercise in "censorship" was still vivid after all the years. "Against the white pillows I saw the black head — I saw that young and beautiful face; and I saw the gracious eyes with a something in them which I had never seen before. They were snapping and flashing with indignation. I felt myself crumbling; I felt myself shrinking away to nothing under that accusing gaze. I stood silent under that desolating fire for as much as a minute, I should say — it seemed a very, very long time. Then my wife's lips parted, and from them issued — *my latest bathroom remark.* The language perfect, but the expression unpractical, apprentice-like, ignorant, inexperienced, comically inadequate, absurdly weak and unsuited to the great language. In my lifetime I had never heard anything so out of tune, so inharmonious, so incongruous, so ill suited to each other as were those mighty words set to that feeble music. I tried to keep from laughing, for I was a guilty person in deep need of charity and mercy. I tried to keep from bursting, and I succeeded — until she gravely said, 'There, now you know how it sounds.'

"Oh, then I exploded! I said, 'Oh, Livy, if it sounds like that, God forgive me, I will never do it again.' Then she had to laugh, herself. Both of us broke into convulsions, and went on laughing until we were exhausted." Clemens also discovered that the children were perfectly familiar with his profanity since they hung over the hall balcony listening while he conversed with the butler George. So much for Mark Twain and language; and the language problem in his work; and for the type of Puritanical and Victorian "censorship" which Livy reputedly, according to many scholars, starting with Van Wyck Brooks, exercised over his behavior, his talk, his writing.

He went on to discuss the game he played with Livy and the children in deliberately inserting passages of writing which he knew would draw their violent protests. "For my own entertainment and to enjoy the protests of the children, I often abused my editor's innocent confidence. I often interlarded remarks of a studied and felicitously atrocious character purposely to achieve the children's delight and see the pencil do its fatal work. I often joined my supplications to the children's for mercy, and strung the argument out and pretended to be in earnest. They were deceived, and so was their mother. It was three against one, and most unfair. But it was very delightful, and I could not resist the temptation."

One could ask, furthermore, if Mark Twain's language was

as severely censored as it has been said to be, by both Livy and Howells, how could it remain so perfectly embedded in our literature, so solid, so fresh, so right, and so definitive? If these things are true, then, somewhat as Lincoln suggested about Grant's drinking, perhaps we could use a little more of that brand of "censorship" in contemporary American writing. It is still true that as regards sex, Sam Clemens maintained a perfect facade of silence — though the *Autobiography* shows some key passages of sexual freedom — about his own views and temperament. The public reasons for this (his popular audience) he openly acknowledged; perhaps the private reason, Livy herself, was worth the price. From the Hartford home Clemens moved backwards to the first meeting of "Mr. Clemens and Miss Langdon" and the whole story of Livy's invalidism, which Clemens himself sensed to be psychological as well as physical. A famous doctor of the period first enabled her to walk, after that curious disabling "accident" (or crisis) of adolescence which in her case, as in Henry James', kept her bedridden for some years. This famous psychological healer Dr. Newton, along with Dr. John Brown of Scotland, were beloved figures in the Clemens household, and from here derived one of the sources of Mark Twain's continuing interest in all phases of spiritualism, faith healing, and psychic phenomena.

There is also the episode of Samuel Clemens' own "accident" which resulted in a prolonged stay in the Jervis Langdon fairy-tale household (to the young provincial ruffian of the 1860s), and then the marriage to the sheltered, cultivated, enchanting, and invalided young eastern heiress of that time. Almost a typical Jamesian romance, but with what a difference! For Livy was not *that* crippled. Sam Clemens remembered Livy's ministrations to his wounded scalp with great clarity. "That was very pleasant. I should have been obliged to recover presently if it hadn't been for that. But under Livy's manipulations — if they had continued — I should probably be unconscious to this day. It was very delightful, those manipulations. So delightful, so comforting, so enchanting, that they even soothed the fire out of that fiendish successor to Perry Davis's 'Pain-Killer.' "

Which Livy's sister, Susy Crane, had poured on Clemens' injured head. And there is the familiar story told all so freshly again of the engagement, marriage, and their early years together almost as part of the Langdon household, and of Livy's remarkable physical endurance in times of crisis or illness in the family.

Then there is a section . . . Another section? By now, in the reading of this remarkable book of free association and stream of (unconscious) consciousness, it hardly bothers us that Twain may be repeating himself, or amplifying an earlier theme, or adding a new section to a previous section. It is almost all fresh; and what we wait for is the sudden turns of his mind, the twist of phrase, the surprise passages, the way he will suddenly repeat an older section and make it appear completely new. Just as when he went back, once more, to lecturing days and that "new and devilish" invention of the period called an Authors' Reading. "This witch's Sabbath took place in a theater, and began at two in the afternoon. There were nine readers on the list, and I believe I was the only one who was qualified by experience to go at the matter in a sane way." Clemens believed that nine times ten are ninety and therefore the average time allotted to each author should be ten minutes, but "There would be an introducer, and he wouldn't understand his business — this disastrous fact could be counted upon as a certainty. The introducer would be ignorant, windy, eloquent, and willing to hear himself talk. With nine introductions to make, added to his own opening speech — well, I could not go on with these harrowing calculations; I foresaw that there was trouble on hand." And most of these authors, like Howells, were ignorant of the speech business. "He couldn't seem to learn it. He was a bright man in all other ways, but whenever he came to select a reading for one of these carousals his intellect decayed and fell to ruin." At the Longfellow memorial in Boston he had brought along a reading selection of seven thousand words which would have taken him an hour and ten minutes to read, said Clemens, not allowing for interruptions such as applause — "for the reason that after the first twelve minutes there wouldn't be any."

Howells' excuse was that he never could find a short enough selection that would be good enough to stand exposure before an audience. "I said: 'It's no matter. Better that than a long one — because the audience could stand a bad short one, but couldn't stand a good long one.'

"We got it arranged at last. We got him down to fifteen minutes, perhaps. But he and Doctor Holmes and Aldrich and I had the only short readings that day out of the most formidable accumulation of authors that had ever thus far been placed in position before the enemy — a battery of sixteen. I think that was the occasion when we had sixteen. It was in the afternoon, and the place was packed, and the air would have been very bad, only there wasn't any. I can see that mass of people yet, opening and closing their mouths like fishes gasping for breath. It was intolerable.

"That graceful and competent speaker, Professor Norton, opened the game with a very handsome speech, but it was a good twenty minutes long. And a good ten minutes of it, I think, were devoted to the introduction of Dr. Oliver Wendell Holmes, who hadn't any more need of an introduction than the Milky Way. Then Doctor Holmes recited — as only Doctor Holmes could recite it — 'The Last Leaf,' and the house rose as one individual and went mad with worshiping delight.  And the house stormed along, and stormed along, and got another poem out of the Doctor as an encore; it stormed again and got a third one — though the storm was not so violent this time as had been the previous outbreaks.  By this time Doctor Holmes had, himself, lost a part of his mind, and he actually went on reciting poem after poem until silence had taken the place of encores, and he had to do the last encore by himself."

An entertaining glimpse of the New England literary circle; and one may note in passing that Clemens' tone of genial comedy about them and about Howells himself is far different from his first and early awe and admiration, his adulation of them, and that altogether excessive shame and horror over the Whittier dinner, now long forgotten.  There is a section in the *Autobiography* devoted to Twain's friendship with President Cleveland and his wife — "the young, the beautiful, the good-hearted, the sympathetic, the fascinating" Mrs. Cleveland.  And talking of women, Clemens recalled one of their German nurses with an innocent penchant for obscenities.  "It brings that pretty little German creature vividly before me — a sweet and innocent and plump little creature, with peachy cheeks; a clear-souled little maiden and without offense, notwithstanding her profanities, and she was loaded to the eyebrows with them.  She was a mere child.  She was not fifteen yet.  She was just from Germany, and knew no English.  She was always scattering her profanities around, and they were such a satisfaction to me that I never dreamed of such a thing as modifying her.  For my own sake, I had no disposition to tell on her.  Indeed, I took pains to keep her from being found out.  I told her to confine her religious expressions to the children's quarters, and urged her to remember that Mrs. Clemens was prejudiced against pieties on week days."

Still reminiscing along, the later Mark Twain recalled a Vassar lecture where his annoyance at his cavalier treatment by the college president did not quite spoil his pleasure in addressing "that great garden of young and lovely blossoms." Girls are charming creatures, he went on to say. "I shall have to be twice seventy years old before I change my mind as to that. I am to talk to a crowd of them this afternoon, students of Barnard College (the sex's annex to Columbia University), and I think I shall have just as pleasant a time with those lassies as I had with the Vassar girls twenty-one years ago." The pagan and plenary strain in this artist still lingered on apparently despite all the "censorship" and "repression" and neurotic "frustration" which we have been told so often were exercised upon him or existed within him. And directly after this episode appears the Mark Twain essay on the killing of six hundred Moros, as authorized by General Wood, and approved by President Roosevelt in the treacherous acquisition of the Philippines. I have already quoted this at some length as one of Twain's most brilliant polemical pieces; it is hardly a surprise that it was omitted in Charles Neider's later and emasculated edition of the *Autobiography*.

There is an interlude in which Clemens described the various letters sent to him (because he represented the conscience of the United States during his lifetime). Among these were letters written to "Mark Twain, Somewhere"; to "Mark Twain, God Knows Where"; to "Mark Twain, Somewhere, Try Satan"; and perhaps the bitterest pill of all, to "Mark Twain, c/o President Roosevelt, The White House, Washington, America, U.S.A." Talking to Howells about the plan of the *Autobiography*, Clemens was prompted to add: "I told Howells that this autobiography of mine would live a couple of thousand years without any effort and would then take a fresh start and live the rest of the time . . . He said he believed it would, and asked me if I meant to make a library of it." Both Twain and Howells were not too far off in their estimates, and then Howells, so Clemens added, was "full of praises and indorsement which was wise in him and judicious. If he had manifested a different spirit I would have thrown him out of the window. I like criticism, but it must be my way."

Nor, in the older tradition of literature, was Mark Twain averse to sentiment or pure sentimentality, in some of these episodes, along with his polemics, his parodies, his touching sense of comedy, and of tragedy. Talking of the Vanderbilts and Mr. Carnegie and of the Roosevelt children, who were distinctly "princely," he remarked that "the things they say are rather notably not worth while." He pointed out that in the remote western villages of his youth, the same attention was paid to the local celebrities. "We recognize that there are *no* trivial occurrences in life if we get the right focus on them. In a village they are just as prodigious as they are when the subject is a personage of national importance." Mark Twain, in the central tradition of American literature, was again binding himself to the aspirations of the masses of men in his central vision of his art; was as interested in the "little" as in the "big" in this *Autobiography,* and in the small things of life as well as in the large. And who knows what is big and what is small, what is great and what is trivial in the end, since, as he asserted, "there are *no* trivial occurrences in life" if we get the right focus on them.

He parodied this grand theme immediately in his account of "The Swangos" — the Swango family riding, visiting, attending auctions, raising cattle, growing turkeys — in Hazel Green, Kentucky. Shades of Sherwood Anderson, who was perhaps the last modern writer to stress this theme in particular. There was the story of Ed Marsh, his wife's counsin, a Civil War hero, and of Calvin H. Higbie, a figure in *Roughing It,* and a

silver-mining friend of Twain's from Nevada. (There is more of
this invaluable material about frontier life and customs.) Then
comes the remarkable sketch of Orion Clemens, the eccentric
and shiftless brother of Sam's, whose history of wild schemes
and terrible failures was the underside of Mark Twain's own
success. Orion's was a curious personality, as Clemens said.
"In all my seventy years I have not met the twin of it." And
perhaps here in this brilliant ne'er-do-well, who was a complete
parody of Sam Clemens while he dogged his heels and lived on
Sam's generosity, was another *personal* source of the twin-fixa-
tion or Twain Myth — which had, in Mark Twain's case, a
much larger generic, communal, and cultural meaning. But
Orion was Sam's unfortunate twin indeed, and contributed to
the pattern; and what curious insight made this artist use the
twin-like phrase for his pen name? Orion is another fascinating
figure among Clemens' portraits, volatile, fragmentary, contradictory, self-defeating, unbearable, and yet oddly charming and
appealing. Clemens was pursued by his dark failure. For Orion
it was always the American dream in fantasy, and always the
American nightmare in reality; and from this grimmer picture
of the frontier life the *Autobiography* moved to Clemens' meeting with the celebrated Russian revolutionary, Tchaykoffsky,*
who old and grizzled as he was still had a Vesuvius inside of
him. "He is so full of belief in the ultimate and almost immediate
triumph of the revolution and the destruction of the fiendish
autocracy that he almost made me believe and hope with him.
He has come over here expecting to arouse a conflagration of
noble sympathy in our vast nation of eighty millions of happy
and enthusiastic freemen. But honesty obliged me to pour some
cold water down his crater."

* Or Tchaikovsky, Nikolai Vasilevich, as spelled today; and not the com-
poser, but the revolutionary populist who founded the St. Petersburg party,
lived in London, returned to Russia in 1905, and became an opponent of the
Bolsheviks' Revolution of October, 1917.

I told him what I believed to be true: that our Christianity which we have always been so proud of — not to say, so vain of — is now nothing but a shell, a sham, a hypocrisy; that we have lost our ancient sympathy with oppressed peoples struggling for life and liberty; that when we are not coldly indifferent to such things we sneer at them, and that the sneer is about the only expression the newspapers and the nation deal in with regard to such things; that his mass meetings would not be attended by people entitled to call themselves representative Americans, even if they may call themselves Americans at all; that his audiences will be composed of foreigners who have suffered so recently that they have not yet had time to be Americanized and their hearts turned to stone in their breasts; that these audiences will be drawn from the ranks of the poor, not those of the rich; that they will give and give freely, but they will give from their poverty and the money result will not be large. I said that when our windy and flamboyant President conceived the idea, a year ago, of advertising himself to the world as the new Angel of Peace, and set himself the task of bringing about the peace between Russia and Japan and had the misfortune to accomplish his misbegotten purpose, no one in all this nation except Doctor Seaman and myself uttered a public protest against this folly of follies.

When Tchaykoffsky said that Mark Twain's talk depressed him profoundly and he hoped Twain was wrong, Twain said that he hoped the same. When Tchaykoffsky pointed out that the United States had sent millions of dollars to help the suffering Russians, and didn't that modify Mark Twain's opinion, Twain said it did not. "That money came not from Americans, it came from Jews; much of it from rich Jews, but the most of it from Russian and Polish Jews on the East Side — that is to say, it came from the very poor. The Jew has always been benevolent. Suffering can always move a Jew's heart and tax his pocket to the limit. He will be at your mass meetings. But if you find any Americans there put them in a glass case and exhibit them. It will be worth fifty cents a head to go and look at that show and try to believe in it.*

Now can you really say that Mark Twain was anti-Semitic, anti-alien, anti-poor people, and in particular against the new urban masses (as Henry James was, and so many other American writers of the period) when he attributed to these new Americans all the traditional old-fashioned American values which he cherished and mourned. But in truth he was correct in realizing that the great American tradition had descended underground, as it were, to the minority groups who nourished and kept it alive during those turbulent years, until a few decades later it would be the young, the students, and the black Americans who carried on the same struggle, under perhaps less hopeful circumstances, and a different historical period, but with great vitality and spirit.

Clemens reached toward the other complementary peak of his temperament when his social concern — or social protest, social polemics, social satire — was directly followed by a late-blooming period of his sexual pleasure. The two human poles of civilizational restraint and biopsychic urges, the outer and inner worlds at war or at peace, agreeing, dissenting, probing, fusing, but always intensely intertwined and creative by the fact of their polar opposition and their polar necessity, were, as I say, at the core of this artist's temperament much more clearly than with most writers.

"Day before yesterday all Vassar, ancient and modern, packed itself into the Hudson Theater, and I was there," Clemens wrote

* This whole passage in the *Autobiography* has been omitted again both in Mr. Neider's modern edition of the book, I am sorry to repeat, and in Mr. Kaplan's modern biography of Mark Twain, just as it has been thought unworthy of mention in contemporary scholarship on Twain; not perhaps so much for its Russian sympathies as for its dim view of the American scene in 1906 — or its prophetic and discerning view?

in that peculiarly affectionate, tenderly comic, mock-ironic tone he used about himself and the ladies. "The occasion was a benefit arranged by Vassar and its friends to raise money to aid poor students of that college in getting through the college course. I was not aware that I was to be a feature of the show, and was distressed and most uncomfortably inflamed with blushes when I found it out. Really the distress and the blushes were manufactured, for at bottom I was glad. I held a reception on that stage for an hour or two, and all Vassar, ancient and modern, shook hands with me. Some of the moderns were too beautiful for words, and I was very friendly with those. I was so hoping somebody would want to kiss me for my mother, but I didn't dare to suggest it myself. Presently, however, when it happened, I did what I could to make it contagious, and succeeded. This required art, but I had it in stock. I *seemed* to take the old and the new as they came, without discrimination, but I averaged the percentage to my advantage, and without anybody's suspecting, I think."

There were half a dozen pretty old girls, also, he added, whom he had met in their bloom at Vassar when he and Susy had visited there so long ago. But then, "Yesterday at the University Club, almost all the five hundred were of the young and lovely, untouched by care, unfaded by age." He had delivered a "moral sermon" to the Barnard girls a few weeks earlier — if they had only realized the true nature of such moral sermons on Mark Twain's part — and now it was like being among old friends. One sweet creature wanted to whisper in his ear and he was nothing loath. "She raised her dainty form on tiptoe, lifting herself with a grip of her velvet hands on my shoulders, and put her lips to my ear and said, 'How do you like being the belle of New York?' It was so true, and so gratifying, that it crimsoned me with blushes, and I could make no reply."

An old man's vanity, yes; a slightly old-fashioned Victorian touch in Twain's language that is not present elsewhere than when dealing with these adoring and delicious maidens — yet it is also remarkably open, tender, and humorous on the part of the aging Mark Twain, play-acting out the sexual comedy to the end. There is a reminiscence here of Ellen Terry as queen of the English stage for fifty years, and Clemens' cable to her:

Age has not withered, nor custom staled, the admiration and affection I have felt for you so many, many years. I lay them at your honored feet with the strength and freshness of their youth upon them undiminished.

And no doubt Mark Twain was well aware of the intent of the original verses dedicated to the dusky Egyptian Queen:

Age cannot wither her, nor custom stale
Her infinite variety; other women cloy
The appetites they feed; but she makes hungry
Where most she satisfies.

There followed a brief account of Tom Sawyer's and Huck Finn's trials and tribulations at the hands of libraries and public institutions. These books, one or the other, or both, had been banned in Concord, Massachusetts, in Denver, Colorado, and by the Brooklyn Public Library in 1905. Just recently, as I say, further attempts have been made to censor *The Adventures of Huckleberry Finn,* without doubt the great epic of childhood in our literature, and whose hero is the old Negro slave, on the grounds that this figure is called "Nigger Jim," rather than "Negro Jim" or "Black Power Jim." When Clemens was informed by the librarian of the Sheepshead Bay Branch of the Brooklyn Library that the familiar discussion had ensued about

Huck's deceit, lies, immoral behavior, and, perhaps worst of all, improper language, Clemens wrote to Asa Don Dickinson, his informant. "I am greatly troubled by what you say. I wrote Tom Sawyer and Huck Finn for adults exclusively, and it always distresses me when I find that boys and girls have been allowed access to them. The mind that becomes soiled in youth can never again be washed clean; I know this by my own experience, and to this day I cherish an unappeasable bitterness against the unfaithful guardians of my young life, who not only permitted but compelled me to read an unexpurgated Bible through before I was 15 years old. None can do that and ever draw a clean sweet breath again this side of the grave. Most honestly do I wish I could say a softening word or two in defence of Huck's character, since you wish it, but really in my opinion it is no better than those of Solomon, David, Satan, and the rest of the sacred brotherhood."

If there was an unexpurgated Bible in the Children's Department of the Brooklyn Library, Clemens concluded, "won't you please help that young woman remove Huck and Tom from that questionable companionship?" There was a newspaper storm a little later about Mark Twain's letter, but he remained comfortably in bed. "Of course I was in bed. I am always in bed." There is another account of Frank Fuller's enthusiastic launching of Mark Twain's first New York lecture, an enormous debacle at the time which was nevertheless a steppingstone to Twain's future success. By now Twain had almost concluded his reminiscences; his mind kept moving around to include last-minute memories of present and past, but his job, his great *Autobiography,* was almost finished, as he thought, and he could not even bear to go back through the mass of material. "I am not glancing through my books to find out what I have said in them. I refrain from glancing through those books for two reasons: first — and this reason always comes first in every matter connected with my life — laziness. I am too lazy to examine the books. The other reason is — well, let it go. I had another reason, but it had slipped out of my mind while I was arranging the first one. I think it likely that in the book called *Roughing It* I have mentioned Frank Fuller. But I don't know, and it isn't any matter . . ."

Such were the ending words of *Mark Twain's Autobiography*, in its first, 1924, edition as edited by Albert Bigelow Paine; the ending that Paine thought Sam Clemens preferred. But this was only the *first* appearance of one of our great books of personal memoirs. There were to be volumes of appendices containing new material, and material omitted by the sometimes over-prudent Paine; there were to be new editions of the *Autobiography* itself, continuing up to the 1960s and no doubt after that. For Clemens had left a huge mass of still undigested, unedited, unprinted material to fill up this book and to make others which were contingent upon it. Ending on the note of laziness, indifference, casualness, even carelessness, viewing the world now from the resting place of his bed, this great voice of our letters would not stop so easily, this great spirit would hardly subside into the silence it pretended to seek.

As a matter of fact, while the last date in the first edition of the *Autobiography* was Wednesday, April 11, 1906, the Autobiography "Dictations" to Paine and a secretary would continue through 1906 at 21 Fifth Avenue, New York, and Dublin, New Hampshire; through 1907 at 21 Fifth Avenue; through 1908 in New York City and Redding, Connecticut; through 1909 when he began what was in effect an extension of his last book, a volume called *Letters from the Earth*.

*Letters from the Earth* would also appear in due course, when the time was ready for it; but meanwhile there was another postmortem supplement to Mark Twain's autobiography, *Mark Twain in Eruption,* published in 1940.

But here we have to discuss what might be called the Ordeal of Bernard DeVoto.

# NINE

# SPY IN THE HOUSE
# OF THE OLIGARCHY

A FTER A LAPSE of over ten years, during which appeared, among other critical studies, the famous study by Van Wyck Brooks, *The Ordeal of Mark Twain,* 1920, revised in 1933, which set the style for a whole school of Mark Twain criticism; which in a different Freudian form has been revived and refurbished in the contemporary period; and during which Brooks, incidentally, moved over toward Bernard DeVoto's "defense" of Twain, while DeVoto in turn moved murkily toward Brooks' original analysis; after this whole period of critical maneuvering, Sam Clemens spoke again in his own voice.

I am also omitting here William Dean Howells' famous eulogy, *My Mark Twain,* 1910, which was partly the focus of Brooks' attack, in a period when this famous and admirable historian of our literature was liquidating all the great talents he was afterwards to rehabilitate in his "usable past." I am also forced to omit *Mark Twain's Notebook,* in 1935, in this discussion for somewhat the same reason that we had to skip *Mark Twain's Letters.* Both of these volumes, fascinating in themselves, are source books of material which is discussed here in other forms.

If in a sense it is true that Mark Twain's life and work comprised one great Autobiography — in a Whitmanesque sense which embraced the world within the soul of the artist, or rather projected the *selfless* soul of the artist upon a boundless outside experience; if Mark Twain is one of those writers whose repetitions never repeat themselves or can be read afresh each time with a new sense of discovery and pleasure — well, there is a certain limit even to this law of non-limits.

Or to put it even more truthfully, I *would* have discussed both *Mark Twain's Letters* and *Mark Twain's Notebook* with great pleasure, surely, if only I had had the patience and the time to do so. And I regret that I can't. Meanwhile still another book, *Mark Twain in Eruption,* edited by Bernard DeVoto in 1940, takes precedence in our discussion. The Albert Bigelow Paine two-volume edition of the *Autobiography,* as DeVoto told us, used "something less than half of the typescript in which everything that Mark wanted in his memoirs had been brought together. This book uses about half the remainder." So the *Eruption* volume is either a sequel or a new edition of the *Autobiography,* and Mr. DeVoto's implication is that the material was too explosive for the earlier Paine edition. This is partly, but only partly true; and while Mr. DeVoto boldly opens the book with another section of Twain's radical social criticism — more boldly, as we've seen, than the intimidated critics of the 1950s — both the new material and DeVoto's appraisal of it deserve some close consideration. DeVoto is not satisfied with either Twain's sense of "formless form" for the *Autobiography,* or Paine's own rendering of this. He has put his selections into related blocks of material, and omitted the "trivialities, irrelevancies, newspaper clippings," the disconnected and planless form of the original book which he had always found "annoying."

He had also, said DeVoto, left out of the new version of the *Autobiography* passages which were "fantastic and injurious," those which contained "violent animosities," and which were crowded with "inaccuracies, distortions, and exaggerations." And very likely this was done at the cost of some of Twain's best passages of writing; since toward the rages and furies and polemical outbursts of genius, DeVoto shows all the cautious and fearful "moderation" of the respectable mind. Twain would hardly be Twain without those distortions, exaggerations, and animosities, as we know — those lurid rages leading into irony, satire, parody, farce, and high comedy. The description of Twain's relationship with the American Publishing Company and Elisha Bliss; with his own publishing company which Clemens entrusted to his nephew-in-law, Charles Webster; the description of Bret Harte — we are cautioned about all these classic sections of the *Autobiography* by the meticulous Mr. DeVoto.

Apart from these superficial "instructions" about reading Mark Twain (which apparently every leading critic of Twain has felt it necessary to impart to Twain's readers: the feeling, in short, that humor is too dangerous a thing to be accepted as humor), DeVoto has several more severe prohibitions about Twain and the *Autobiography* which have colored a large part of modern criticism.

He warns us, for example, that the *Autobiography* is not so much an autobiography as "a kind of table-talk" about the men and events which Sam Clemens was interested in. He took this from Twain's ironical self-deprecatory description of his book. Now this may be true of DeVoto's book, which being an appendix to the *Autobiography* (rather than a new edition) lacks all the marvelous range and depth of the original memoirs. And DeVoto points out that Twain, while being "the most autobiographical of writers," does not ever even try to reveal himself — forgetting the basic assumption that Mark Twain, like Walt Whitman, was one of those pantheistic poets whose "I" was the world's "I," whose rare temperaments reflected universal life, and could not be separated from it. "I contain multitudes," said Walt. Moreover the whole *Autobiography,* according to DeVoto, was written under the shadow of Twain's financial bankruptcy and domestic sorrow and was a dark and obsessional and phobic document — whereas we have just seen that in fact it is one of the great *daylight* books of the world! Bearing indeed all the scars of a wide, high, and full life, as Mark Twain did, always touching the opposite extremes of great success and deep failure, of intense joy and the depths of sorrow, of happiness and misery — and forgetting nothing, with that total recall which extended most vividly back to his earliest years — he was perhaps the most open of all the major writers in North America. Aware of the vicissitudes of human experience, the complex interaction of a life force which is continually in flux, never to be counted on, always variant but with the one certain element of change and surprise and final loss, as Twain well knew, he yet, in the final period of his work, was able by the sheer touch of his genius to transcend and to re-create his whole life in that one last book, that one last illuminating and enchanting chronicle.

The rages, furies, and searing indictments of Mark Twain; the long-remembered and even intensely treasured scores to be evened up; the curses and maledictions that brighten these pages; the exaggerations and obsessions that DeVoto scolds Twain for and points his reproving finger at — what are these but the marks of that open-ended genius whom we have been describing in this book? Of that Mark Twain to whom love and hate were equally valid, and to whom perhaps only one thing in the world — the "moderation" which Mr. DeVoto advocates; or the "consensus" which Twain himself so violently decried; or the conformity and "normalcy" of life; or the sensible and "reasonable" thing — was despicable and tedious.

It is quite true that DeVoto corrects some dates and titles that in the range of his inimitable narrative Sam Clemens guessed at, forgot, didn't care about, or, as he frankly said, was too lazy to check. It is here also, in the famous Introduction to *Mark Twain in Eruption* (a lecture or essay which DeVoto spent much time in writing and revising as one of his own major critical documents), that we come upon the source of another central error of contemporary Mark Twain criticism. I mean the silly notion that Mark Twain's whole creative life and his best literary work were confined to the narrow limits of his frontier childhood in Hannibal. "When he wrote fiction," adds Mr. DeVoto, "which is to say when the bases of his personality were finding instinctive expression, the human race was the race he had known in Hannibal. Life was confined within the circumstances of his boyhood. There is a profound difference between Tom Sawyer and Huck Finn, but one or the other of them is holding the pen in the best, the deepest, and the truest of Mark's work."

Now Mr. DeVoto is treading on very subtle and mysterious ground here — a deep and profound quagmire of misunderstanding into which he then plunged over his head. This is a half-truth which, getting at the cause of Twain's greatness which has been described in these pages, mistakes its true nature only to end up in total error. "His artistic creativeness, his phantasy-making, was rooted in his boyhood," says Mr. DeVoto. "Why this should be so is a question not germane to this Introduction; one, furthermore, which could be answered only speculatively and only in analytical psychology." But it is indeed germane not only to Mr. DeVoto's introduction, but to Mark Twain's work as a whole, as we have described it. It is the essence of

Mark Twain's genius. And it is clearly perceived not indeed in "analytical" or Freudian psychology, but in the cultural psychology of Otto Rank who continually related the Artist — remembering human nature in all its plenitude, its generosity, its happiness, its sense of love and affection and play — to that "Fall" which was the beginning of civilization, with all its repressions and discontents.

Mr. DeVoto is so close to the truth at times, it is depressing to see him always reach the wrong conclusion. Mark Twain's memory of his childhood was indeed lyrical, as "a memory of freedom, irresponsibility, and security, islanded in a countryside and a society as pleasant as any in the American past." But this unique vision of pagan splendor and ease in the Sam Clemens of Hannibal was not at all beaten down by his memories of "anxiety, violence, supernatural horror" so much as it was always present in his vision of maturity and society. His vision of human life was hardly restricted to these childhood environs so much as it was always compared with it. The lost Eden was the shining remembrance in, so to speak, man's everlasting day of atonement. In fact, what happened was just the reverse of Mr. DeVoto's concept. The remarkable thing about Mark Twain's work is not that it stopped with childhood, but that *he carried his childhood* — his sense of play and pleasure, ease and irresponsibility, humor and affection — throughout his maturity.

All big artists do this; this is just what makes them artists — but never perhaps so clearly as in the case of Sam Clemens. In the fiction itself, it is quite true that he balanced off the early Tom Sawyer–Huck Finn parables of "innocence" (a satanic innocence to be sure) with the dark fables of *Pudd'nhead Wilson, Hadleyburg,* and *The $30,000 Bequest* in a kind of polar opposition of evil within the same familiar setting. But this duality, so familiar also in Melville and other writers, found its ironic

resolution in *The Mysterious Stranger*; just as Clemens' own deep
conflicts and wounds in life were resolved in the final complex
but essentially satirical and comic tone of the *Autobiography*
itself. By contrast, and through sheer error, one must infer,
Mr. DeVoto links together *What Is Man?*, *The Mysterious
Stranger*, and the *Autobiography* as examples of Mark Twain's
defeat and despair. (We have seen just how *The Mysterious
Stranger* used the raw material of *What Is Man?* for a much
more sophisticated and fulfilled artistic purpose.) Mr. DeVoto
claims that the crisis period in Twain's life broke his career in
two, and left him only with a shattered talent at the end.

But the plain fact is, as I hope the pages of this book illustrate,
that Mark Twain not only survived and surmounted life's worst
things, but that his later work far surpassed his earlier in knowledge and insight, in its range and complexity of artistic vision.
It too is a celebration of life but with all its tragic depths; much
more aware and complex than the rather simplistic innocence
of Huck and Tom. The Fallen Angel in Mark Twain himself
is still the supreme and satanic observer of the world; and all the
better for his fall from that innocence he always cherished and
never quite lost.

Even in fiction one might put *The Mysterious Stranger* in the
same literary category as *Huck Finn*. But of course Mr. De-
Voto's fatal mistake, from which all his other errors spring,
is the insistence about Mark Twain "that fundamentally he was
a novelist." Only a critic unaware of a novelist's temperament
could say that. Fundamentally Mark Twain was *not* a novelist
or a fiction writer at all. As I am forced to repeat, he was a
poet-prophet on the model of Walt Whitman even more than
that of Melville. And he used the fiction form, carelessly in
many instances, as a kind of parable dumb show for certain aspects of his temperament and vision that could best be described
in that medium. But even as to Twain's bardic role, as the ac-

knowledged prophet and conscience of his country at the end of
the Old Republic, a role no writer has since assumed with
Twain's singular splendor, Mr. DeVoto is curiously critical.

The merit of *Mark Twain in Eruption* is that it brings together
another collection of Mark Twain's brilliant socio-historical commentary. In precisely that late, or last period of Mark Twain's
work which he had just finished depreciating, Mr. DeVoto as-
sembled enough important material to refute his own thesis. But
was this captious critic aware of this, was he pleased with his own
book? Not completely. "What is added to the portrait of Mark
Twain by this book is the citizen of the first Roosevelt Era looking toward our own time with a strong foreboding. I have said
elsewhere that when *The Adventures of Huckleberry Finn* is examined from a point of view much recommended to criticism
since I wrote, that of social implications, it may be seen as the
American democratic hope colliding with a realization of the
limits implicit in American democracy." Mr. DeVoto writes as
though he had pioneered in the "social implications" of literature. And isn't this a narrow and pedestrian view of a literary
work whose larger and deeper theme is that of the pagan splendor of life confronted by the prejudices, superstitions, and repressions of *all,* not merely democratic forms of civilization?
And Mr. DeVoto continues with an even more surprising eval-
uation of Mark Twain's social criticism.

"In what Mark has to say about the government and the plutocracy at the moment when the American empire is achieved he
typifies his generation's confused surprise at finding contradictions in the American axioms. The man of good will, the
Mugwump, not only perceives that there is something wrong
but wonders, against his belief, whether something may not have
been wrong from the beginning."

Now it is hard to imagine a more numerous and profound
series of misconceptions about Mark Twain than that contained

in these two sentences of DeVoto's. Mark Twain certainly did not belong to "his generation" in this sense at all — a generation indeed of financial barons and titans who felt not "confused surprise" but active pleasure in contradicting all the hitherto accepted axioms of American democracy and the American Dream. (Twain *did* belong to that artistic hierarchy of Melville and Whitman, and Thoreau and Emerson, as we've seen, who before and during his own time had discovered these contradictions.) Nor was Mark Twain any longer "surprised" at such fatal contradictions in the democracy which he had been writing about directly since the mid-nineties, and implicitly long before that. Nor were his marvelous polemical essays directed only at the "plutocracy," as DeVoto implies here; long before the *Autobiography* he had discovered the far worse evils of imperialism, both in the old world and the new. Imperialism is a key word of modern history from the nineteenth to the end of the twentieth century, at least — and a word that DeVoto never once mentions! Nor was Sam Clemens, finally, a "man of good will" in that conventional sense; but an edenic-satanic genius, as we know, on a far more complex level of human feeling; and his Mugwump period was really the sign of a very youthful and provincial phase before his true literary education began.

Let us remember the brilliant and eloquent defense of the French Revolution that runs through Mark Twain's work before and after *A Connecticut Yankee*. The man who could, after each rereading of Carlyle's apoplectic history of that revolution, declare himself more of a Jacobin than ever, and not just an ordinary Jacobin, but a Sansculotte and Marat Jacobin — can hardly be classified as a Mugwump. The artist who was attacking imperialism in 1895; and who in the 1900s was proclaiming the advent of the "American Empire," while he brilliantly attacked its colonialism and its racism alike, could hardly have

been so naive and confused as was stated in the introduction to
*Mark Twain in Eruption.*

It seems more likely that Mr. DeVoto himself was poorly prepared either to recognize the radical depths of Mark Twain's social criticism, or, more important, to accept it. It was this same
western critic, first approaching Mark Twain as the epitome of
"Frontier Individualism" — that Turneresque American Frontier which has since become subject to so much qualification —
who had just a little earlier rebuked the major American writers
of the twenties and thirties for having lost hope in the American
Dream itself. For if DeVoto had really understood and accepted Mark Twain's revolutionary premises about the end of
old-fashioned American democracy, about the advent of "Monarchy" and the imminence of a native dictatorship in one form
or another, then his own literary values and his work would have
had to undergo a deep change. It was easier to blame Mark
Twain's confusion and ignorance than to accept Twain's profound insights — as a later generation of more radical critics
would do. It was easier to focus the criticism on Mark Twain's
"broken career" and the "diminution" of his talent in just those
areas where Twain's prophetic genius would go beyond his personal life, and would achieve its final triumphs.

Perhaps indeed it was DeVoto's own confusion and ignorance
and frustration that this critic attributed to the great master
whose custodian he had become. But that is not to say there
were not some confusions and contradictions in Twain's description of the oligarchy and the monarchy which opens *Mark
Twain in Eruption* — and perhaps this came out most sharply
in the commentary on Theodore Roosevelt which DeVoto chose
to begin with. It was true that Clemens' friendship with Rogers,
even his adoration of Rogers, made him defend the Standard
Oil trust at times even while he was attacking it. His attitude was

ambiguous here, but hardly mute, as Justin Kaplan claims. And the attack on Roosevelt veered from seeing him as the figurehead of the great corporations which he was ostensibly attacking — though Clemens caught this *at the time,* long before the historians recorded it — to seeing him as the villainous creator of the business panic of 1907. The Roosevelt commentary was another example of Twain's compulsive hatreds but — perhaps because he was too close to his subject and too angry — one of the least engaging. Nor was Twain altogether right in evaluating the great corporation and the finance capitalism which Thorstein Veblen was more accurately describing during the same period. But this is hardly the same as accusing him of a blind ignorance in this field, some aspects of which he spotted so acutely, and some personalities among the oligarchy whom he described so intimately, in terms that no merely "proletarian" author would have known about.

And just here, despite his abiding affection for his financial savior, Rogers, Sam Clemens was not diffident about pointing out some facts concerning the Standard Oil trust. "Mr. Roosevelt is easily the most astonishing event in American history, if we except the discovery of the country by Columbus. The details of Mr. Roosevelt's purchase of the Presidency by bribery of voters are all exposed now, even to the names of the men who furnished the money and the amounts which each contributed. The men are great corporation chiefs and three of them are Standard Oil monopolists. It is now known that when the canvass was over a week before election day and all legitimate uses for election money at an end, Mr. Roosevelt got frightened and sent for Mr. Harriman to come to Washington and arrange measures to save the State of New York for the Republican party. The meeting took place and Harriman was urged to raise two hundred thousand dollars for the cause. He raised two hundred and sixty thousand and it was spent upon the election in the last week of the campaign — necessarily for the purchase of votes, since the time had gone by for using money in any other way."

Now that is a pretty well-informed and precise account of a typical American election, and despite the irregularities of the Roosevelt commentary as literature it is still useful to have it in print as history. And DeVoto underestimated — for once — the depths of Mark Twain's bitterness and despair about the new American empire when Twain closed this essay by saying he would vote for Taft and the continuation of the "monarchy." "The monarchy is here to stay. Nothing can ever unseat it . . . Things will go along well enough under this arrangement so long as a Titus succeeds a Vespasian, and we shall best not trouble about a Domitian until we get him. All in good time he will arrive. The Lord will provide — as heretofore. My humble vote is for Titus Taft, inherited insane policies and all, and may it elect him! I do not believe he will appoint a Domitian to succeed him; I only know that if he shall disappoint us and appoint Domitian, Domitian will be elected. But I am not personally concerned in the matter; I shall not be here to grieve about it."

To later historians the comparison with the early Roman emperors would seem a very apt reference as delivered by Mark Twain in 1906. On Andrew Carnegie, Clemens was even more vitriolic; on Carnegie's unabashed, unconscious, unblushing egoism, Clemens was murderous.

"He never has any but one theme, himself . . . He is himself his one darling subject, the only subject he for the moment — the social moment — seems stupendously interested in. I think he would surely talk himself to death upon it if you would stay and listen . . . He talks forever and ever and ever and untiringly of the attentions which have been shown him. Sometimes they have been large attentions, most frequently they are very small ones; but no matter, no attention comes amiss to him and he likes to revel in them. His friends are coming to observe with consternation that while he adds new attentions to his list every now and then, he never drops an old and shopworn one out of the catalogue to make room for one of these fresh ones. He keeps the whole list, keeps it complete; and you must take it all, along with the new additions, if there is time and you survive. It is the deadliest affliction I know of. He is the Ancient Mariner over again; it is not possible to divert him from his subject; in your weariness and despair you try to do it whenever you think you see a chance, but it always fails; he will use your remark for his occasion and make of it a pretext to get straight back upon his subject again."

\* \* \* \*

In view of what followed, however, DeVoto's strictures appear rather more beneficial than not. At least DeVoto *presented* the best aspects of Twain's social commentary even while he devalued them. Charles Neider, in 1959, simply repressed and deleted this whole area of Mark Twain's work for the most dubious reasons. Moreover, while DeVoto's *Mark Twain in Eruption* was clearly a kind of supplement to the *Autobiography,* Neider's *The Autobiography of Mark Twain* claimed to be, and was in certain aspects, a new edition of the famous book.

In his introduction Neider pointed out that "for the first time the whole manuscript is being used as the source, not parts or selections of it." But he neglected to say that his new version was the most severely streamlined edition of the *Autobiography* to appear yet. (Neider also describes DeVoto's *Mark Twain in Eruption* as a new edition of the *Autobiography,* which it surely is not.) More accurately, Neider rejects DeVoto's psychologizing on the "failure" of the *Autobiography*: "When he invoked Hannibal [that is, his early years] he found there not only the idyll of boyhood but anxiety, violence, supernatural horror, and an uncrystallized but enveloping dread. Much of his fiction, most of his masterpiece [*Huck Finn*], flows from that phantasy-bound anxiety." So Neider quotes DeVoto, and surely Sam Clemens was no stranger to these psychic states which he himself described so openly in the *Autobiography*.

But we have seen how Mark Twain's laughter could wash away those somber strains of his temperament which any great writer must be aware of; laughter which Mr. DeVoto did not seem to appreciate or understand. Nor is *Huck Finn* the *only* masterpiece of Twain's, as DeVoto and his successors have continually proclaimed, not realizing the "broken childhood" of Mark Twain was never broken, and is the key element, indeed, of his temperament and work. But I have reverted to Mr. De-Voto only because Mr. Neider quotes another key passage of the supposed "indictment" of Twain's later, and obviously more interesting, mature and complex work. Neider correctly sees that Twain wrote the *Autobiography* for his own pleasure, which is always the secret of a writer's best writing, and not out of some impulse to examine his own deep core of dread . . . that De-Voto invented.

Neider goes on to examine Twain's various reasons for writing the *Autobiography* the way he did, and Paine's reasons for selecting or editing out various sections of the book, and for keeping Clemens' stream-of-consciousness form. And he (Neider) describes his own method of editing the *Autobiography*. "Working with the autobiographical manuscript as a whole, both unpublished and published parts, I weeded out a variety of material. I did this for several reasons: in order to make a wieldy volume which would meet certain requirements of the general reader (for whom this book is designed); in order to unburden the excellent parts of the dated, dull, trivial and journalese sections of the work; and in order to concentrate less on opinion and second-hand recollection amd more on the truly autobiographical, the more purely literary and the more characteristically humorous material. My volume is to a high degree anecdotic, but I believe this to be a virtue rather than a defect in that it correctly represents the creative slant of Mark Twain's mind."

Neider continues with a more or less detailed selection of what he has used in his version of the *Autobiography,* and what has been omitted. But isn't this a curious kind of general statement about the book — which becomes much more curious after we have read the book. A wieldy volume, yes, of course; by all means omit the dated dull and trivial journalese; although it is not so often that Sam Clemens, and especially the later Clemens, wrote any purely dated and dull stuff. But to do this "in order to concentrate less on opinion and second-hand recollections and more on the truly autobiographical." Are we then to omit Twain's *ideas,* and opinions about life, and that is to say, the central core of Mark Twain's writing? Are we to equate this equivocal "opinion" with "second-hand recollections," as Neider seems to imply — and opinion and recollections of *what?* And finally, are we to assume in Mark Twain's case that the truly autobiographical parts of his last book are the "more purely literary" (whatever that means); are *only* the "characteristically humorous" material, and to a high degree "anecdotic"?

What a medicinal-sounding word Mr. Neider uses instead of the more familiar "anecdotal," and as we read along in his version of the *Autobiography* the real import of his introduction becomes clear. Now let me say at once that he has performed a valuable service in arranging the *Autobiography* in chronological order, and that his edition is highly readable. It is even, within its arbitrary limits, another good book by Mark Twain; it surely serves as an obvious refutation of DeVoto's thesis that the later Mark Twain was crushed and broken and full of dark forebodings which the *Autobiography* tried to deal with and failed. Nonsense! We have already demonstrated that just as Sam Clemens was a "daylight writer" of the Old Republic, despite all those darker elements of temperament and experience every major writer must have, so the *Autobiography* itself is a "daylight book," a triumphant conclusion to Twain's human existence and literary career, a celebrating of life despite all of life's tragedies. In Neider's pages is the whole chronicle of Clemens' boyhood and youth in Hannibal, again. Neider has put it all together, instead of the original broken form of Twain's reminiscences, and the whole experience of Twain's rebel youth is even more impressive.

\* \* \* \*

But the closing selection on the Anglo-Saxon race, in Neider's *Autobiography,* intended perhaps as a sop or a solace, really gives the whole game — and the book — away. Neider's Mark Twain is indeed a folklorist, a genial satirist, a patriot, an anecdotal teller of tall tales. But that is all. Why, Paine himself, cautious and conformist Victorian that he was, had more respect for Twain's central values and vision of life than to omit this whole side of Twain's genius. Possibly Paine overdid, in the first and what is still the standard edition of the *Autobiography,* the running account of "the Morris case" which Clemens used as an indictment of the haughty arrogance and disdainful manner of the new American oligarchy. But the Morris case (which Neider also omitted) led into Mark Twain's further commentary on the state of affairs which the United States, as a whole, had arrived at.

Now that is the real key to all of Neider's omissions of Twain's social criticism, and also of Justin Kaplan's negation of Twain's achievement in this area. During the Cold War period of the 1950s which conditioned the thinking of both Neider and Kaplan, there was to be very little criticism, in effect none, of a democracy which was considered to be struggling for its very survival against the so-called Russian Frankenstein. As revealed in a series of sensational disclosures in the year 1968, this intellectual stance was formulated by the CIA-funded "Congress for Cultural Freedom," — which dominated the cultural activities of both Europe and the U.S., and became the prevailing ideology for the "Free World's" leading intellectuals. And as further revealed in a series of books by young revisionist historians of the 1960s, the whole concept of the "Cold War" and the "Free World" was highly ambiguous, if not totally erroneous, and simply another ideological product of our own CIA's Frankenstein monster. Its real effect was to enslave *American* culture.

From Paine's original edition of the *Autobiography,* we remember that the Morris case led directly into the great insurance company scandals of the period; into the Standard Oil Corporation, into the Panama Canal Commission scandal; into the Russian revolution and the mystery of why American troops were being dispatched to China; into General Funston and the Philippines; and into Twain's blistering attack against the arrogant, ruthless, deceitful Theodore Roosevelt himself — the imperialistic, blustering, and warmongering President of the new American Empire.

None of this is in what we may now call Neider's censored version of Mark Twain's *Autobiography,* as I have already suggested in discussing Paine's *Autobiography.*

Nor does Neider include Clemens' famous satirical essay on Thanksgiving as printed in the Paine edition. To satirize a national holiday might be construed, in the Fatal Fifties, as giving comfort and aid (and classified information?) to the monolithic conspiracy of atheistic communism organized to destroy the very center of democracy — which in the 1900s Mark Twain was already having those dark doubts about. Better to simply ignore that little gem on the genocide of the American Indian. Far better not to remember that in 1906 Clemens had himself wished to ignore Thanksgiving on the grounds that nothing had happened to be thankful for except several vicious and inexcusable wars, and King Leopold's usual slaughters and robberies in the Congo, and the resurgence of the Russian Czar. Far far better for Charles Neider to omit *all* of Mark Twain's antiwar polemics and parodies which the naive and unpoliticized Paine had so innocently included in the book of an earlier, an older American world; not realizing that such literary gems were not "art" and were merely "tasteless and transient journalism."

The revival of this material in the radical resurgence and reaction against the Cold War period during the American sixties, and the emergence of the "New Left" in our universities did of course indicate a certain permanency and lasting relevance in Twain's old-fashioned social satire. Some of the essays we have discussed here have appeared almost continuously in New Left periodicals and programs, and were clearly among the best-written and freshest sounding satires, parodies, and polemics of the new period. And a period which was in fact only reverting to an older and major strain of social criticism and social justice in American literature and culture alike. It was the Cold War period which was the exception in our history — with the exception of the fact that at times the Cold War threatened to be the norm in our future history. What was the real future, indeed, of the Old Republic and the Democracy, which in those later essays Mark Twain himself saw as reverting to a proto-fascist "monarchy"?

In Paine's "antiquated" edition of the *Autobiography* also, there was the now-famous essay on "The Killing of 600 Moros" in our treacherous acquisition of the Philippines: another unflattering event in the New World's history deemed to be invidious, and doomed to exclusion by the Cold War historians, scholars, and biographers. We remember Clemens' direct statement of his real position in his period as the *conscience* of America; and what indeed he himself considered his true role as social prophet: a theme one hardly meets in the "anecdotal" Neider book. Where is the account, again, of Nikolai Vasilevich Tchaykoffsky, the revolutionary populist who came to visit Clemens, as did radical and revolutionary figures from the whole outside world where Twain's name was perhaps even more revered than in his own country? Tchaykoffsky's (or Tchaikovsky's) name is as absent from Mr. Neider's index as the event is from his narrative. And Twain's response, so vivid, clear, eloquent, that I will just reproduce it here again for the sake of the *style,* the writing craft that Mr. Neider says is the true base of his omissions:

> I told him what I believed to be true: that our Christianity which we have always been so proud of — not to say, so vain of — is now nothing but a shell, a sham, a hypocrisy; that we have lost our ancient sympathy with oppressed peoples struggling for life and liberty; that when we are not coldly indifferent to such things we sneer at them, and that the sneer is about the only expression the newspapers and nation deal in with regard to such things.

But it is obviously quite true that such a description of the American spirit would hardly be consoling to a nation whose national psyche was being constrained again to the so-called Christian struggle of "containing" (or suppressing) an international surge of communism and "atheism." It might just arouse the Americans; it would not be consoling to our allies in the Cold War consortium; it might give away our true view of those mainly non-Christian Asian and African peoples who were adopting various (and non-monolithic) forms of native communism and socialism in their liberation struggles against the Western European and American "Free World." A Free World just then obsessed by spiritual censorship and demonology.

Twain concluded (we know) by saying that Tchaykoffsky's only real support would come from the immigrants, the poor, and the Jews: those who had not yet had time to become "Americanized." What heresy! Unspeakable; unprintable! and surely unprinted in the Mark Twain material published in the 1950s. Now, as we know, if it was Bernard DeVoto who started this contemporary trend of denigrating Mark Twain's social criticism in the *Mark Twain in Eruption* of 1940 — for whatever personal reasons we have suggested — at least DeVoto *published* the Twain material which he was so niggardly in praising. But in Neider, once more, where are the glowing personal portraits of Carnegie, Roosevelt, the Rockefellers, and the other members of the new American oligarchy? From this whole firsthand view of his own country and society, which had changed so much for the worse in Clemens' own lifetime, a change which he was in the center of and which he recorded so intimately and eloquently — from this whole rich historical treasure in *Mark Twain in Eruption,* there is not a single selection in Mr. Neider's later version of the *Autobiography.*

It has been said that the reason for such a startling omission was simply that the DeVoto volume was so lately published; and Neider had stated (or pretended) that his edition was altogether "new." But what was the purpose of such originality

when there was already one well-established version of this famous book, and one recent and almost invaluable supplement
to it? What was the need — and what was the cost of such
"originality"?

We have just come from the description of *Mark Twain in
Eruption*: there is hardly any reason to recall the virtues that
shine out from beneath the curious editorial assumptions of Mr.
DeVoto. But it was Mr. Neider who carried DeVoto's direc-
tives to the final and logical conclusion of liquidating this whole
area of Mark Twain's work. Was the latest editor of the *Autobiography* altogether blind about such Twain essays as the description of Andrew Carnegie's ego? Or on Carnegie as the
epitome of the whole new oligarchy of industrial barons and titans
who had so radically changed the nature, the being, the essence of the old democracy into the portentous and ominous
shadow of the new "monarchy"? Or the prophetic comparison
of American monopoly capitalism and ancient Roman de-
cadence? Or the savagely brilliant description of the "Montana
jailbird," Senator Clark? Or the profile of Jay Gould as the
worst robber baron of them all; Jay Gould as "the mightiest disaster which has ever befallen this country." How could any
editor omit such choice items of Mark Twain's literary achievement? And the analysis of Jay Gould's "gospel," in rather the
same literary tone that Clemens had used for Mary Baker Eddy's
gospel?

Not to mention those corrupt magnates like the McCurdies,
the McCalls, the Hydes, and Alexanders — "and the rest of that
robber gang who have lately been driven out of their violated
positions of trust in the colossal insurance companies of New
York" — whom Sam Clemens had pilloried so magnificently
in his letters from the grave. Not to mention Clemens' blistering
strictures on the American press as "the palladium of our lib-

erties," in the course of his vivid profiles of Colorado's Senator
Simon Guggenheim, and then the Rockefellers, father and son,
as Christian ministers and teachers of the young. And then
Clemens' wholehearted and hilarious attacks on the Bible itself
as the source of Christian morality and Christian culture, and
indeed of Western civilization.

But enough. What is missing in Charles Neider's "modern"
edition of Mark Twain's *Autobiography* is not merely what I have
been describing as Twain's "radical social criticism" as a central
theme in his work. What is missing in Neider's book is, in effect,
the whole *public aspect* of an artist whose chief interest, whose
whole value, whose true literary position was exactly in such
public utterances, as expressed through the various modes of
his own writing from the satirical essay or the sardonic parable
to the realm of fiction itself and back to his genius for direct re-
portage. If Mark Twain was the acknowledged conscience of
his nation — to the outside world its great literary and almost
religious prophet in Tolstoyan terms — how can this version of
his autobiography dare to reduce him to the simplistic status
of a "humorist." And quote mainly, almost exclusively from his
"anecdotic" or autobiographical passages! The most social of
all our writers, as should be clear by now; the most "public" — to
the point of having almost no psychic core that was not entwined with all of nature, and all of the culture surrounding him;
and the most "open" — to the world surrounding him, to all of
human experience — has been reduced to a purely private rac-
onteur.

Mr. Neider is trying to make another Simon Wheeler ("The
Celebrated Jumping Frog of Calaveras County") out of the
artist whose career started with the famous parody of a garrulous narrator. But it won't work. It can't work with Mark
Twain. Even the most personal reminiscences in Neider's *The*

*Autobiography of Mark Twain* carry with them all the flavor and color of an age and a culture and a public personality beyond compare. And what is needed obviously is still another edition of this book — now really becoming the "whole library" that Clemens prophesied it would be — using Mr. Neider's chronological structure (which is the contribution of his edition) but including in its scope the whole central matrix of Mark Twain's temperament and career which Mr. Neider chose to exclude. In this sense Neider's is hardly so much a new "edition," again, as another kind of appendix to the original Paine edition. And what is really needed is a comprehensive *Autobiography,* based on the central material of Paine and using both Neider's and particularly DeVoto's supplementary material.

# TEN

# ETERNAL LIFE,
# LIGHT AND LAUGHTER

MEANWHILE in 1962, there appeared still another DeVoto volume of Mark Twain's writing, called *Letters from the Earth,* with another curious bit of background history. In the book's introduction, Henry Nash Smith, who was then literary editor of the Mark Twain papers, and a leading Twain scholar, explains that DeVoto, before his sudden and tragic death, had recommended that three volumes be published from the balance of Mark Twain's unpublished work. These were: one, further selections from the autobiography (*Mark Twain in Eruption*); two, a volume of letters; and three, a collection of essays and sketches.

DeVoto actually began work on the third volume first, and

had it ready for the printer in March, 1939, when Clara Clemens objected that certain parts of the manuscript presented a distorted view of Mark Twain. "The project was accordingly dropped," says Mr. Smith, "and the work has lain unpublished for more than twenty years in the successive depositories of the Mark Twain papers, at Harvard, the Huntington Library, and the University of California, Berkeley." Since 1960, the fiftieth anniversary of Twain's death, we are told, at least a dozen books about him had been published; and Clara Clemens (Gabrilowitsch Samossoud) withdrawing her objections, the book was published in 1962 in its original 1939 form.

Perhaps that is why, and certainly when compared to the glittering and spectacular social commentary of *Mark Twain in Eruption,* this "new" volume appears slightly old-fashioned and slow-moving at first. It is a collection of early and late essays and fragments, of good and bad things, and of some innocuous material that Mark Twain never published, with good reason, during his own lifetime. The opening chapters of religious satire may or may not include the "finest didactic chapters of the *Autobiography*" which a little earlier Charles Neider was not able to reprint because of Mark Twain's daughter's objections. It seems reasonable to suppose that these chapters were Clara's main concern; but they are really very unimportant in a modern context, and rather tedious. It is still interesting to notice that Neider refers to them as "good" didacticism, while Twain's social satire is "bad" didacticism; and DeVoto himself attempts to enclose Twain's social and moral radicalism within his religious radicalism. What is it there at the core of Sam Clemens that so terrifies these commentators and obliges them to indulge in such verbal gymnastics?

It could be the plain truth which is always so hard to face. In any case the opening of *Letters from the Earth* includes ten letters from Twain's Satan who has been exiled again and has chosen to reside upon the earth. This was a work which Clemens had initiated for his own pleasure during the last period of his life. Within its loose framework of religious fantasy and irony (some of it reminiscent of *The Mysterious Stranger*) he poured a random selection and a loose summary of all his familiar ideas.

Satan was being punished, to be sure, for "his too flexible tongue," a trait he shared with Tom Sawyer and Sam Clemens. And again Satan and Twain waxed lyrical about the human race. "This is a strange place, an extraordinary place, and interesting," Satan wrote to Saint Michael and Saint Gabriel. "There is nothing resembling it at home. The people are all insane, the other animals are all insane, the earth is insane. Nature itself is insane. Man is a marvelous curiosity. When he is at his very very best he is a sort of low grade nickel-plated angel; at his worst he is unspeakable, unimaginable; and first and last and all the time he is a sarcasm. Yet he blandly and in all sincerity calls himself the 'noblest work of God.' . . . Moreover — if I may put another strain upon you — he thinks he is the Creator's pet. He believes the Creator is proud of him; he even believes the Creator loves him; has a passion for him; sits up nights to admire him; yes, and watch over him and keep him out of trouble. He prays to Him, and thinks He listens."

In this sense "Letters from the Earth" (from which DeVoto took the title for the book) was the explication for some — though not all — of the mysteriousness in *The Mysterious Stranger*. It contains both man's view of God and God's view of man. "For there is nothing about man that is not strange to an immortal. He looks at nothing as we look at it, his sense of proportion is quite different from ours, and his sense of values is so widely divergent from ours, that with all our large intellectual powers it is not likely that even the most gifted among us would ever be quite able to understand it." And now man is a mystery in truth, rather than God; and Clemens went on to describe man's notion of heaven in his familiar way — but with an unfamiliar twist. For here heaven, unlike that visionary scene of sardonic horrors in *Captain Stormfield,* consisted not merely of psalm singing, praying, church-going, removable wings and halos, but concerned itself with both the biological and social aspects of man. "For instance, take this sample: he has imagined a heaven, and has left entirely out of it the supremest of all his delights, the one ecstasy that stands first and foremost in the heart of every individual of his race — and of ours — sexual intercourse."

This was a new note in all of Twain's reflections on man, God, and heaven. It was to be amplified in "Letters from the Earth," and perhaps it was the outspoken sexual content of these letters, as much as the religious satire, which caused Clara Clemens to hesitate so long about having them published.

To leave out the notion of sexual intercourse in heaven, said this Satanic Twin of Twain's, was as if "a lost and perishing person in a roasting desert should be told by a rescuer he might choose and have all longed-for things but one, and he should elect to leave out water!" And this later Satan went to further extremes in depicting the role of the sexual passions in mortals, and even more so in immortals. "First of all, I recall to your attention the extraordinary fact with which I began. To wit, that the human being, like the immortals, naturally places sexual intercourse far and away above all other joys — yet he has left it out of his heaven! The very thought of it excites him; opportunity sets him wild; in this state he will risk life, reputation, everything — even his queer heaven itself — to make good that opportunity and ride it out to the overwhelming climax. From youth to middle age all men and all women prize copulation above all other pleasures combined, yet it is actually, as I have said: it is not in their heaven; prayer takes its place."

Now this is not altogether as ironical as it sounds, since sexual intercourse *is* placed at the center of certain more ancient, more pagan, and perhaps wiser religious thinking.  But this is certainly the most direct, overt, and illuminating — perhaps almost astonishing — statement of Mark Twain's about the most taboo subject in what still amounted to the end of the Victorian epoch. And note that Sam Clemens included women equally as man's *partner* in sexual desire — another unheard of concept in Victorian culture — and there was still more to follow on this subject.*

Pausing to observe that this Christian heaven hadn't a rag of intellectuality in it, Clemens returned to his favorite historical couple, Adam and Eve, and their sin. "Very well, Adam and Eve now knew what evil was, and how to do it.  They knew how to do various kinds of wrong things, among them the one principal one — the one God had his mind on principally.  That one was the art and mystery of sexual intercourse.  To them it was a magnificent discovery, and they stopped idling around and turned their entire attention to it, poor exultant young things!"

What Twain was really writing, in these fragmented and uneven pages which still contained such brilliant things, was his own newly revised version of the Bible; and such a book would have been a sensation. In his reconstruction of our primal myth, Clemens pointed out that "Adam and Eve entered the world

---

* I am reminded of Leslie Fiedler's notion of a homosexual love affair between Huck and Jim on the Mississippi River. Readers of this book will have long ago concluded that Fiedler's "thesis," if it deserves that name, is both sensational and silly; but perhaps if Mr. Fiedler had known about the later statements of Sam Clemens about sexual matters, he would hardly have dared to formulate such an absurd hypothesis.

naked and unashamed — naked and pure-minded; and no descendant of theirs has ever entered it otherwise. All have entered it naked, unashamed, and clean in mind. They have entered it modest. They had to acquire immodesty and the soiled mind; there was no other way to get it. A Christian mother's first duty is to soil her child's mind, and she does not neglect it. Her lad grows up to be a missionary, and goes to the innocent savage and to the civilized Japanese, and soils their minds. Whereupon they adopt immodesty, they conceal their bodies, they stop bathing naked together."

But Twain's "New" Testament was also a stirring attack upon Christianity itself and upon Western Christian civilization in its entirety — despite all of Mr. Neider's involuted rationalizing on this subject, and the complete expunging of this aspect of Twain's work in Neider's *Autobiography*. For there followed a savage denunciation of the Judeo-Christian Jehovah himself, whom Clemens, incidentally, never identified by name.

And, after further commentary on the flourishing of sexuality in the pagan period of the Bible, and the visitations upon the lovely sex by the primitive gods, and the multiplying of the human race, we are treated to Mark Twain's version of the Flood. "By help of those visiting foreigners [the pagan gods] the population grew and grew until it numbered several millions. But it was a disappointment to the Deity. He was dissatisfied with its morals; which in some respects were not any better than his own. Indeed they were an unflatteringly close imitation of his own. They were a very bad people, and as he knew of no way to reform them, he wisely concluded to abolish them. This is the only really enlightened and superior idea his Bible has credited him with, and it would have made his reputation for all time if he could only have kept to it and carried it out. But he was always unstable — except in his own advertisements — and his good resolution broke down."

For some strange reason God still took pride in man, Twain said. "Man was his finest invention. Man was his pet, after the housefly, and he could not bear to lose him wholly, so he finally decided to save a sample of him and drown the rest . . ." Nothing could be more characteristic of God, Twain said, and he proceeded with a meticulous analysis of Noah's Ark; and a description of certain things not commonly known. "All these facts were suppressed in the Biblical account. You find not a hint of them there. The whole thing is hushed up."

There is a description of God's small-mindedness, including jealousy as one of his central traits; and of the microbes, who in this version actually constituted the main population of the Ark. Shem was full of hookworms, and God was especially generous in contributing his disease to the poor. "It is wonderful, the thorough and comprehensive study which the Creator devoted to the great work of making man miserable. I have said he devised a special affliction-agent for each and every detail of man's structure, overlooking not a single one, and I said the truth. Many poor people have to go barefoot, because they cannot afford shoes. The Creator saw his opportunity. I will remark, in passing, that he always has his eye on the poor. Nine-tenths of his disease-inventions were intended for the poor, and they *get* them. The well-to-do get only what is left over. Do not suspect me of speaking unheedfully, for it is not so; the vast bulk of the Creator's affliction-inventions *are* specially designed for the persecution of the poor."

Thus spoke Twain's Satan in "Letters from the Earth" — a Twainish Satan, however, who made some social discriminations in describing man's earthly condition, unlike the totally sardonic Satan of *The Mysterious Stranger*. And so much for the "anecdotic" and purely personal Mark Twain whom Charles Neider created out of Cold War fantasy and aberration. Published just three years after Neider's "new" version of the *Auto-*

*biography,* the volume called *Letters from the Earth* completely refutes every aspect of Mr. Neider's narrow and blinkered vision of Mark Twain himself.

I repeat these statements for the sake of history and Mark Twain scholarship rather than for my own interest, but I think Sam Clemens is entitled to the pleasure of seeing such a swift and ironical case of historical retribution. (History was always awarding such entertainments to this favorite child.) And here Twain began alternating his satire between the Deity and the Pulpit. His main point was that God never invented a single human or social reform, but immediately rushed to get the credit for any good deed that men achieved. The Creator was indeed "the one that never sleeps when there is a chance to breed sorrow for somebody." Speaking of the sleeping sickness in Africa caused by the tsetse fly, and the Pulpit's praise of science as being god-given, Clemens concluded: "He is surely a curious Being. He commits a fearful crime, continues that crime unbroken for six thousand years, and is then entitled to praise because he suggests to somebody else to modify its severities. He is called patient, and he certainly must be patient, or he would have sunk the pulpit in perdition ages ago for the ghastly compliments it pays him."

Man, commented Clemens again, is without any doubt the most interesting fool there is. Also the most eccentric. He went on to describe the central civilizational conflict in human evolution: the conflict between the laws of God and those of man. But in this case he viewed God as pagan and plenary nature, the true source of all animal and human temperament and drives, which "man" (society, civilization) had attempted to suppress and inhibit. (Perhaps the reverse is true; or rather God obviously embodies both strains of the human temperament.) He traced his argument to its central core of sexuality, again. "Temperament is the law of God written in the heart of every creature by God's own hand, and *must* be obeyed, and will be obeyed in spite of all restricting or forbidding statutes, let them emanate whence they may." He compared the sexual temperaments of the goat and the tortoise. "The excitable goat, the emotional goat, that has to have some adultery every day or fade and die; and the tortoise, that cold calm puritan, that takes a treat only once in two years and then goes to sleep in the midst of it and doesn't wake up for sixty days. No lady goat is safe from criminal assault even on the Sabbath day . . . whereas neither the gentleman tortoise nor the lady tortoise is ever hungry enough for the solemn joys of fornication to be willing to break the Sabbath to get them. Now according to man's curious reasoning, the goat has earned punishment, and the tortoise praise."

More boldly still, Clemens asserted the sexuality of the (Victorian!) woman when compared with the often limited and unreliable male sexuality; and the fact that female sexuality had been repressed to conform to man's view of it — that women were in fact the sexual slaves and sexual property of a "master" who could hardly compete with them. In these pages of sexual comparison Clemens was frank and funny to the point of obscenity; he was convulsed by the notion of female sexuality all but overcoming the inadequate and restricted male. "Now there you have a sample of man's 'reasoning powers,' as he calls them. He observes certain facts. For instance, that in all his life he never sees the day when he can satisfy one woman; also, that no woman ever sees the day that she can't overwork and defeat, and put out of commission any ten masculine plants that can be put to bed to her. He puts these strikingly suggestive and luminous facts together, and from them draws this astonishing conclusion: The Creator intended the woman to be restricted to one man."

Perhaps women were even more of a damned fool to Clemens than man was. But certainly this was open and frank and remarkably bold sexual commentary on the part of an artist who has been so often, so continually, so tediously described as "censored" and "neurotic" and "frustrated" and "repressed" at the very core of his being. This "core" remained constant with Clemens, as we've seen, from his youth to his age, during poverty and wealth, success and failure, sickness and health, joy and tragedy. And it actually flourished and grew freer and bolder and more luxurious in the final phase of his life. He described a buxom royal princess of the Sandwich Islands whose harem included thirty-six splendidly built young native men. By comparison he thought that Solomon's harem of seven hundred wives and three hundred concubines was poorly serviced. "To save his life he could not have kept two of those young creatures satisfactorily refreshed, even if he had fifteen experts to help him. Necessarily almost the entire thousand had to go hungry years and years on a stretch. Conceive of a man hardhearted enough to look daily upon all that suffering and not to be moved to mitigate it. He even wantonly added a sharp pang to that pathetic misery; for he kept within those women's sight, always, stalwart watchmen whose splendid masculine forms made the poor lassies' mouths water but who hadn't anything to solace a candlestick with, these gentry being eunuchs. A eunuch is a person whose candle has been put out. By art."

From time to time, Clemens concluded, "I will take up a Biblical statute and show you that it always violates a law of God, and then is imported into the lawbooks of the nations, where it continues its violations. But those things will keep; there is no hurry." This was in all ways a brilliant view of the long tradition of Judeo-Christian morality which lay at the base of man's development in Western European culture. It was a view whose essential soundness, if not the entertaining and deliberately ludicrous details, has been supported by modern depth psychologists searching for the key to culture and civilization, to evolutionary progress and/or societal reversion. The key to a fuller and happier human existence, and a less tortured and sickly life, *within* society.

The Old Testament, continued Clemens, gave us the Deity as he was before he got religion. "The other one gives us a picture of him as he appeared afterward. The Old Testament is interested mainly in blood and sensuality. The New one is Salvation. Salvation by Fire." The first time the Deity came down to earth, said Clemens — excuse me, I mean the Satan of these "Letters from the Earth" said, or Satan-Twain — he brought life and death. "When he came down the second time, he brought hell." And Clemens embarked upon another of his passages about the meaning of life in death.

> Life was not a valuable gift, but death was. Life was a fever-dream made up of joys embittered by sorrows, pleasure poisoned by pain; a dream that was a nightmare-confusion of spasmodic and fleeting delights, ecstasies, exultations, happinesses, interspersed with long-drawn miseries, griefs, perils, horrors, disappointments, defeats, humiliations, and despairs — the heaviest curse devisable by divine ingenuity; but death was sweet, death was gentle, death was kind; death healed the bruised spirit and the broken heart, and gave them rest and forgetfulness; death was man's best friend; when man could endure life no longer, death came and set him free.

Thus Twain in the tragic mood; and hard upon it Twain in the ironic mood. For in time the Deity perceived that death was a mistake. "A mistake in that it was insufficient; insufficient for the reason that while it was an admirable agent of the inflicting of misery upon the survivor, it allowed the dead person himself to escape from all further persecution in the blessed refuge of the grave." This was not satisfactory to the Deity, said Clemens, and a way must be contrived to pursue the dead beyond the tomb. "The Deity pondered this matter during four thousand years unsuccessfully, but as soon as he came down to earth and became a Christian his mind cleared and he knew what to do. He invented hell, and proclaimed it."

Thus Jesus Christ, who replaced the jealous and cruel Jehovah of the Old Testament, and became a symbol of all that was gentle, merciful, and forgiving, was in Mark Twain's eye, a crueler and more malign figure. It was in Christ's name, not Jehovah's, that hell was invented and proclaimed. But there was not that much difference between the two Deities, and the chronicle continued with a detailed account of Jehovah's crimes against mankind. "The Biblical law says: 'Thou shalt not kill.' The law of God, planted in the heart of man at his birth, says: 'Thou shalt kill.' The chapter I have quoted shows you that the book-statute is once more a failure. It cannot set aside the more powerful law of nature . . . According to the belief of these people, it was God himself who said: 'Thou shalt not kill.' Then it is plain that he cannot keep his own commandments. He killed all those people — every male. They had offended the Deity in some way." And Clemens went on to illustrate all of the possible offenses to the Deity that he could imagine, except that of being guilty. "The Lord slew Onan for that, for the Lord could never abide indelicacy. The Lord slew Onan, and to this day the Christian world cannot understand why he stopped with Onan, instead of slaying all the inhabitants for three hundred miles around — they being innocent of offense, and therefore the very ones he would usually slay. If he had a motto, it would have read, 'Let no innocent person escape.' "

In these passages indeed Sam Clemens was pursuing the Lord himself with the same fascinated concern, and almost obsessional curiosity, and wrathful malice which he had used in the case of Mary Baker Eddy; who herself had had some thoughts of replacing the Virgin Mary.

There followed a sort of bawdy exchange with the Lord, developing from Onan's sin in sexually withdrawing from his brother's wife. And again there was the related commentary on God and the Pulpit. "Human history in all ages is red with blood, and bitter with hate, and stained with cruelties, but not since Bible times have these features been without a limit of some kind. Even the Church, which is credited with having split more innocent blood, since the beginning of its supremacy, than all the political wars put together have spilt, has observed a limit. A sort of limit. But you notice that when the Lord God of Heaven and Earth, adored Father of Man, goes to war, there is no limit. He is totally without mercy — he, who is called the Fountain of Mercy. He slays, slays, slays! All the men, all the beasts, all the boys, all the babies; also all the women and girls, except those that have not been deflowered."

This was in connection with the campaign against the Midianites in the Old Testament. And Clemens, in wrathful tones reminiscent of King Leopold's Congo — for injustice and cruelty five thousand years ago were just as fresh and searing to him as yesterday's event — went into another savage discourse on the Lord's treatment of the 32,000 Virgins and their induction into sexual slavery under the divine guidance. "It was the Father that inflicted this ferocious and undeserved punishment upon those bereaved and friendless virgins, whose parents and kindred he had slaughtered before their eyes. And were they praying to him for pity and rescue, meantime? Without a doubt of it . . . These virgins were 'Spoil,' plunder, booty.

He claimed his share and got it. What use had *he* for virgins? Examine his later history and you will know."

Clemens concluded once again — like Beethoven he had so many chances to end his compositions which he ignored — by comparing the peaceful moral preachings of the Judaic-Christian Biblical God with his actual behavior. "Would you expect this same conscienceless God, this moral bankrupt, to become a teacher of morals; of gentleness; of meekness; of righteousness; of purity? It looks impossible, extravagant; but listen to him. These are his own words." And then Clemens-Twain suggested that the Beatitudes and the chapters from Numbers and Deuteronomy which he had just been quoting should always be read from the pulpit together. "Then the congregation would get an all-round view of Our Father in Heaven. Yet not in a single instance have I ever known a clergyman to do this."

There is no doubt that if Mark Twain had ever completed and published his satanic version of the Bible, it would have been a remarkable book. Meanwhile we are glad that Mr. DeVoto rescued these fragments for publication, and they were much better than the next section of *Letters from the Earth,* called "Papers of the Adam Family." These were "translated from the Adamic," according to Clemens and Paine and DeVoto, throughout Twain's career, starting as early as the 1870s, and were obviously intended as another testament of Biblical times. The first translations were extracts from "Methuselah's Diary," which preceded the publication of "Adam's Diary" by some fifteen years, and, according to Paine, there was an even earlier version of "Shem's Diary" which has been lost.

How Clemens enjoyed conversing with primitive and edenic human nature in the Bible before the Fall — or the first coming of morality, society, and civilization — as DeVoto remarks here, concerning Twain and the Adam Family, but without recognizing the source or true meaning of this communion. DeVoto did realize the analogy in Twain's mind between the Flood and the imminent destruction, as he (Twain) felt, of his own American democracy. "In Methuselah's time as in Mark Twain's time, a great civilization had reached the point when the destructive forces it contained were beginning to dominate. He appreciated its greatness; he also appreciated the inevitability of its collapse. He and Methuselah lived in eras which they both loved and hated but in which they were never quite at home, eras with a doom on them, eras when the world was spinning toward the abyss."

Here indeed DeVoto, under the guise of analyzing the historical crisis in Mark Twain's religious chronicle, was himself far more direct and open in the analysis of his own society than anywhere else in his public writings — although the lingering traces of his belated frontier optimism persisted in the generalized vagueness of his statements; in the romantic use of Twain's formulations; and in the addition of some rather peculiar social commentary of his own. Now we know that from the very start of his career, Sam Clemens had been critical of many of those democratic institutions which so much later DeVoto still supported without doubt and without question. But it was only in the mid-nineties, as we have seen, that he met at first hand the conditions and consequences of western imperialism upon those "backward" and "pagan" and "pigmented" countries whose great champion in America (and for the whole world) Mark Twain became.

The breaking point in Clemens' personal career, to which DeVoto earlier had attributed the deterioration in his talent, was in fact the dividing line which gave a new force, power, eloquence to Twain's later writings — which now, quite belatedly, and still in another (religious) guise DeVoto paid tribute to. For he does note that around 1906, the "Father of History" became the "Mad Prophet" — as Twain's social discontent persisted and increased. "The year 920 After Creation was fateful for Adamic society," so DeVoto paraphrased Twain, "and he saw the same forces at work round him, the same softened people, the same corrupt plutocracy, the same venal and bewildered government, the same chaos." That *was* the symbolic content which Twain intended to convey in "Papers of the Adam Family" — even though a more sophisticated historian would not use DeVoto's description of a "bewildered government" — as Twain did not — a "softened people" (softened from or by what?) and the almost meaningless word "chaos."

The twentieth-century United States Government of the military-industrial-scientific complex, of world monopolies and super-conglomerates; this corporate state of armed imperialism and colonial wars of extermination was not "bewildered." Only its own people (and some historians) were. What Mark Twain was describing in both his direct social commentary and his religious parables was much more accurate, pointed, and particularized than DeVoto acknowledged. I only wish I could say as much in favor of the Adam Family papers as literature as has been said about their meaning and purpose. Despite DeVoto's inclusion of them as such a large block of *Letters from the Earth,* they are really quite boring to read. Partly because Clemens had started them so early as the 1870s as a desultory sort of self-entertainment, they are difficult and confusing to read, and some of them are written in a falsely archaic style. Maybe DeVoto used them to *obscure* Twain's direct social criticism; or at least they were more congenial to him.

In the 1900s Clemens also wrote a variation on "Eve's Diary" called "Eve's Autobiography," which was much more theoretical and pseudo-scientific and even pseudo-historical than the published version of "Eve's Diary" already discussed in these pages. It is true that Twain was writing of the world's rising birthrate which would concern the thinking of the twentieth century; and that he Swiftianly proposed war as the only solution for the population explosion. And it was here he developed the notion of the "Shoemaker-Dictator" who would sweep "the Double Continent with fire and sword" to purge its commercialism and moral corruption. But his descriptions of the North American nation's final phase had been done better before. (These papers were probably the false inspirations or first drafts or poorer formulations of what Mark Twain said more forcefully elsewhere.) And his elaborations of the "Law of Periodical Repetition" and the "Law of Intellectual Averages" were not only historically untrue but monotonous.

These were mainly either preliminary or repetitious fragments of Mark Twain's best work which were gathered together in *Letters from the Earth*; yet they still contained such brilliant passages as Twain's indictment of the Philippines war (once again) in phrases completely appropriate to the Vietnam war of the 1960s. "I pray you to pause and consider. Against our traditions we are now entering upon an unjust and trivial war, a war against a helpless people, and for a base object — robbery. At first our citizens spoke out against this thing, by an impulse natural to their training. Today they have turned, and their voice is the other way. What caused the change? Merely a politician's trick — a high-sounding phrase, a blood-stirring phrase which turned their uncritical heads: *Our Country, right or wrong!* An empty phrase, a silly phrase. It was shouted by every newspaper, it was thundered from the pulpit, the Superintendent of Public Instruction placarded it in every schoolhouse in the land, the War Department inscribed it upon the flag. And every man who failed to shout it or was silent, was proclaimed a traitor — none but those others were patriots. To be a patriot, one had to say, and keep on saying, 'Our Country, right or wrong,' and urge on the little war. Have you not perceived that the phrase is an insult to the nation?"

In the early years of the Nixon Administration — just as in the epoch of President Theodore Roosevelt — when the inglorious "little" war in Vietnam (which had turned out to be larger and longer than the Pentagon had estimated) was still being pursued under the deceitful guise of making peace; and when so many replicas of the American flag had blossomed forth in every area of the Empire as to make the lack of showing the flag very conspicuous — those words *were* appropriate. And Clemens' prophetic words applied directly to those who claimed it was "impossible" to end the war without honor. "Only when a republic's *life* is in danger should a man uphold his government when it is in the wrong. There is no other time. The Republic's life is not in peril. The nation has sold its honor for a phrase. It has swung loose from its safe anchorage and is drifting, its helm is in pirate hands. The stupid phrase needed help, and it got another one: 'Even if the war be wrong we are in it and must fight it out: *we cannot retire from it without dishonor.*' Why, not even a burglar could have said it better. We cannot withdraw from this sordid raid because to grant peace to those little people upon their terms — independence — would dishonor us. You have flung away Adam's phrase — you should take it up and examine it again. He said, '*An inglorious peace is better than a dishonorable war.*' You have planted a seed, and it will grow."

The source of Mark Twain's "compulsive" hatred for Theodore Roosevelt is thus tracked down. It was Roosevelt whom he blamed for the collapse of the Old Republic; the advent of the American Empire which was to lead to the Monarchy, and to the Dictatorship. Now this process of the Oligarchy and Imperialism — after the American heartland had been exploited, despoiled, and enchained by the new breed of financial barons and titans in the post-Civil War epoch — had started long before, as Clemens knew and described. But it was during the Rooseveltian era that Mark Twain saw the *outward* expansion of this process until it did in fact lead to something like the American world imperium in the 1950s and 1960s. Twain saw the brutal and ruthless beginnings of this right at home in the 1900s, and he foresaw how it would destroy the democracy.

"But it was impossible to save the Great Republic. She was rotten to the heart. Lust of conquest had long ago done its work; trampling upon the helpless abroad had taught her, by a natural process, to endure with apathy the like at home; multitudes who had applauded the crushing of other people's liberties, lived to suffer for their mistake in their own persons. The government was irrevocably in the hands of the prodigiously rich and their hangers-on; the suffrage was become a mere machine, which they used as they chose. There was no principle but commercialism, no patriotism but of the pocket. From showily and sumptuously entertaining neighboring titled aristocracies, and from trading their daughters to them, the plutocrats came in the course of time to hunger for titles and heredities themselves. The drift toward monarchy, in some form or other, began; it was spoken of in whispers at first, later in a bolder voice."

And from monarchy, the lost republic called upon the Shoemaker-Prodigy from the Deep South to take control. The standing army — another innovation of American democracy — refused to obey the Congress, and the Dictatorship set in.

This apocalypytical vision was at the center of the posthumous DeVoto volume called *Letters from the Earth;* and its publication was another service from a badly harassed critic, even though he only allowed Twain's social criticism to filter through the religious parables.

The rest of the collection included stray and casual pieces of minor interest; yet, as always with Mark Twain's prose, there were some other interesting or entertaining passages to be noticed. There was another children's story ("A Cat-Tale") he had invented for Susy and Clara whose main distinction was the hilarious Mark Twain line drawings and his "analyses" of these works of art. (A special volume should be published of Mark Twain's drawings and his descriptions of them.) The front end of one of his cats, for example, was peacefully asleep, the rear end was ferociously active. There was another essay on "Cooper's Prose Style" adding some further remarks on that early American master's craft. "I beg to remind you that an author's way of setting forth a matter is called his Style, and that an author's style is a main part of his equipment for business. The style of some authors has variety in it, but Cooper's style is remarkable for the absence of this feature. Cooper's style is always grand and stately and noble. Style may be likened to an army, the author to its general, the book to the campaign. Some authors proportion an attacking force to the strength or weakness, the importance or unimportance of the object to be attacked; but Cooper doesn't. It doesn't make any difference to Cooper whether the object of attack is a hundred thousand men or a cow; he hurls his entire force against it. He comes thundering down with all his battalions at his back, cavalry in the van, artillery on the flanks, infantry massed in the middle, forty bands braying, a thousand banners streaming in the wind; and whether the object be an army or a cow you will see him come marching sublimely in, at the end of the engagement, bearing the more preferable fragments of the victim patiently on his shoulders, to the stopping-place. Cooper's style is grand, awful, beautiful; but it is sacred to Cooper, it is his very own, and no student of the Veterinary College of Arizona will be allowed to filch it from him."

Menckenesque? One might add that while the New Criticism of the mid-twentieth century has made important discoveries in respect to the technique of writing, it hasn't yet approached the effects of Mark Twain's studies of his own craft. There was a little postscript to the Gorky incident in which Clemens attempted to rationalize his and Howells' behavior in terms of human custom as the rock of society, and law as the only pure reason. But the fact remains that these two American writers had behaved badly in cutting Gorky because he had arrived for a tour of revolutionary lectures with his mistress. (The fact was that this "mistress" was Gorky's common-law wife; and the Russian embassy had spread the slander.) But then Clemens followed this with a remarkable little essay (originally meant for the *Autobiography*) written in 1908 and called "Something About Repentance." It was curious, he said, about the misassociation of certain words:

"For instance, the word Repentance. Through want of reflection we associate it exclusively with Sin. We get the notion early, and keep it always, that we repent of bad deeds only; whereas we do a formidably large business in repenting of good deeds which we have done. Often when we repent of a sin, we do it perfunctorily, from principle, coldly and from the head; but when we repent of a good deed the repentance comes hot and bitter and straight from the heart. Often when we repent of a sin, we can forgive ourselves and drop the matter out of mind; but when we repent of a good deed, we seldom get peace — we go on repenting to the end. And the repentance is so perennially young and strong and vivid and vigorous! A great benefaction conferred with your whole heart upon an ungrateful man — with what immortal persistence and never-cooling energy do you repent of that! Repentance of a sin is a pale, poor, perishable thing compared with it.

"I am quite sure that the average man is built just as I am; otherwise I should not be making this revelation of my inside." And note again perhaps the most original spirit of them all drew all his faith and strength and power — in that older tradition of nineteenth-century American writing from Emerson and Thoreau, Whitman and Melville — from an absolute identification with the people, the masses, and that "average man" who was both the mask and the true source of strength for Clemens' art. This was the source of our literature's greatness in its high period; and the lack of this was the cause of contemporary American literature's failure. "I say the average man," Clemens continued, "and stop there; for I am quite certain that there are people who do not repent of their good deeds when the return they get for them is treachery and ingratitude. I think these few ought to be in heaven; they are in the way here. In my time I have committed several millions of sins. Many of them I probably repented of — I do not remember now; others I was partly minded to repent of, but it did not seem worthwhile; all of them but the recent ones and a few scattering former ones I have forgotten. In my time I have done eleven good deeds. I remember all of them, four of them with crystal clearness. These four I repent of whenever I think of them — and it is not seldomer than fifty-two times a year. I repent of them in the same old original furious way, undiminished, always. If I wake up in the night, they are there, waiting and ready; and they keep me company till the morning. I have not committed any sin that has held me like this save one; and have not repented of any sin with the unmodifying earnestness and sincerity with which I have repented of these four gracious and beautiful good deeds.

"Possibly you who are reading these paragraphs are of those few who have got mislaid and ought to be in heaven. In that case you will not understand what I have been saying and will have no sympathy with it; but your neighbor will, if he is fifty years old."

This is surely one of the best and shortest of all informal essays. Not a word is wasted, not a word could be cut, not a word is wrong; this is implacable prose, riding high with mature wisdom. (Twain the frustrated adolescent!) One is reminded of those pages in the *Autobiography* concerning Clemens' earlier sense of sin and doom — at night in the dark hours — which somehow never survived the light of day. What has happened to Mr. DeVoto's thesis of the split Twain, the frustrated Twain, the tragic and dark Twain who was so unresolved and tormented, unfulfilled to the end of his life? As we said originally, the *Autobiography* is not such a work. Full of torment, tragedy, sorrow about the human lot, it is still one of the great *daylight* documents of literature (I repeat) where the artist is immersed in the communal experience, and where finally all of the pain and suffering of human experience is recognized and acknowledged in beautiful art — and dissolved by the laughter of genius.

A rare thing even in the upper brackets of literature, for Twain was not being merely entertaining, either. What was being described in "Repentance" was the consuming vanity of the human heart, so much larger than conventional morality. And what Clemens was celebrating was his own release from conventional worldly obligations — the free soaring of spirit in the very last of his years. Talking of form, this barely page-and-one-half sermon must be counted among his best things. There followed a purely Dadaistic extract from the earlier days of Clemens' repudiation of the Victorian taboos; an unfinished burlesque of the etiquette books of the period which preached "good manners" — refinement, gentility, sexual repression —

to a supposedly crude and ignorant American audience. Apparently Clemens worked on this unfinished book from the 1880s on; and I have space only to quote a little from still another collection of essays of philosophical speculations about man's nature. This was called *The Damned Human Race* and written mainly in the years from 1900 to 1909, and could just as well have been included in the *Autobiography*.

Twain devoted a good deal of time to proving that if the Lord had intended the earth only for man's use, he had certainly taken his time about it, and tried many other experiments and failures before reaching this conclusion. This essay was notable for the range of his thought and knowledge in geology, astronomy, biology. Darwinism was at the center of these speculations, and pulpit religion was the target. In a section titled "In the Animal's Court" he showed again that none of the lower animals could escape the law of his own makeup. The lion was bold because he was bold, the wolf was savage, the sheep was tame and sacrificial, the fox was cunning, the machine was a machine. And what was Man, Clemens wondered, if not a mixture of all these elements, along with the pretense of free will. But in "The Lowest Animal" he was even more direct and sardonic; and one remembers Clemens' affinity, from the very start of his career, with the animal world. "I have been studying the traits and dispositions of the 'lower animals' (so-called) and contrasting them with the traits and dispositions of man. I find the result humiliating to me. For it obliges me to renounce my allegiance to the Darwinian theory of the Ascent of Man from the Lower Animals; since it now seems plain to me that that theory ought to be vacated in favor of a new and truer one, this new and truer one to be named the *Descent* of Man from the Higher Animals."

In brief space Clemens then went on to catalog his familiar

complaints about man, and the familiar virtues of the higher animals. Perhaps because his space was shorter, his complaints more varied and vivid, his comparisons with the animal world so generously in their favor, this becomes almost one of his unbearably savage — Swiftian — essays. And so we come to the last section of *Letters from the Earth,* in the last — well, almost — of Mark Twain's books we can discuss here. This was another fragment of narrative, written in the late nineties, at the peak of Sam Clemens' domestic troubles, which DeVoto titled "The Great Dark," and to which he gave so much editorial study and analysis.

Perhaps too much. This was an interesting fragment of work, at best, illuminating as to the depths of Clemens' despair, to the point where he felt he could no longer distinguish between illusion and reality in life (as other works of this period also recorded) — to the point that he believed his whole lifelong domestic idyll of love and pleasure with Livy and their children was in fact an illusion; an illusion which the Livy figure in "The Great Dark" does not remember as a fact.

But the central point of the present book is that Samuel Clemens was not a major talent frustrated at midpoint. Not in the least; not at all; not possibly so. And I think that we have more than amply refuted the old and recurrent thesis of Twain's "frustration," his "failure," his final "bitterness." On the contrary we have seen just how Clemens recovered his talent intact from the pit and quagmire of disaster. The whole point is that he surmounted the crisis of mid-life; he survived it and he transcended it.

He entered his mature and later periods of writing quite triumphantly indeed, with all his old powers enhanced, rather than broken or diminished, by his own central tragic experience; by his depth realization of life's pain and evil. He retained to the end the central source of his artistic virtue: that untouched spring of pagan, plenary, and edenic innocence, that full sense of joy and pleasure in life, which sprang up even more freely in his final decades — which came to a second and later flowering despite all those civilizational discontents which he, perhaps more than any other American writer, also felt so directly and personally at the center of his being.

It was only certain Twain critics, from the youthful Van Wyck Brooks, who came to change his mind, to Bernard DeVoto and Charles Neider and Justin Kaplan, as we've seen, who refused to acknowledge — or who were perhaps ignorant of — the value of his later writing. Mark Twain was more correct in his own estimate of that work, his joy in writing it, and yes, his pleasure in receiving the world's acclamation then (and yet again today) for having written it. The last periods of his writing were indeed younger in spirit if wiser in essence than much of his earlier and middle periods of work. *Huck Finn* as his single great classic — what nonsense! His whole career was a classic. He was not merely the artist of American youth and the past; he was surely our most mature and wisest of artists whose acerbity and profundity alike were ringed about with the imperishable comic spirit. In his age he only became freer, bolder, more open and honest, more emancipated both socially and sexually, from the taboos of his epoch which, at base, his spirit had never accepted.

To the critics' discomfort at times (and perhaps this was the true cause of their discontent), he became even more satanic and savage in the social commentary of his last period. But was he not also, as we have seen during the same period of his work, more touching, tender, and lyrical, bringing forth our tears when he wielded that magical wand; this genius who was wedded to both the tragic deeps and the great peaks of the human comedy.

Presently, even more Mark Twain material is being opened up

for public inspection — the bonanza of his genius is still being tapped. Sponsored by the Modern Language Association, the University of California Press is publishing some fourteen volumes of Twain's hitherto unpublished papers. While most of this material has already been studied by Mark Twain scholars, and while some of it — like the dreadful extract of Huck Finn and Tom Sawyer "Among the Indians," published for no good reason in *Life* magazine in 1969 — was rejected for publication by Sam Clemens himself, or by his subsequent literary editors, still, I have no doubt that out of these fourteen volumes of unpublished papers at least one more valuable Mark Twain book will emerge. And perhaps, as one must hope, another one. And maybe another.

Nobody should discount anything that Samuel Clemens wrote, as I said earlier, and as I hope this book has demonstrated. At least it has presented the various levels of Mark Twain's art in all its range, scope, depth, and variety — of a talent which seems as fresh and sharp and enchanting today as when the ink first flowed from its inspired pen. It is with some sense of personal loss (at least momentarily) that I write these closing pages about such an unearthly, yes, and divine spirit which was so firmly rooted in the earth. These notes and letters and parables and commentaries from the older world of the American democracy, which appear so often as if written by some visitant from another planet . . . and concerned above all with the mysterious soul of man. And that old-fashioned bardic and runic American artist who now belongs to all the world, to the history which he meditated upon, to whatever future, uneasy, dark or dubious as it appears from here, may still hopefully prevail.

# Index

**Catalog**

If you are interested in a list of fine Paperback
books, covering a wide range of subjects
and interests, send your name and address,
requesting your free catalog, to:

McGraw-Hill Paperbacks
1221 Avenue of Americas
New York, N. Y. 10020